BLACK EYES AND BLUE BLOOD

. date shown.

ɔv.uk/library

Norman Johnson was born in Merseyside in 1933 and now lives quietly in Stafford, close to his daughters and grandchildren.

Michael O'Rourke was born in 1955. He has been a close friend of Norman Johnson's for over 20 years and lives in Yarnfield.

BLACK EYES AND BLUE BLOOD

The Amazing Life and Times of Gangster 'Scouse' Norman Johnson

Norman Johnson
and Michael O'Rourke

MAINSTREAM
PUBLISHING

EDINBURGH AND LONDON

First published in Great Britain in 2008 by
MAINSTREAM PUBLISHING COMPANY
(EDINBURGH) LTD
7 Albany Street
Edinburgh EH1 3UG

ISBN 9781845963552

A catalogue record for this book is available
from the British Library

Typeset in Champion and Concorde

Printed in Great Britain by
CPI Mackays of Chatham Ltd ME5 8TD

Contents

Introduction

People often ask me: do you class yourself as a Liverpudlian or a cockney? Well, I was born on Merseyside and spent my formative years there, but from my late teens London was the place where the winds of fate took me. The truth is, both cities have had a profound effect on my life. I have witnessed the people's unique humour, kindness and particular ways of living in both places. Of course, finding 'bad apples' in either metropolis didn't require a detective, so confrontation was a natural occurrence.

Once I was established in London, I was universally known as 'Scouse' Norman, and that became my nickname. To help readers understand how I became the man I am today, my story starts with the struggles endured by my parents, through 'the seven ages of man' and up to the present day. I make no excuse for the violence, none of it gratuitous, as it was simply a way of life. I can hold my head up high – I never exploited my undoubted reputation. Now, at the age of 75, I find myself on the strangest retro-journey. My head is spinning with memories, good and bad.

What do I write and what do I omit? I have made many mistakes in life, but I wouldn't change any of it for the world: fist, knife and gun fights; black humour, laughing and crying; good times and not-so-good times; romance, affairs and dalliances; the Mafia, Special Branch, Customs and Excise, and Scotland Yard; gangsters, scum of the earth and rough diamonds; sportsmen, showbiz celebrities, MPs and royalty. All are featured.

Through three continents, my roller-coaster life roared on at breakneck speed, seldom slowing. The journey was so varied, I didn't know myself what each up-and-coming day would bring. The quest certainly wasn't for the shrinking violet.

I give you my life story.

Norman Johnson
August 2008

1

•••••••

Early Daze

In the twilight hours of 10 August 1933, yours truly came kicking and screaming into a world that was as turbulent and uncertain as at any time in history. That year a certain little ex-painter and decorator from Austria had somehow risen to the top of the Nazi Party tree and was a cause for concern for people all over Europe. The Germans appointed him chancellor, but if they thought that his ambition would plateau at that position they were woefully mistaken.

I was born in a very working-class area on Merseyside called Toxteth. I didn't know my grandparents, but I was fascinated by my father's account of how he had left them to settle on Merseyside. My grandfather was Ronald Derbyshire, a quite wealthy businessman from Crewe, Cheshire. He owned The Crown Hotel and had his fingers in a number of pies. He married Minnie Johnson, a local girl, whose family had a thriving business selling coal at Crewe Railway Station, so money was never a problem.

My father was christened Ralph William Derbyshire. He was the youngest sibling of four, with two older brothers and a sister. Through his early years, he didn't want for anything, and he was not unloved by his parents, although his father Ron was not overtly affectionate, a trait that was to rub off on the young Ralph. Minnie adored him but always seemed too busy in the hotel to give him the time he deserved. When his brothers and sister were about, they would play with Ralph and take him on trips and outings. These were the happiest times of his childhood. Unfortunately, they did not last long, as his elder brothers left the roost to join the air force,

BLACK EYES AND BLUE BLOOD

where one was later tragically killed, and his teenage sister married a Harley Street surgeon and emigrated to California.

As a result, Ralph now seemed to spend more time with the servants and staff than with his parents. It wasn't a happy childhood from that point onwards, and sullen Ralph didn't suffer fools gladly. He was on his own much of the time, so he retreated into his shell and became moody and taciturn.

In his teens, Ralph noticed his father's behaviour changing. Whether it was because of business problems or marital stress, Ronald was drinking copious amounts of alcohol. He was talking down to Minnie, and their relationship seemed strained. It came to a head one night when Ralph heard screaming coming from the parlour. The fifteen year old careered into the room to encounter his father in a drunken frenzy, knocking seven bells out of his mother. Ralph was a large teenager, taller than his father, with a bull neck and powerful biceps, and he was not at all intimidated by Ron. In a split second, he snatched a heavy brass poker from the hearth and with a high looping action brought the shining implement down with great velocity onto Ronald's head. His father crashed onto the hearth rug like a lead zeppelin. Blood was gushing from his injured skull, staining the fabric. 'God, Ralph. You've killed him,' cried his mother. A servant rushed in and checked the wound. 'No, ma'am. He's breathing, but unconscious. We must fetch the doctor.'

Ralph left the room. He knew that he had a hair-trigger temper, but the ferocity with which he had intervened had surprised him. He flew upstairs and packed some clothes. When he sloped back down, his father was coming round, but Ralph knew that he had no choice but to leave the nest. He kissed his tearful mother goodbye. She implored him not to go, but he had made his decision and insisted that he had to leave. Minnie pressed some paper money into his palm, and he walked out of the hotel. Ralph never saw his parents again.

Even before the incident, Ralph had been unhappy in Crewe. He had considered joining the army, knowing that they were turning a blind eye to underage enlistment. However, he was drawn to the lure of the sea. He fancied a life on the ocean waves, sailing under the Merchant Navy's Red Duster. After the confines of Crewe, the attractions of the seven seas, with their far-flung, exotic ports, were irresistible to him. That night he crossed his own Rubicon and ventured north, destination Liverpool.

Briskly walking through the darkness, trying to cadge a lift, Ralph walked hour after tedious hour until daybreak. He was plodding along, a sorry state. He must have put 20 miles behind him by the time dawn broke through. And with the new day came a welcome change of luck. He heard the clip-clop of horse's hooves on the cobbles, and turning around he beheld a grizzled farmer's horse and cart full of root vegetables. It wouldn't have looked any finer to Ralph if it had been the king's state coach and carriage. The farmer helped him up and enquired where he was heading. 'Liverpool docks, mate,' answered the bedraggled youth.

'It's your lucky day, son. I'm dropping off at Liverpool Market,' said the farmer. 'The docks are a short walk from there.'

Good fortune was shining at that moment. Ralph kept his fingers crossed that the day was picking up, and on reaching the market helped the farmer unload his produce. Ralph then bade him farewell and headed down to the docks.

He arrived at the gates and took in the cosmopolitan vista with all its hustle and bustle. There were Lascar sailors from the East Indies, Yankee cotton merchants, French *matelots* and Spanish fishermen. It seemed as though the whole world had descended on Liverpool that day. The local dockers were busy moving all the freight and cargo to and from the ships. The scene resembled a gigantic ant colony.

Ralph was directed to the Merchant Navy's employment offices, where he was rebuffed twice before being accepted as galley boy on a medium-sized steamer due to sail for Argentina. Even though he was three years shy of the minimum age, he was a stocky lad and convinced the company that he was eighteen years old. He was there for the long haul and signed on for five years as Ralph William Johnson, rejecting his surname in favour of his mother's maiden name.

He loved his life at sea and experienced many cultures and lifestyles when docking abroad. In the end, he stayed on in the Merchant Navy for a lot longer than his original five-year stint.

After a few years, while on a long voyage, he befriended a middle-aged man named Henry Hall, who had been a top amateur boxer in his youth. Ralph was now a six footer and weighed in at around fifteen stone, so Henry suggested that he might take up boxing and started training him with some light sparring. Henry Hall turned out to be a good teacher, and Ralph listened intently and learned fast.

Whilst on shore leave, Ralph joined a local Liverpool boxing club and quickly gained the district heavyweight boxing title. Throughout his boxing career, he did lose a few bouts on points, but he was never knocked out in the ring, although a pretty young local girl called May Evans did have a knockout effect on him when they were first introduced. They had a short courtship and decided to get married. May was impressed by Ralph's strong, disciplined character and he by her kindness and love, which he hadn't experienced for many years.

In 1928, they married at the local registry office. He was 26, and she was sweet 16. After the wedding, May wanted Ralph to work ashore; Ralph tried but couldn't adapt and was enticed back to sea. He made sure that he only accepted short-haul work but was still away for periods of two or three months in the early years. Every time he came home, there seemed to be another hungry mouth to feed. May certainly had her hands full.

2

·······

Malpas and Back

I was the third of six children. My elder brother, affectionately known as 'Snowy', was born in 1930, and he was quickly followed in 1931 by my sister Minnie, who was named after my grandmother. My father was an archetypal man of the day: a disciplinarian with a short temper and no great sense of humour. He enforced a strict regime, in which children were to be seen but not heard. Snowy and Minnie were well behaved, but I was a different matter. My father didn't seem to have the same control over me, and as I grew from an infant, the spankings and their severity increased.

Baby Rose came along when I was two. My mother May had her work cut out with four children under the age of five, especially with little room, so we moved to larger accommodation in Berkeley Street, Toxteth. My mother had a much softer nature than my father. She was a devout Roman Catholic and attended church every Sunday come rain or shine. There were biblical pictures on every wall of the house and a large crucifix over the marital bed. She was a wonderful mother but had a hard life.

When my father was at sea, my mother could not control me, and I was frequently told, 'Wait till your father gets home.' I took absolutely no notice of this and grew to hate my father instead of fearing him. My behaviour was deteriorating, and I was spiralling out of control, staying out late and running wild.

Then, out of the blue, tragedy struck. Snowy was playing football at school when the ball bounced over some metal railings. Snowy clambered onto the fence but was startled by a teacher's whistle, which caused him to lose his balance, and he was impaled on the spikes. He screamed out as two of them punctured his ribs. His classmates struggled to get him to the ground, but being a tough kid he didn't show the extent of his injuries and staggered home in pain. He didn't tell a soul about his ordeal, but that night in bed he was moaning in agony, which prompted my mother to discover his injuries. She immediately rushed him to the local hospital, where he stayed overnight. She had to leave him with the nurses, as we were all at home alone.

On returning to the hospital the following morning, the doctor informed my mother that Snowy's internal injuries had been so severe that he had passed away during the night. May was heartbroken. It was a very black day. She told us all the bad news, and even though I was very young, I knew that I had to look after my two sisters, as I was now the eldest boy.

It was approaching 1939, and the black clouds of war were looming over Europe. Baby Leonard appeared just before Hitler's Panzer battalions started to reduce Europe to rubble. Len was to have a massive effect on my later life, but for the moment I was one of four again.

As Hitler's jackboots were crushing weaker nations, my father's boot was making its own impression on my behind. At the time, I wasn't winning our personal battle, but I was becoming harder and more cynical.

Due to the worsening war situation, Liverpool council took a pre-emptive decision to evacuate children to the surrounding countryside, most going to North Wales or Cheshire. It was a rare well-thought out plan by the politicians, as Liverpool was later blitzed by the Luftwaffe – only London had it worse.

The powers that be didn't always make it a priority for brothers and sisters to be housed together, and in some cases siblings never saw each other again. As a result, our family was split up. Minnie and I were evacuated to Derbyshire to stay with strangers who were not the friendliest people we could have wished for. The situation became unbearable, so I ran away, but I was quickly retrieved by the authorities.

My mother couldn't tolerate us being apart and pleaded with my father to arrange for the family to be together. Ralph contacted a certain Major Ramsbottom, who was a director at the shipping company he worked for, and asked him if he could help. The major had a soft spot for my father and suggested that my mother take us all to a small lodge in Malpas, Cheshire. This was on the major's private grounds, and although it was a little bit isolated, being three miles from a school or shops, it was much better than what we had been used to. The lodge had two bedrooms, and a coal and wood fire, but the only lighting was from paraffin lamps, drinking water was procured by an old outside water pump and we had to boil a large cauldron over the fire for hot water.

Until we got to know the route, my mother took me and Minnie to school every day. The country school was just like being back in Liverpool: full of snotty noses, scuffed shoes, tatty shirts and torn trousers (and that was just the teachers). Over the months, I got into many scrapes with the other children, and things came to a head one day when the schoolmaster accused me of hitting another pupil. I'd been at the school for about a year and was all of seven years old. If I'd hit the other lad, I would have admitted it! But, in this instance, I hadn't. The master took me out in front of the class for a caning. He told me to hold out my hand, but I refused. He then lost his temper and damned me for my impudence. I refuted his claim again and kept my hands down by my side. He grabbed me by the back of my shirt collar, to which I reacted by giving him a powerful kick to his shins. It made his eyes water, as I was wearing wooden clogs with metal toe rims. He had a demented look in his eyes and swiftly lashed down with his cane across my legs and chest. He held me tight as he was thrashing my body, and I tried to kick both of his legs from under him. We were grappling for about a minute, and the class was screaming and out of control when another teacher came in to stop the melee.

I didn't cry, even though I was young and he had given me a good beating. Back home that afternoon, my mother saw that my legs and upper body were covered in black-and-blue weals. My skin had also been punctured in places from the ferocity of the caning. She burst out crying and asked me what had happened, and I recounted the whole incident. She then took me to the house of a well-to-do lady whom she had befriended. The lady was horrified when she saw the state I was in. She told my mother that she would make extensive enquiries, which culminated in the master being sacked or moved

15

on to another school. I never did find out. Afterwards, I was the talk of the school, and teachers and older pupils appreciated that I was a tough kid.

In 1941, there was another ankle biter in the family when my youngest sister Sylvia was born – she was a real war baby. Outside of school, I was getting on better with my father, as there wasn't so much mischief to get up to in the country. When he was on leave, he took me rabbiting and taught me how to use nets and snares. I also went scrumping for apples and stole potatoes and carrots from the local farmers, which wasn't exactly condoned by my mother, although the extra food was always appreciated, as she had to fill the bellies of five hungry children. I even persuaded her to come scrumping with me one day, and I don't know who was more embarrassed when the farmer caught her eight foot up a Bramley apple tree.

The war years passed quickly, and six years seemed to go by in six minutes. In 1945, we headed back to Liverpool. I had learned a few new tricks in the Cheshire countryside, and it wouldn't be long before I began to go off the rails again.

3
· · · · · · ·

Teenage Angst

We were back in God's country. There was a sense of optimism in the air, but times were still hard. I was 11, going on 12, and enrolled at St James School, Mount Pleasant, off Parliament Street. I got in with some wrong 'uns, and my attendance at school suffered. Most days, we would head for the docks to see what we could pilfer. We would cut open sacks of sugar and make off with our ill-begotten gains by riding on the back of tram cars. Fruit and veg lorries were also fair game, as were corner shops. As a result, I was frequently falling out with my father again, who took to hitting me with a rope, although I had absolutely no fear of this and continued to do exactly as I wanted.

Liverpool had a large Catholic population, so poverty and large families went hand in hand. It wasn't unusual for some people to have ten or twelve children. In fact, some women had so many kids that they had stretch marks on their family allowance books. My mother always seemed to be short of money, and every week she went to the pawn shop and put in three of our best blankets to raise cash, leaving us to keep warm at night under army overcoats. She would then receive something called allotment money, and although this didn't stretch far she would always redeem the blankets. At Christmas, she managed to get us a little present, even if it was mostly fruit and sweets.

I was still getting into plenty of fights, be it at school or on the streets. I'd had a recent scuffle with a local black youth named Michael Barton and thought no more of it when he invited me around to his house. Being naive, I walked in and was confronted

17

by his dad and older brother, who gave me a good pasting, although nothing too serious. In retrospect, it taught me a good lesson – to be more worldly wise. The next day, an older relative of mine, Davey Evans, enquired how I'd got a shiner. I told him I'd had a scuffle with Michael Barton and that his family members had got their own back on me. Davey said, 'I'm not having that,' and took me back to the Barton household. He went in, and they proceeded to knock him all around the room. He came out in a worse state than me. I had to laugh, as he had meant well.

Being a boxer himself, my father decided that if I was fighting all the time, I should at least fight properly and arranged for me to go to the St Patrick's Boys Boxing Club on Park Road in Toxteth. I was placed in the charge of Father Mean, the local parish priest who trained all the young lads. At last I had something to concentrate on, and I trained every night. Father Mean was right behind me, and I had quite a few fights in my time at St Patrick's, winning them all.

In the midst of this upturn, I was still at loggerheads with my father. Neither of us would bend, so I decided to move out. At 13 years of age, I hit the road to Blackpool and slept rough for a week. I befriended some locals who were members of a boxing gym and was encouraged to go along. The trainer there was Ronnie Clayton, who was the ex-British featherweight champion. He could see that I had potential and found me occasional work, which included selling seaside rock along the promenade. With my first wages, I rented my own place near to Blackpool Tower. I was training religiously and doing well in the gym against lads four or five years older than me.

I became good friends with a local hot prospect named Ken Regan. He'd had 12 professional fights and a dozen had hit the canvas. At that time, Ken was about 18 years old and used to wear a leather jacket sporting his picture and the words 'KO Ken' on the back of it. Every time we went into a pub, there would be comments such as 'Who the fuck d'you think you are? Joe Louis?' or 'See if you can fucking knock me out'. Most of the time we would honour the last request, but we always had to be very wary, and I told Ken that the jacket would have to go.

One night, Ken was boxing at the tower, which was a popular fight venue at the time. I would usually watch Ken fight, but that night another boxer didn't turn up, and I volunteered to take his place. My trainer knew that I could look after myself, and I got kitted up. Ten minutes before the fight, the promoter walked in and asked me, 'How old are you, son?' I told him that I was 18. He laughed and said, 'Sorry, son. I can't risk it.' I so nearly had a professional fight at 14 years of age.

Around the time that I was growing tired of Blackpool, news reached me that my father had left the Merchant Navy for a period to take a job as caretaker in the NALGO (National and Local Government Officers Association) union building in London, near to the House of Commons. I'd been hearing a lot about the capital and decided that I wanted to experience life down there for myself. My whole family had moved into a top-floor flat with three bedrooms, and every night we were put to sleep by Big Ben's chimes. My father and I agreed to an uneasy truce for my mother's sake.

I was now a competent young boxer and joined the famous Battersea Boxing Club under the tutelage of trainer Harry Groves. I was knocking a few opponents over and was hailed as a good amateur prospect, regularly getting my picture into the south London papers. I did a lot of sparring with another young boxer who was about the same age as me named Peter Waterman, elder brother of Dennis Waterman the actor. A class act, he was later to become Great Britain and European welterweight boxing champion. I was learning all the time with sparring of this calibre.

Again, things were looking up – until I returned to old habits, that is. Money was short, and I was at an age when I was beginning to appreciate the finer things in life. To fast track this appreciation, I burgled an affluent residence in Chelsea. The house must have been alarmed, because as I dashed into the street with the purloined jewellery I ran straight into the arms of the law. The next day, I was taken to the local magistrates' court and given six months at the remand home in Shepherd's Bush, from which I absconded twice.

After that, I was in and out of trouble and spent my middle teens at St Christopher's Approved School in Middlesex. The headmaster was a Mr Westgate, and the first time I met him he marked my card. 'There's the bus stop, Johnson,' he said, pointing towards the window. 'If you want to go, you'll not get far.' I always loved a challenge. Later that afternoon, I leaped over the fence and got as far as Leicester, where I was apprehended in a farmer's barn and taken back.

The one thing that was constant in my life was my boxing, so I decided after my excursion to give it 100 per cent, and Westgate gave me his full backing. We had really good facilities for boxing at St Christopher's, and the lads from Hayes Boxing Club used to come over to our gym for sparring and training. A guy called Dickie Gunn ran the Hayes Boxing Club, and he took me under his wing. I had seventy-eight fights in two and a half years and won seventy-seven. I don't really know how good the boys I was up against were, but all I could do was beat whoever was put in front of me. My one loss was to a lad called Roy Squibbs. There were reasons for my defeat that I won't go into, but I did beat him in a return match.

At the All England Approved Schools Championships at Chelsea barracks, I won a medal in my weight category, which was presented to me by the eminent soldier, Field Marshal Slim. There was a big picture of all the winning boxers mounted in the school corridor. Mr Westgate gave me two days off to visit my parents as a reward, not knowing that they had already returned back to Liverpool. I had a nice couple of days out in London.

Eventually, my time at St Christopher's came to an end. I was approaching 18 and was conscripted into the army. Mr Westgate bade me farewell. He hadn't done a bad job, and I'd like to think that the responsibility he had given me had helped me to get through my teens. But it was now time to serve king and country – my army career was beckoning.

4

· · · · · · ·

King and Country

On my 18th birthday, I was told to report to the army base in Aldershot, as I was now regarded as an adult. On the first day, me and 30 other sorry-looking conscripts picked up our kit and were directed to our new home in the barracks. A red-faced, big-mouthed corporal was screaming at everyone, getting in people's faces and covering them in saliva. 'Right, you pathetic specimens. Get your kit in the lockers. I want your boots and brasses blancoed and polished. I'll be back in two hours.'

I wasn't having any of this nonsense, so I got up, left the barracks and went into town. I decided to get a tattoo on my arm of two hands shaking over a heart. I returned to the camp about three hours later and entered the barracks to find that all of my fellow conscripts had fully prepared their kit for inspection. A little cockney guy on the next bed warned me, 'The corporal's on the warpath. He wants your guts.'

I said, 'Fuck him. He's an airhead,' and lay down on the bed. Two years of this bullshit wasn't going to be an option!

He arrived ten minutes later, heading full pelt in my direction, shouting and gesticulating. 'Johnson. I'll bring you down, boy. Stand up. I'm going to sort you out.'

I stood up and butted him in the face. He was curled up on the floor holding his bloodied nose. I told the astonished onlookers, 'Nobody leaves the barracks or says a word.' With that I left and caught a bus to the railway station, where I boarded a train to London's West End.

I headed towards Piccadilly Circus. It was good to be out and about. At around midnight, I ended up in an all-night café called the Corner House in Leicester Square. It was a large place that could seat hundreds. Whilst sitting alone, drinking a cup of tea and minding my own business, six brasses (prostitutes) and two men sat down at the next table. After a while, they started taking liberties with a poor old destitute fellow who was slurping soup through his beard. The stockier of the two men started degrading the old man by flicking fag ends at him. The women encouraged him by laughing uproariously.

'Why don't you leave him alone?' I said. The stockier man reacted by jumping to his feet and approaching me in a threatening manner. I launched out of my seat and butted him right in the teeth. He went in the direction of downwards. The man turned out to be Ronnie Fryer, a well-known face locally, also known as 'Mad Ronnie'. His pal came over, stating that he wanted no trouble, picked Ronnie up and left.

One of the brasses marked my card: 'I think he's gone to fetch Tommy Smithson.' She then informed me that he was a big name in the West End. Smithson was apparently very heavy and had a reputation as a ferocious fighter. She implored me to leave.

'I'm not interested,' I replied. 'Let him come.'

Half an hour later, a guy who was just under six-feet tall walked in. His black Crombie could not disguise his wide shoulders. The brasses were all over him. This was my first meeting with the legendary Tommy Smithson. He asked one of the brasses, 'Who was it that hit Ronnie?' She nodded in my direction. Smithson glanced over at me. He had to look twice. 'God, he's only a kid,' he said.

'Less of the kid,' I retorted. Tommy grinned and came over. I got to my feet.

'Cool down, son,' Tommy said. 'You're from Liverpool, then.' He'd obviously clocked my accent. It transpired that Tommy was also a Scouser. He asked whether I lived locally, and I told him that I'd just come to London on the off chance. He sat down and said, 'You'd better come back to my place. You can get cleaned up there.'

Tommy's drum (flat) was off Bayswater Road in Leinster Gardens. I had a quick wash and shave, then joined Tommy at another all-night café called Theo's in Wardour Street. Tommy was meeting his girlfriend there, another well-known face named Fay Richardson.

She was universally known as the 'Black Widow', as her two previous husbands had met with premature deaths. We drank until five in the morning, and then returned to Tommy's place. It must have been a good session, as I didn't wake until two in the afternoon.

Tommy supplied me with a suit and some shirts, which fitted OK, and took me around some afternoon drinkers, where I was introduced to more faces. Tommy left at about six in the evening on a business matter, but before he went he gave me £50 in white fivers and arranged to see me at 2 a.m. at Theo's. As I drank that evening, I heard Tommy's name mentioned repeatedly. He was certainly well known in the West End.

On my travels that night, I bumped into a guy called Terry Kenny, another Scouser, in Aggy Hill's club in Archer Street. He was with his girlfriend, and I joined their company. Later that evening, in another club, Terry battered two Yanks who had made disparaging remarks about his woman. I didn't have to move a muscle; Terry took them both out easily. We eventually arrived at Theo's, but shortly afterwards Terry's girlfriend wanted to go home, so I told Terry where he could get hold of me in future before he left. Tommy Smithson arrived and suggested going to his own spieler (illegal club) across the road. We played cards until six in the morning. I wasn't a card shark, but it was a great pastime for socialising.

During the following days, I got really pally with Terry Kenny, and he turned out to be a right diamond. Most nights we would go greyhound racing at Park Royal, White City or Hackney, followed by drinking sessions with Tommy. The good life was starting to add inches around my middle, so to keep myself in shape I started training at a gym owned by boxing promoter Jack Solomon. It was one flight over a down-at-heel billiard room on Great Windmill Street, quite near Raymond's Revue Bar in Soho. My previous experience as a very good amateur came to the attention of some shrewd judges. One or two trainers advised me to turn professional, but this was out of the question under the name 'Norman Johnson', as I was still on the run from the army. So, I swapped names with another lad who frequented the gym and signed professionally as Benny Lloyd under the guidance of trainer Billy Clueless, a very accomplished ex-boxer. Billy would take me to his home every night, where his wife would cook giant steaks. I felt on top of the world. Billy was either very rich or he knew a good spiv. It turned out that neither was the case. I wondered why I wanted to jump fences and was drawn to Royal Ascot: Billy had been feeding me horse meat. I wasn't happy with him, and the situation was made worse when I discovered that he'd been going around all the nightclubs asking the bouncers to refuse me entry. I now know that he was looking after my best interests, but we fell out big style and went our separate ways.

One night in Theo's I had a huge row with a local hard man named Harry Hilton, aka 'Harry the Savage'. While we grappled, he ripped my shirt to shreds. We punched each other black and blue, until I eventually knocked him down. He struggled to his feet and left. He had got the message, but Harry Hilton would turn up again at a later date.

A few nights later, my luck ran out. The freedom I'd gained by absconding from the army came to a close. I was just going into Chez Toni's for a drink when somebody grabbed me by the arm. He said, 'We want a word with you,' and swung me around. It later turned out that the two men in front of me were plain-clothes coppers, but I didn't know that at the time. I didn't ask any questions and flew at one of them, butting him in the face. He went down but was able to drag me on top of him. The second detective jumped on my back and pulled me off, leaving the other to get up and boot me four or five times in the body. He obviously didn't acknowledge the Marquess of Queensbury rules. In the furore, two more uniformed officers turned up. I was arrested, handcuffed and taken to West End Central Police Station off Regent Street. In the police car on the way to the cells, the injured copper, who was holding a handkerchief to his face, said, 'You'll get five years for GBH.' I just ignored him.

At West End Central, I was thrown into a holding cell. My shirt was a bit torn, and I had a few bruises, but if I played my cards right, I could accentuate my injuries to my advantage. I forcefully punched myself in the left eye socket, which immediately swelled up like a golf ball. I then ripped open my shirt and drew blood with criss-cross movements across my chest with my nails.

I rang the buzzer in my cell, and a copper looked through the spyhole and scornfully asked, 'What do you want?'

'I want you to contact the newspapers. I want photos taken.'

He left without responding. Half an hour later, the cell door opened, and an inspector and two uniformed officers came in. 'How did you get in that state?' he exclaimed.

'Your men have given me a right pasting,' I replied. 'I'm going to the papers.' He responded by saying that he would look into it and ordered one of the uniforms to get me another shirt and clean me up. As they were leaving, I said, 'As soon as I get in court tomorrow, I'm going to say that the police beat me up.' The inspector didn't say a word, but I could tell that I'd got to him.

The next morning at 7.30 a.m., the inspector and a different uniform came in. The inspector said, 'Put your shirt on, Johnson. Go to court, don't speak and we won't charge you with any offence. You'll just be sent straight back to the army.' I'd got a result. The assault accusation was going to be dropped.

I was accompanied into court between two large sergeants. The magistrates were told that I was AWOL from His Majesty's Armed Forces and that it had been arranged for me to be taken to the army detention centre holding cells in Whitehall, near to 10 Downing Street. At the end of the proceedings, the chief magistrate responded by telling the police to get me out of his sight!

Arriving in Whitehall, the police escort handed me over to two large redcaps. I changed into army fatigues and was placed in a small cell. Half an hour later, two military policemen (MP) even larger than the first pair walked in. One was carrying an old bucket. 'Polish this so that we can see our faces in it,' one of them said.

'No chance,' I replied.

The redcap said, 'You will. I need to shave.'

As soon as they left, I jumped on top of the bucket and completely flattened it. On their return a few hours later, they saw the squashed bucket and went ballistic. They were screaming and shouting threats. 'Right, Johnson. You're gonna clean the toilets.'

'No fucking way,' I retorted.

At that stage, I was sitting on the floor, so each MP grabbed an ankle and dragged me down the highly polished corridor. I gave them no resistance and lay in the toilet for three hours, during which time they kept popping in and giving me loads of verbal. Eventually, they got tired of this and shouted, 'Get up and go back to your cell.' I continued to ignore them, so they dragged me back along the corridor and threw me in the cell. I knew that I had beaten them psychologically. Their mind games would not work on me!

A day later, four military policemen came down from Blackdown army barracks to take me away. Blackdown was an establishment for the internment of criminal and problem army personnel. It was a place where the army would try to break you. At the base reception, I changed back into civvies, and the sergeant said to me, 'You'll be sorry for this, Johnson.' It was all water off a duck's back to me. I was charged with assaulting a corporal and absconding from the army. An officer was assigned to defend me, and I was placed in yet another cell – they were all starting to look the same to me. But I still wasn't playing ball. When MPs told me that I had to exercise, march or go on work detail, I refused. I was driving them mad.

One of the decent MPs started giving me newspapers and got me swapped to the dormitory, which I shared with 20 other offenders. I still continued to refuse work detail, and, in my boredom, I thought that it would be a good idea to put some itching powder, which some joker had brought in, into everybody's trousers and shirts when they were out one day. I made sure that I was on parade that hot summer's day as the well-drilled marching machine started to look like a disco for St Vitus's dance sufferers. Soldiers were scratching the back of their legs, underneath their arms and around their genitals. It was hilarious! It soon became obvious who had engineered the phantom powder plot, and I was returned forthwith to my beloved single cell.

Dickie Gunn, my old boxing trainer, had traced me down to Blackdown and was sending correspondence. A certain Captain McGuiness, a former army boxing champion, read one of the letters and declared an interest in me as a result of his love of the noble art. 'I hear you do a bit, Johnson,' he said. 'Would you like to glove up?' I was always game for pugilism, so I took him up on his offer, and he escorted me down to the gym, where we sparred for three rounds. He wasn't bad, and although I gave him a black eye and a split lip, he was over the moon and asked me to box for his team. I later discovered that the other MPs were made up with his injuries, as he was unpopular on account of his strictness, although he was always fair with me.

I was now going outside during breaks and walking around the exercise yard. There was one large Glaswegian prisoner from the wrong side of the Gorbals named Alec Beatty, a Scottish hard man who was a right Neanderthal and forever flying off the handle and clumping the MPs. At the time, I had no use for cigarettes but had been given a couple by Captain McGuiness. I offered them to a group gathered in the yard: 'Does anybody want a fag?'

Beatty came over aggressively. 'Give them to me, boy,' he said and tried to snatch them out of my hand. I just walked around him and gave them to somebody else. 'I'm gonna fuckin' do you,' screamed Beatty, and he ran at me. We must have tussled for two minutes, but it seemed like an hour. The MPs stood back and let us get on with it. They were hoping I'd give him a good hiding as retribution for his past indiscretions against them. I eventually knocked him to the floor. He'd come off worse, and the MPs jumped in to stop the fight from going any further. I was locked back up in my cell, and he was taken to the hospital.

A fortnight later, I was in the charge room, up in front of the camp's commanding officer (CO), Donald Thomas, for my brawl with Beatty and for my earlier altercation with the red-faced corporal when Captain McGuiness walked in. He must have been a man of some influence, because he told the CO that Glaswegian Beatty had attacked another MP and that I had intervened, saving the redcap from a good hiding. McGuiness then told the MP that he had spoken to me and that I had said, 'I want to do the right thing – do my army time and box for the regiment.' I couldn't believe my ears. It was all fabricated.

The CO retired to consider his options, returning half an hour later. 'Johnson,' he said. 'Against my better judgement, all charges are dropped. Do not let Captain McGuiness down. He has shown great faith in you.' I was one relieved man, as I had been expecting at least six months in Shepton Mallet Military Prison. McGuiness then took me to the guard room and passed me a stripe. 'I'm going to give you some responsibility with MP duties,' he said. (I might be wrong, but I've been told that I was the only man ever to have been enlisted in the British Army and get a chevron without ever wearing the uniform or appearing on the parade ground.)

I was due to get kitted up a couple of hours later. In the

meantime, I sat on the bed in my new quarters, gazing at my new stripe. I'd only been in the forces a few weeks and was already a lance corporal. Could this be the beginning of a brilliant military career? Would I make brigadier? I made my decision. I thought, 'Nah! Fuck it,' and walked out of the back gates and absconded again to the West End.

5

•••••••

Trouble in the Smoke

After arriving in the West End, I continued to indulge myself in a life of drinking and gambling. I was meeting new people, many of them important faces. Tommy Smithson introduced me to a heavy gangster named Jack Spot on a visit to his new drinking club in Soho. Tommy was to have trouble with Spot later on, but at that time everything was cordial.

That night, there were three men drinking at a table in the club: two guys about my age and one who was older. The elder guy turned out to be Bobby Ramsey, who did some minding for Spot. The younger two were twins Ronnie and Reggie Kray. They were softly spoken and told me that if I ever needed help, to give them a call. They were very friendly, unlike Ramsey.

In a club one night, I met 'Maltese' Joe Ferrugia, who I already knew on nodding terms. We quickly hit it off, and he asked if I wanted to get involved in a robbery near Baker Street. I was always game for some extra money, but the plan didn't turn out to be that good. While we were on the premises, the police came and arrested us, and we were both taken to Swiss Cottage Police Station. On arrival, we were interviewed in the facing room by a detective. I looked at Ferrugia as if to say 'Let's make a run for it', but he just stared down at his shoes, so I took unilateral action. I spotted a map on the wall, which gave me an idea. I pointed up to it, and the detective stuck out his chin. Bing. I hit him right on the button and dashed out of the room. I burst in and out of the foyer and leaped over a wall into a churchyard. There were half a dozen police chasing me. The closest one tried to cut me off, but when

29

I threatened him he feigned injury and went down on one knee, saying 'Aah, my leg.'

I had a good head start on the rest of them so decided to lie low for a few minutes. I noticed that two patrol cars were out and about, so I decided to double back towards the police station, as they wouldn't be expecting that. I went down a nearby alley and got into the back of an unlocked fruit-and-veg van, where I lay down on some sacks of spuds for a couple of hours. It was all quiet on the western front until the back doors suddenly flew open. I thought that it must be the police, but it turned out to be the veg man. 'What are you doing?' he enquired.

'My bird's took me to the cleaners, and I need a lift to the West End,' I lied.

'Well I'm going towards Hatton Garden,' he said. That would do me quite nicely. He dropped me off, and I made my way safely home.

That night, Tommy told me, 'The Old Bill are after you. You've made them look bad.' I told Tommy I'd keep my head down and adopt a low profile for a couple of weeks.

Before long, Joe Ferrugia's girlfriend, Shirley, got in touch. She'd been to see Joe in Brixton, and he'd asked me to visit him. I went incognito, using another name. It was a bold move to visit Ferrugia, as the police were looking for me all over the West End. At that time in Brixton, all prisoners were on 'closed visits', and I spoke to Joe in a cubicle through a glass partition. 'Scouse [all the cockneys were now referring to me as Scouse because of my Merseyside connections], thank God you've come. You've got to give yourself up. They're gonna keep me on remand until you do. I could be here for months.' I said, 'No can do, Joe. You should have made a run for it with me when you had the chance.' I felt genuinely sorry for him, but if he'd have been in my shoes, I'm sure he would have done the same thing. He accepted the situation and got his head down.

A few months later, Joe went to court and got three years for robbery. This didn't bode well for me, and when I was arrested three weeks later I feared the worst, especially because I'd hit the detective and was on the run from the army. They took me back to Swiss Cottage, but this time there was more security. I was handcuffed and thrown in a cell. The case went to the Crown court at Southwark, where I was expecting a similar outcome to Joe's, possibly more. It was a no-win case, so I pleaded guilty.

The army were represented at the trial and informed the judge that I was also facing a military court martial for violence. On top of that, a detective from Swiss Cottage revealed that his colleague had been severely traumatised and had been off duty for two months. He really laid it on thick, and I thought to myself, 'Here comes a long 'un.' The one chink of light was provided by my probation officer, who told the judge, in mitigation, that I'd become a professional boxer, even though it was under a different name, and that he thought I could lead a respectable life.

Now, I've been in court many times over the years, and the judges have seldom demonstrated any compassion, but on that day the judge was influenced by the probation officer. 'Johnson, I'm going to give you a chance. You seem to have ambition to become a boxer, so I'm going to send you to borstal for six months.' What a result – six months. I'd been expecting a lot longer.

I was sent to a borstal in Hull. By God, it's grim up north, as they say, but by and large the time passed quickly and was trouble and incident free. Then, out of the blue, I received some good news in the form of a letter just before the end of my sentence. It was a dishonourable discharge from the army. Things were going my way.

Arriving back in the West End, I decided to pay a visit to Tommy Smithson's gaff and was greeted at the door by Fay Richardson. She was in a terrible state, 'Norman, Tommy's in hospital. He's been beaten up real badly.' I rushed to the infirmary and found Tommy in intensive care. He'd been cut up, was sporting 300 stitches and had been pummelled black and blue. I asked him who was responsible. It turned out the main protagonists were Jack Spot and Billy Hill (both legendary names in the gangster world). I said to Tommy, 'Let's get them.'

Tommy reasoned with me: 'No, Spot and Billy will fall out, then we'll take them.' This prediction turned out to be 100 per cent correct. Jack 'Spot' Comer, who was born in 1912, was the son of Jewish-Polish immigrants and was the self-styled 'King of Aldgate'. He was not known as Spot as a result of having a large mole on his cheek, as a lot of people thought, but by being on the spot with his Jewish hard men when fascist Oswald Mosley marched through the East End. Spot's reign of terror was coming to an end thanks to his ambitious partner Billy Hill. Born in the same year, Hill was ruthless enough to take over Spot's big-time activities. And unlike Spot, Hill would live through the period and die a natural death as a wealthy man.

Now that Tommy had enlightened me about his attackers, I wanted to know the ins and outs of the carnage and why he had been so savagely put upon. What happened has been documented a few times, with different scenarios being described, but I can only relate what Tommy told me. A couple of days earlier, Tommy had gone to a club, where a well-known face called Slip Sullivan was having a drink and becoming lairy in the company of some of his cronies. He was making an old Maltese guy perform a ridiculous dance on a table and was treating him like a fool. Tommy said, 'Come down, dad,' and helped the old guy off the table. Slip Sullivan took umbrage to this and snarled at Tommy, 'Don't spoil our fun. Keep your nose out.' There was no way Smithson would be taking that verbal off Slip. Tommy whacked him and cut him up. It was all over as quickly as it had started.

The next day, Spot's right-hand man, Moisha Blueball (real name Morris Goldstein), started making himself busy. He told Tommy that Billy Hill and Spot wanted Tommy to have a straightener – a fair fist fight – with Slip's brother Sonny Sullivan, which would then draw a line under the whole affair. The Sullivans were good friends with Spot and Hill, and Tommy didn't trust them. He thought that it was all coming on top and got himself a shooter.

Meanwhile, Hill and Spot changed their tactics by getting in touch with Tommy's old trusted pal Dave Barry from Paddington, a very well-known face from a family with influence. A meeting was arranged. Moisha Blueball and Spot picked up Barry and Tommy in an Austin 1100. They drove to an area near Mornington Crescent. At all times, Dave Barry was under the impression that it was to be a fair fight. After the car came to a standstill, Spot jumped out and opened the door for Tommy. As Tommy alighted, Spot smashed an iron bar onto his head, knocking him to the ground. At the same time, the back doors of an old ambulance parked nearby burst open and six tooled-up heavies jumped out. They performed a deadly sabre dance on Tommy. After they had finished, he was in a sorry state and close to death. He was rushed to hospital, which is where I now found him. Amazingly, he walked out of the ward a few days later, still covered in bandages, having recuperated in record time.

We all went back to the old routine for a few weeks. Tommy was biding his time. One night, Tommy and I went to Barney Fellow's restaurant in Aldgate. Guess who was in there when we walked in? Yes, Moisha Blueball with a couple of brasses. If we'd have been the grim reaper and the devil incarnate themselves, he couldn't have looked more terrified. He turned as pale as a ghost. I lurched forward, to give him a good hiding, but Tommy grabbed my arm and whispered in my ear, 'Now's not the time or the place.' We sat down at the next table and eyeballed him instead. Our constant stares were burning through him. He couldn't eat a scrap of food or talk even. He was suffering more than if he had been taking a physical beating and eventually slunk out in a manner that suggested his bowels had malfunctioned.

By that time, Spot and Hill had fallen out. Hill was now king of the underworld, and Spot was a broken man. Hill promised Tommy a spieler and money to bring the current feud to an end, but Tommy declined the offer and waited to make his move. Other people might have thought that that was a sign of weakness, but Hill knew that Tommy was an extremely dangerous enemy.

Johnny Carter, a very serious villain, athough not as bright as Hill, thought he could take liberties with Tommy. Thinking Tommy was out for the count like a wounded animal, he started to brag to all and sundry that he was going to finish him off. To be fair, Carter had a massive reputation and plenty of people feared him. He'd had rows with 'Mad' Frankie Fraser and his in-laws, the Brindles, and had often dished out violence with vicious intent. It was also known that he was not to be trusted, as he would use underhand methods. He rarely smiled and never laughed. He was a man of few friends, a lone wolf who didn't seem to fear any man or gang.

Word got back to Tommy that Carter had been slagging him off in Theo's. Tommy told me that he wouldn't waste his time looking for Carter and left a note at Theo's stating where he would be that week if Carter wanted to face him. Tommy left Theo's, but I was itching for a fight. I'd had enough of all this diplomatic bullshit. I asked Theo for the note back. I rewrote it as follows: 'Dear John, you are nothing but a woman beater, and you've got no bollocks. I'm looking for you.' I later told Tommy the SP (starting price; to give somebody the lowdown), as I thought it would liven up the proceedings.

Early the next evening, Theo gave Carter the note. He was now looking for me as well. I said to Tommy, 'Let's sort the toerag out.' Tommy agreed but had meetings that night and the following day with some Maltese guys.

The next day, I was gagging to 'Get Carter'. Terry Kenny and I went to Woolworth's and bought two hatchets. We then travelled all over Elephant and Castle, which was Carter's manor, telling everyone who would listen that we wanted a serious word in his ear. Nobody seemed to know where he was. We searched all week to no avail. Eventually, Terry said, 'Fuck this, Norm. Let's have a night off.' So we left the tools in Tommy's flat and went to The Grantchester Hotel on Bayswater Road. More than a few beers were sunk, and after a long night we caught a taxi back to the Leinster Gardens flat. Half a mile from home, Terry shouted excitedly, 'That's Carter there on the corner.' I looked round to see a guy standing with his hands in his pockets with a large hat masking his face.

'Are you sure, Terry?' I asked.

'That's fucking Carter,' he replied.

'Pull over and don't move a fucking yard,' I ordered the taxi driver. With that I leaped out and ran over to him.

'You're only a boy. Fuck off or I'll cut you to pieces,' Carter warned me. I knew he would be carrying a blade, but before he could use it I had butted him twice and was on top of him. However, he managed to pull a knife from his coat and tried to stab me. Terry who had now arrived, tried to kick it out of his hand, and I eventually managed to wrench it away from him. I cut him on the back of his head, chest and ribs and stabbed him several times in the buttocks. He was a dirty fighter and deserved to have the tables turned on him. In the meantime, Terry was sticking the boot in. The trouble was that in his drunken state he was kicking me more than Carter.

It was all over in a couple of minutes. Lights came on in the adjacent buildings, and local women began to scream and shout.

Terry noticed two policemen running down the road, so we dived back into the taxi and got out a street before Tommy's flat. It must have taught Carter a lesson, as he never came back for me.

The next morning, I looked at my side and chest in the mirror. Thanks to my mate, I was bruised all over. Terry had a strange sense of humour – he thought it was hilarious.

In the meantime, Tommy had been talking to Mickey Duff the boxing promoter. 'I've got a boy who can really bang, Mickey,' Tommy said. 'He's turned pro.'

'Great,' Mickey replied. 'Bring him down so I can have a look at him. I'll find him a suitable opponent for sparring.' Tommy took me to Pop Kearn's gym in Warren Street, a famous boxing haunt, and introduced me to Mickey. 'Go into the changing room, son,' he said to me. 'There's some kit in there for you. I'd like you to spar with one of my boys.'

I climbed into the ring. In the opposite corner was Al Wilburn, a stunning prospect and contender for a title. There was no bell or referee. Mickey Duff just said, 'Off you go, boys.'

My opponent's left hand was like a cobra. I took numerous jabs to the face and soon realised I could never outbox him. I changed my tactics and surged forward, throwing as many punches as possible to knock him off his stride and make the fight less one-sided. After calling time on the first round, Mickey Duff came to my corner and said, 'Box him, box him. No rushing in and don't get wild.'

I said, 'I'll fight the way I want to.'

The second round started with more of the same. Wilburn was jabbing me to death, so I decided to rough him up. I walked through the jab and got in close and personal. Mickey Duff called a stop to proceedings. 'I've seen enough,' he cried. I implored him to let me have another round, even though I knew the other bloke was a superior boxer. It had got to the stage that I wanted to nail him with a good shot. 'No, that's it. You've got to learn to control your temper.' I told him to fuck off and went to get changed.

Tommy Smithson was laughing uproariously. 'What d'you think, Mickey?' he asked.

'No, Tommy,' Duff replied. 'He's too bad-tempered for the pro game. I wouldn't be able to control him.' Tommy insisted that I was only young and could be trained, but Duff was having none of it.

I wouldn't be teaming up with Mickey Duff's boxing machine any time in the near future!

Since I'd been with Tommy Smithson, he'd persuaded me to make up with Mad Ronnie Fryer, the guy with whom I'd had the altercation whilst I was on the run from the army. We were now on good terms, so I was a bit shocked when one night he walked into Theo's with a split lip and his arm in a sling. 'Jesus, Ronnie. What's happened to you?' I asked.

Ronnie enlightened me: 'I've just been up the Edgware Road and had a row with Bobby Ramsey.' He also told me that the sling was the result of an incident the week before when somebody had tried to glass him in the face and he had instinctively raised his right arm to protect himself – as a result, his arm and hand had been badly cut.

'So I take it Ramsey smacked you one whilst you were handicapped?' I asked. Ronnie nodded and stated that Ramsey wouldn't have tried it on otherwise, and in the circumstances would I make one with him, meaning would I help him tackle Ramsey. I said, 'You're injured. You won't be much help with your arm in that state. I'll sort it out.'

I got up and hailed a cab. I couldn't resist helping friends who'd had liberties taken, and I'd harboured a dislike for Ramsey from the first moment I'd met him. Ramsey – a wide-shouldered ex-boxer with a flat nose – was a minder for Billy Hill and was another one who was very handy indeed. Arriving at the all nighter where Ramsey was drinking, I walked in and ascended the stairs to the restaurant where he was entertaining some ladies of dubious virtue. He spotted me before I could reach his table. I shouted, 'Try me. I've got two arms.'

'Come outside, boy,' he replied. 'I'll teach you a lesson.' I followed him to the restaurant door. He opened it for me and in a split second swivelled round and butted me straight in the mouth. I was groggy for a moment but instinctively pulled him through into the narrow passageway landing, which restricted our movement. A lot of close-range punches were landed until I got a good grip on his trouser belt and tried to lift him over the banisters and throw him down the stairs. If he'd gone over, it would have half-killed him, but he was hanging on for dear life with one arm around the back of my neck.

'You're a game kid,' he was screaming. 'Don't let other people use you.' I took it as a compliment, even though he just wanted me to haul him back onto the landing.

We were face to face, and I could clearly see all the red capillaries in his nose – they looked like tributaries of the Amazon. His eyes were crazed with fear, and I could smell his boozy breath. Despite his imploring, I decided he was still going over. Luckily for him, Mad Ronnie had phoned Tommy Smithson and told him I'd gone looking for Ramsey. At that moment, Tommy arrived and, with the help of two waiters, pulled me off Ramsey. We were shouting insults at each other while Tommy tried to be the peacemaker. I wanted to carry it on, but Ramsey, still screaming threats, left with the two frightened women.

Tommy quipped, 'You do like picking on the top boys.' My answer was unrepeatable. We caught a cab back to Theo's. It wasn't the last I'd see of Ramsey. He'd turn up a few years later, like the bad penny that he was.

It was during that period of my life that trouble was rearing its head most weeks. As for most young men, fear was in another dimension to me. A short time after my spat with Ramsey, I was involved in a more serious incident. The guy involved was a stranger to me, but he turned out to be a local tough guy named Leo Carney. I'd gone to a West End café for a nice quiet drink with a lady friend when in marched Carney dressed in a winter overcoat. He started ranting and raving at another young lady at the bar. I was going to intervene when out of the blue he punched her to the floor. As far as I was concerned, that was totally out of order, so I jumped up and chinned him, bouncing him against the wall. There weren't many people in the café, but they managed to get between us, and Carney, now recovered, suggested carrying on the argument downstairs in the basement, as it was snowing outside. I gave my lady friend money for a cab and arranged to see her later on.

Carney beckoned me down into the basement, but not before I had told all of the people in the café, 'Do not follow us down. Let us do what we've got to do.'

Apart from a few tables and chairs, the basement was empty, and it took me a few seconds to accustom myself to the lighting, which revealed Carney standing in front of me with a knife in his hand. I saw red – he was another one who was brave with a blade. I hit him with a lightning right, which knocked him backwards, and as he hit the wall I grabbed his right arm, at the same time rapidly butting him twice in the face and also managing to wrench the knife from his grip. He responded by throwing a limp-looking left swinger and overbalanced. I was not happy that he thought he could cut me up and turned the tables on him by puncturing his sides and buttocks with his own knife. He collapsed to the floor, his face cut up as a result of my butts and punches. There was blood seeping through his clothes – he was in a sorry state. I was covered in splatters of his blood, and although I had a few superficial injuries, Carney had come off very much second best.

I got off home, where I cleaned myself up. Tommy came over a couple of hours later and said, 'I've heard about your fight with Carney. He's in intensive care, you know. It could be bad. He's lost a lot of blood.' Tommy told me to stay put and he'd see what more he could find out. He managed to establish that Carney had lost a dangerous amount of blood. In the end, he stayed in intensive care for two weeks, hanging to life by a thread.

In the meantime, the Old Bill were looking for me all over London for attempted murder, but I was lying low, safe in the knowledge that only Tommy Smithson and Terry Kenny knew where I was. Thankfully, Carney pulled through, but the police still wanted to nail me on a serious assault charge. So, when he came out of hospital on crutches a month later, Tommy met him and suggested that he meet with me. I knew Carney had been interviewed by the West End police whilst in hospital, and I wanted to know if he had made a statement, and if so, what had been said.

Tommy brought Carney over to the pad, and he hobbled in on his crutches. I asked him what he had told the police. It transpired that he had informed them that he didn't know who his attacker was, but the police had put up the name Scouse Norman to him. Carney had replied, 'The name doesn't mean anything to me.' The police wouldn't let it go and tried to coerce him into dropping my name into the hat. He refused again, and the police suggested that he was scared to tell the truth. I decided that the only thing I could do in the situation was to hand myself in and be arrested in Carney's company. So, we caught a taxi to the West End, where, having walked only twenty yards, four CID officers pounced on me. 'Norman Johnson, we are arresting you for the attempted murder of Leo Carney.'

'Don't talk silly,' I replied. 'He's standing right there. He's a pal of mine.' As I was being dragged away along the pavement, I shouted to Carney, 'Tell them I didn't fucking stab you.' Carney, worryingly, remained silent. Had I been set up?

I was taken into the police station and thrown into a cell for a few hours. I thought it was all coming on top. A uniformed copper then opened my cell door. 'Johnson, the governor wants a word with you.'

I was taken to an office, where the police commissioner who ran the West End was standing behind his desk. He said, 'You fucking bastard, Johnson. I know you've done this, but Carney won't implicate you. I can't have any more of this going off on my patch. If I catch you carrying so much as a nail file, I'll put you away for a very long time. Now fuck off out of my sight.' Without Carney's statement, there was no evidence, and, reluctantly, they had to let me go. I was still on the side of the angels.

It was like I was wearing a four-leaf clover. I knew I'd been extremely lucky, so I tried to keep on the straight and narrow. However, an incident occurred about a month after the Carney confrontation. I escorted a young lady named Selina to Theo's for a meal. We were having a pleasant evening, drinking and chatting, when Selina excused herself to go to the ladies. Two Maltese gentlemen were seated by the entrance. As she passed their table, one of them grabbed her arm and wouldn't let go. She was struggling to free herself and screamed over to me for help. I ran across and hit the groping Maltese with a haymaker that came from the next county. I then proceeded to chin the other one, who had risen to his feet, with an uppercut. They were both down on the floor, and I carried on punching them until I was pulled off.

Theo's quickly cleared of customers, and as if by magic filled up again with the boys in blue – somebody must have alerted them. I was arrested and taken down to my second home, West End central, where I had a stroke of luck: the detective sergeant was in Tommy Smithson's pocket. George Webb always let Tommy know when one of his spielers was going to be raided, and the bent copper took charge of my problem, as he was the only CID officer in the station at that time. He told me that he had alerted Tommy, who was on his way down, but I would have to stay the night, as it was now past two in the morning.

Tommy arrived and said, 'Not again. Why can't you keep your hands in your pockets? Luckily, I don't think we've got too much of a problem.' In court the next morning, George Webb gave a favourable account, and my brief said that I'd been out with female company to the theatre and that we were having a quiet meal afterwards. Selina had been accosted and I had rushed over to help, at which point I had been assaulted. I'd had no option but to defend myself. George Webb also asserted that this was his understanding of the matter. My brief applied for bail, but surprisingly the magistrate refused and put me on remand, as he wanted to hear the Maltese guys' versions of events. I appeared before the magistrates for three weeks running with no sign of them.

The magistrate eventually lost patience and demanded that the police find the two men, who were traced to Manchester, but they would not return to London for any amount of money in the world. Then, in the fourth week, the magistrate received a letter from the absent witnesses. George Webb related the crux of it to me:

> Dear Sir,
> We are two Maltese waiters working in London. We cannot continue in our current work, as we are still in shock. We suffered multiple injuries and were badly beaten and scarred. The man in front of you is a vicious nasty person, and we are very scared, so we would like to see him in prison for a long time.

The magistrate immediately announced, 'Case dismissed. Letters are irrelevant.' I again walked out of the court, acquitted by the law.

As a rule, on weekdays Jack the Lads, small-time felons, bully boys, con men and even top villains stayed in their own manor, but Fridays and Saturdays were a different matter and hordes would descend on the West End for fun and frivolity. A lot of these characters accepted that violence would often rear its ugly head and were prepared for such an eventuality. One weekend night, a mob came down six-handed from the Elephant and Castle. They came to sink a few jars and enjoy the West End atmosphere but weren't averse to putting themselves about if trouble arose. They turned up at Theo's and were quite rowdy. Terry Kenny was drinking at the bar. He didn't suffer fools gladly and for some reason got involved in an argument with them. When he knocked one over, the rest retaliated with fists, boots, bottles and chairs, injuring Terry badly enough for him to be hospitalised.

When I visited him in hospital, he told me, 'They were like a pack of animals, and I didn't recognise any of them.' I told him not to worry. This wouldn't be forgotten and our turn would come.

The chance came sooner than I had anticipated, as two weeks later four geezers walked in to Theo's on a Saturday night. The barman whispered in my ear, 'That's four of the guys who did Terry over.'

I got up and approached them. 'Outside. I want the best one of you four.'

The biggest one stood up and replied, 'I'll fucking have you.'

I then told them, 'No police involved, whatever happens.'

We all went outside, and the big lump lunged towards me, but he ran onto my fist, which connected with his chin, and he went down like a sack of potatoes. The other three took exception to this and pulled out a crowbar and two coshes. The crowbar caught me a pearler on the head, cracking open my skull and covering me in a fountain of blood. For a few seconds, I was out of it. After regaining my senses, I shouted, 'So you want to play games, do you? Stay there. I'm going to fetch a tool.' I ran over the road to Tommy's spieler, where a card game was in progress. As I passed the table, one of the players fainted from the sight of the blood. I went into the back room and grabbed a hatchet. Returning to the street, I found that the mob from the Elephant had gone.

I didn't go to the hospital for stitches but got patched up locally and returned to Theo's. Terry was released from hospital a few days later, and one of his mates told us that the unknown gang were regulars at The Lyceum Ballroom. They were now on borrowed time. I acquired a gun, and Terry got suitably tooled up for our ballroom visits. Night after night, we looked down from the Lyceum's balcony onto the dance floor and bar but could not spot any of them. They shouldn't have been hard to find, as one was ginger and another was a tall bald guy. However, it turned out that one of them had clocked me and Terry early doors, and they had been too scared or too sensible to stick around. At least they now knew that we were looking for them.

Days later, I was in the billiard hall in Windmill Street when a guy came running in and exclaimed, 'Scouse, there's a mob looking for you down at Theo's.' I turned to Alec, the billiard hall manager, and asked what tools he had, whereupon he produced a large butcher's knife accompanied by some choice words: 'Fuck me, Norman. You must be off your fucking head.' I grinned and went off to face the mob.

I walked down the middle of the road, so that no one could jump me from a doorway. The shout went up – 'There he is' – and a score of men closed in on me from the front. There were a few brasses about, and one of them rushed off to fetch Tommy. I screamed, 'Come on then. Who's got the bottle for a row?' That stopped them in their tracks, and while they were looking at each other Tommy burst out of the spieler to join me.

'Which one have you got the hump with?' he shouted. I pointed to the guy who'd hit me with the crowbar, who suddenly didn't look so brave. Another one of them tried to sneak around the back of us, but I went for him, and he backed off.

Somebody in the crowd then shouted, 'If one of us gets hurt, we all get hurt.'

Tommy countered, 'You've come down team handed, just for one man.' It transpired that they didn't want to come down in ones or twos and be picked off.

I noticed a guy called Tony Reuter, so called 'King of the Teds', in the mob. It was obvious that the Elephant crew had been calling in many favours. I must have got under their skins. We were determined to stand our ground and not run from these bullies, and we were not deterred by their superior numbers. They could see that we were up for a ruck, and none of them seemed to have the bottle to make the first move. They looked extremely sheepish, and when one of the ringleaders cursed and turned on his heel, prompting a mass exodus, I said to Tommy, 'Come on. I'll buy you a drink.' Little did I know that those pints would be some of the last drinks we would have together.

6

•••••••

Unlucky Seven

I was beginning to sense that Tommy Smithson was having misgivings about taking me under his wing. To be fair, I had brought a certain amount of aggravation and police activity onto his manor, but I had no idea that I was such a headache to him. Looking back, he had obviously decided a break from each other was the only solution. The way he went about it was both unbelievable and unnecessary.

I had just moved into my new London flat, which must have been a relief to Tommy. Only he and Terry Kenny knew my address. One night in Theo's, Tommy told me that he had some blinding information regarding a top jeweller and his wife. The plan was to get into their north London home, tie them up and extract the jewellery-shop keys. While the shop was being emptied, one raider would stay behind with the couple. That was the plan; the reality was somewhat different.

Tommy had arranged for three of his men to go to the house: two to extract the keys and one to act as a lookout. Me and Tommy were waiting in a car near to the front door. Minutes after the men had burst in, I heard screaming, so I jumped out of the car and ran inside. The lights had been smashed, and the room was in darkness. A man and woman were laying face down on the floor being threatened. Tommy's two men were shouting and screaming, 'Where's the keys?'

I pushed my way through and said, 'Keep the fucking noise down.' One of Tommy's guys was a Pole and took exception to the way I'd spoken to him, shoving me against the wall. I lost my temper and went for him, and he retaliated. I broke his nose in the melee, covering us both in blood. I told his mate to get him out of the house, and they disappeared with the lookout. I jumped back into Tommy's car and shouted, 'Drive. That's been a right fuck-up.'

Tommy half apologised and drove me back to my new flat. 'Get cleaned up and get rid of those bloodied clothes,' he said. 'I'll see you later at Theo's.'

Within 30 minutes, half of London's Metropolitan Police force had smashed through my front door. A plain-clothes detective pushed a badge in my face and said, 'Norman Johnson, you are under arrest for attempted robbery.'

I swore under my breath. 'Bloody Tommy Smithson.'

They took me to old Scotland Yard in Whitehall, where I was put in a cell for an hour. Later, I was shown to an office by three CID officers – my bloodied clothes were on the table. I was bang to rights. I was put on remand and spent nine months in my own cell at Brixton, where I had plenty of time to ponder my relationship with Tommy Smithson. Like I said, there were only two people who knew my address, Smithson and Terry Kenny, and I could trust Kenny with my life.

After I had been in Brixton for a month, Albert Dimes, the well-known gangster, found himself banged away for cutting up Jack Spot in a row. I knew Albert quite well and had always liked him. Albert also knew Tommy Smithson, so when I got the chance to walk round the exercise yard with him I told him, 'If you see Smithson before me, tell him I'm definitely going to hurt him.'

He replied, 'That won't be a problem, Scouse.'

Not a lot happened on remand. It was the same dreary routine every day. We slopped out in the morning, had just one hour of exercise a day and ate three meals, which were hardly cordon bleu fare. The seconds, minutes and hours dragged. And, surprise, surprise, Tommy never visited or sent me any correspondence, which only reinforced my suspicions that he had set me up.

The nine months culminated in a guest appearance at Chelmsford Crown Court, where I was represented by Legal Aid and pleaded guilty. In the meantime, the police hadn't arrested anyone else in connection with the robbery. The man in the street might have thought that I would implicate Tommy Smithson in the first ten seconds of an interview, but I never grassed on anybody in my life and preferred to do the time, sorting out the situation later in my own way. The Old Bill had been trying to nail me for some time, and this was their chance. One man after another went into the witness box and stated that I had not cooperated at all and would not reveal the names of any of my accomplices.

At sentencing time, I was expecting to get about three years, which wouldn't have been too bad, as I had already served nine months on remand. With remission, I'd be out sooner rather than later. However, the right honourable judge didn't agree with my calculations. By his way of thinking, my silence and misguided loyalty were perverting the course of justice, and if I wanted to act the strong silent type, he'd give me plenty of time to practise. He announced, 'You will go to prison for seven years. Take him down.'

I was shattered, I was only 22 years old, and it was a stiff sentence by anyone's standards. Even the prison officers were shocked at its severity. One of them muttered, 'He had it in for you, son.'

I nodded. 'I'll just have to grin and bear it.'

I was taken straight to Wandsworth Prison and put in a single cell. However, I was pleasantly surprised when I went on exercise for the first time and found that I knew half the inmates in there. It was like being home from home, although the conditions were only just habitable.

I arrived as winter was approaching, and for three months lived in a cell that was at the end of a block, exposed to all the elements. I didn't usually wear a tie, but in the circumstances putting one on helped to keep the heat in. I even took the cork cover off the table in my cell and put it on my bed every night. Consequently, I asked the landing screw if I could swap cells, and he told me that I could only if someone wanted to swap with me. So, I hatched a plan and put it into action the next day in the workshop.

I sat next to a guy called Lenny Cullen, sewing mail bags. 'Lenny, where's your cell?' I quizzed him.

'Down the centre,' he replied.

'What's it like?'

'Fine, but it's a little bit cold.'

'Mine's lovely. I'm like toast in mine. There's no draughts, and I can't sleep in the heat.' I then told him that I wouldn't mind being down the middle near to a couple of my mates. He was up for a swap. I told him to grab his gear and his name card out of the door to his cell. He could then run up to mine, and I could run down to his. Result or what?

The next morning, he came into the workshop and shouted, 'You cunt. It's fucking freezing.' The whole workshop burst into laughter. He refused to return to the cell under any circumstances, and I think he eventually found one to his liking. At least it wouldn't have been as cold as the fridge-like cell at the end of the block.

Just as I was settling into a routine, the authorities decided to move me. The chief screw at Wandsworth was a guy from Merseyside, His name escapes me, but he was a very fair and decent man. He knew that there were only really two choices for a sentence of seven years: Dartmoor or Parkhurst. He said, 'Scouse, I think you're too young for those nicks. I'll try and get you across the city to Wormwood Scrubs. I'm not promising anything, but I'll do my best.'

He must have had some pull, because I found myself transferred to the Scrubs. Again, I was placed in a single cell. It wasn't exactly the Ritz, and my bed was a wooden board with a thin, coarse mattress, two blankets and a sheet. There seemed to be as many faces in the Scrubs as there were in Wandsworth, so I settled in quickly, and I was given a job in the tailor shop, which wasn't the worst labour in the prison. In my cell, there was a high window, which I could see through if I stood on the wash basin, so I had a clear view of the nurses' block at the back of the hospital nearby. The nurses weren't shy or slow at displaying their attributes when getting changed or having a bath, and although they were a fair distance away I could just about see enough to make it worth the effort. In my imagination, they were probably doing a lot more than they actually were.

Bobby Warren, a well-known and popular face in London, was in the next cell to me. He was regularly visited by Albert Dimes, whose case had been thrown out. Albert told Bobby to relay to me that he had informed Tommy Smithson of my intention to sort him out. It gave me great satisfaction to know that Smithson was aware of my displeasure and would always need to be looking over his shoulder on my release.

However, by a strange stroke of fate, I was beaten to the punch. One day, the landing screw showed Bobby Warren a national newspaper. The front-page headline read 'London Gangster Shot Dead'. It was the demise of Tommy Smithson. The screw said to Bobby, 'Have you seen this about your mate?'

Bobby replied, 'I knew Tommy a bit, but he was a big friend of Scouse next door. Show it to him.'

The screw opened my cell door and threw the newspaper on the table, saying, 'Your mate's on the front page.' I read the article and was gutted that someone had got to him first. However, I was also glad that he was dead, as I couldn't forgive him for his involvement in my seven-stretch.

It turned out that Tommy had been involved in an argument over money with three Maltese guys that had turned nasty. As a result, he'd been shot in a Paddington premises by a guy called Phillip Alou. Afterwards, Tommy had staggered out into the street and collapsed in the gutter. Looking up at passers-by, he'd said, 'Good morning. I'm dying.' Those famous last words have gone down in gangster history. Although Tommy had helped me a lot when I first came to London, he had lost my friendship by informing the police of my whereabouts after the robbery.

The governor at the Scrubs was a very religious disciplinarian who encouraged the inmates to turn to God, and going to church on a Sunday morning was compulsory. I wasn't too bothered on my first visit, as it at least got me out of my cell. However, after about an hour I was cheesed off listening to the boring sermon and declined to sing the hymns. I vowed never to go again. The following Sunday, everybody left their cells to go to church except me. I was sitting on my bed when a screw popped his head round the door. 'Come on, Jonno. You've got to go to chapel.'

'I'm not going.'

'You've got to.' I reiterated what I'd first said, and he replied, 'If you don't go, you'll be put on a charge.'

I said, 'Do what you have to,' and lay down on the bed.

Early the next morning, I was taken in front of the governor. 'I'm disappointed in you, Johnson. You will go to church.'

'I won't go.'

His face turned scarlet. 'Right, seven days' loss of privileges and loss of remission. Take him out.'

The next Sunday went much the same way: no show for church,

up before the governor, and a loss of remission and privileges. This went on for eight weeks consecutively. I got to know the governor well on my visits. He was a religious zealot, the kind of man who could bore for England. He reminded me of the guy who relates his best dart finishes, or the bloke who knows all the numbers and times of the buses. We've all met them, but I was a captive audience while I was in the Scrubs. I must have got to the governor, though, as he seemed to run out of patience and decided to take a different tack. The following Sunday morning, the prison padre walked into my cell and started to speak. I cut him short. 'Get out of my cell. I've lost two months' remission. I'll lose two years if I have to. I'm not going to your church.' The padre turned on his heel and left. He returned an hour later with a form, indicating where to sign. I was now an atheist. The padre told me I could return to his flock at any time. I had lost eight rounds, but in my own mind I had beaten the authorities on a knockout.

The nurses were still keeping us entertained by carrying on their nightly striptease, and I reckon most of our block were turning into voyeurs, craning their necks to watch the free burlesque show. Bobby Warren took it a stage further by persuading Albert Dimes to smuggle in a small pair of binoculars, and on exercise one Monday he filled me in about the magic lenses. He said, 'We'll have these alternately, Scouse. You have them tonight, I'll have them tomorrow and so on.' I thought it was a magnificent gesture on Mr Warren's part to give me first crack with them.

That night, I birdy watched for about two hours – not even a glimpse of ankle. I smelled a rat. Bobby had realised that bath nights were Tuesdays and Thursdays in the nurses' quarters. I thought, 'You crafty bastard. No wonder I've got them tonight.' Operation Night Nurse had failed.

I remedied the situation by pulling the binoculars apart to create two mini-telescopes, and the next morning I passed one to a gobsmacked Bobby, saying, 'I can't believe it. I've sat on the binoculars. We might as well have one each.' Bobby's reaction wasn't, 'Never mind, dear fellow, accidents happen,' but from then on we both looked forward to Tuesday and Thursday nights. Thank God for the national health – it certainly made us feel better. The only drawback was that on Wednesday and Friday mornings we'd each come out of the cell with one eye closed and the other red and squinting.

I got into a few more minor scrapes, but after three years, ten months I was offered a place on a new hostel scheme, where I was joined by other well-known faces, Bobby Warren, ex-boxer Billy Ambrose, Ronnie Malloy, Billy White and about ten others. Just inside the front gate of the prison, there was a hostel building, where we were all given a room. The building was unlocked, and there was no supervision by the screws. It was a lot more civilised, and we wore our own clothes. Most of the men left the prison at seven in the morning to go to their allocated jobs. The faces all had friends outside who would vouch for them on the matter of employment. Dave Barry, my friend from Paddington, notified the authorities that I was working for him as a painter and decorator. As if! There was never going to be a paintbrush in my hand unless it resembled a pint glass!

I was more interested in other forms of rehabilitation. On week days, we all had to return by 10 p.m. at the latest, and at weekends we were off from Friday evening until 10 p.m. on Sunday night. The faces were supposed to be going to their jobs in the morning just as the screws were clocking on, but we all wore top-quality clothes and shoes, and they knew that we weren't doing manual labour, especially when we jumped into top-of-the-range motors outside the gates. They really had the hump knowing we were going on the razz, and we would rub it in as much as we could. For instance, Bobby Ramsey would pass me a large wad of notes in front of them all and say, 'Here you are, Scouse. That's the 100 quid I owe you.'

During the scheme, I frequented a few clubs, and if the owners were having any trouble, they would offer me a stake in the club in return for helping them out. Billy White and Ronnie Malloy were in the car trade, Billy Ambrose had his fingers in a few pies and Bobby Warren went to Soho to work with Albert Dimes. On my first Friday night off, I went to an all-night drinker on the Portobello Road, run by my good friend Billy Manning. He was doing well, and the club was heaving. I hadn't touched any grog whilst in prison, so it was pleasant to experience alcohol again. I said to Billy, 'You've got it sussed here.'

'Yeah, but I'm having a lot of aggravation and trouble with some

BLACK EYES AND BLUE BLOOD

of the locals,' he replied. 'It's getting out of hand. Would you mind coming down at weekends, and I'll put you up as a partner.'

I accepted Billy's offer, and he brought me up to speed with what had been happening. We hadn't been talking for more than 20 minutes when a petite blonde at the bar started screaming. Her venom seemed to be directed towards three guys to her right. It transpired that they were men about town, Terry Donnelly, Selwyn Cooney and one Billy Gardener (who was later arrested for the infamous 'Mr Smith's' incident). Blondie was shouting, 'I'll bring my old man down.'

Billy turned to me and said, 'Oh no, we don't need that. She's going out with Ronnie Nash.' Ronnie was one of six brothers in an up-and-coming firm from Islington. Billy was shitting bricks. I'd never met the Nashes but had heard accounts of them in prison.

I told Billy not to worry and went over to calm her down. 'Come over here, babe. Have a drink and relax.' I took her by the hand and sat her down next to Bill. I asked her if she was all right and she nodded. I then said, 'You don't need Ronnie, babe.'

The altercation had occurred as a result of Selwyn Cooney bumping her car and refusing to pay up. I went to the bar to get a round of drinks in, and while I was waiting to be served I overheard Cooney say, 'He doesn't fucking worry me!' I wouldn't have normally let that go, but this time I gave him the benefit of the doubt. I turned to walk past them with the tray of drinks when Cooney grabbed my arm and yanked me round, causing the drinks to spill over. 'Are you with the Nashes?' he asked. I gave him my answer with a head-butt straight in his face. The impact knocked him back into the wall. He was half gone, but I jumped in and butted him again, just for good measure.

I spun round and addressed the other two, 'D'youse want it as well?' They didn't reply, so I took their silence as a no!

Cooney had now unsteadily risen to his feet and was shouting repeatedly, 'Who is he? Who is he?'

I thought, 'He does ask some stupid questions,' and chinned him with a beauty. He was down and out.

At that moment, four faces entered the club: one of the Nash brothers, Joey Pyle and two others. One of them said, 'We'll give it to him now.' He was talking about Cooney.

I intervened. 'No you won't. If you've got an argument, have it another time. Nobody else is touching him tonight.' They shouted a few threats at the prostrate Cooney and left. I hadn't saved Cooney for kindness; I wasn't going to allow a gang to attack a defenceless man.

It had been an eventful night. Reverberations were sure to follow. On the Sunday afternoon, I was having dinner at my brother Len's flat in Maida Vale when the phone rang. It was Dave Barry, who told me that he'd just taken a call from the *Sunday People*'s crime reporter, Tom Bryant. Apparently, the Old Bill were looking for me for the murder of Selwyn Cooney. I told Dave that it was all bollocks and asked him to find out as much as he could. He came back to me a couple of hours later, saying that Cooney had been shot in The Pen Club late on Saturday night by Jimmy Nash, accompanied by Joey Pyle and Johnny Read.

I decided it was time to go back to the hostel, where I was confronted by the chief officer at the main gates. He told me that there were two officers from Scotland Yard waiting to talk to me. As I sat down in a side room, one of the detectives opened up with, 'We've heard about your row with Cooney. We believe you got Jimmy Nash to shoot him.'

'You're going daft,' I replied. 'I've been locked up for nearly four years.'

'Your forehead's in a mess.'

'It would be. I butted him twice in the face on Friday night.'

There were a few more inane questions before the detectives left, stating that they had more enquiries to make. The chief officer then said, 'Jonno, you won't be going out again until this is all sorted.' I wasn't sweating, because I knew I hadn't done anything, and the truth did indeed emerge.

Apparently, the three went to The Pen Club, where Selwyn Cooney was drinking. Cooney said, 'Lock that door. I'm going to have these three.' Fists and bottles started flying, and Billy Ambrose, who was my hostel buddy, was wounded in the stomach by a bullet. A lot of people were hurt in the fracas. It was a case of the wrong people being in the wrong place at the wrong time. The upshot of it all was that Selwyn Cooney took one in the nut, killing him instantly. Months later, Jimmy Nash was charged with manslaughter, and after a painstaking trial he received five years. As for my part in the Cooney episode, after a two-week inquiry I was totally absolved of any wrongdoing and returned to the hostel scheme.

7

········

Showdown at the O'Kray Corral

Back on day release, I continued my business affairs. The advantage of being out of prison on a daily basis was that if any of my friends were in trouble, I could help them out. At that time, my good mate Terry Kenny was serving a five-year sentence under appeal at Wandsworth for an altercation with a Paddington club owner named 'Belgian' Johnnie. By coincidence, Reggie Kray was also serving at Her Majesty's pleasure at Wandsworth at that time. I don't know if there was a personality clash, but one day trouble flared up between them in the visiting area whilst Ronnie Kray was there to see Reggie. Terry and Reg were going at it hammer and tongs on their side of the cubicle, trying to knock each other senseless, while Ronnie was trying to get involved by kicking down the glass partition in an attempt to aid his twin brother. The two inmates were eventually separated by the screws and put in chokey (solitary confinement).

A short time after this incident, Terry's wife Dolly got in touch and gave me a visiting order to see him. When I went to see him, we discussed his row with Reggie and debated his appeal. Later on that evening, I returned to the hostel, where there was a message for me to get in contact with Jimmy Nash's older brother Billy. We met the next day in a Paddington club. 'Scouse, could you help with our Jimmy?' Billy asked.

'What can I do?' I replied. Billy Nash was going to see his brother's brief and set up a meeting, as Jimmy was now on remand after the recent murder of Selwyn Cooney. The following Friday, Billy came back to me, 'Could you meet me and Jimmy's brief tonight at The Double R Club?' I told him I would.

The Double R Club was owned by the Krays, and because of Terry and Reggie's row, being careful was the order of the day. I got a shooter from another club owner by the name of Ginger Randall. If there was going to be any monkey business, I wanted to be prepared, as the Krays were aware that I was Terry's best friend. That night, I went to the club. Benny Stewart was on the door. The Scottish hard man was a well-known face associated with the twins and several others. Benny said, 'Cor, Scouse. You've got some balls.' I gave him a friendly laugh and walked past.

Billy Nash came over and apologised profusely. 'I'm sorry to drag you down here, Scouse, but the brief's just phoned. He can't make it.'

I shrugged and said, 'Let's have a drink.'

Ten minutes later, Ronnie Kray came over. 'I'm glad to see you're out and about, Scouse. Is there anything I can do for you?' He then tried to slip me a couple of hundred quid.

'No, Ron. I'm all right for money. Thanks anyway.'

The three of us had a few drinks for about an hour; the incident with Terry Kenny was never mentioned, and the night passed peacefully. Before I left, Billy Nash said, 'I'll see the brief again on Monday, and I'll let you know what's happening.' He contacted me on the Monday morning. 'Scouse, with your record, the brief didn't think it wise for you to be a defence witness.'

'OK. You know where to find me if you want me.'

Brothers Ray and Brian Mills, two old prison buddies of mine, had just been released and invited me down for a drink at The Rainbow Club in Balham Crescent, Notting Hill Gate. We were catching up on old times when we were joined at the table by one of the club's owners. He was a real flash bastard and was starting to rub me up the wrong way. He went past the point of no return when he insulted me with a cheap shot, so I butted him and gave him a good hiding. We left the club and continued drinking elsewhere.

The next morning, Ray Mills came down to the hostel gate as I was coming out and told me that the club owners were planning to do me a mischief. He knew where one of the owners lived, so we went straight round to his house. His wife came to the front door and informed us that her husband was not at home. I told her, 'Tell him Scouse Norman's looking for him.'

The following Friday, I walked into The Rainbow Club at opening time. The club's other partner was standing there looking sheepish. 'Where's your cunt of a mate?' I asked.

'He's gone,' he replied. 'Can I talk to you? I'm not involved in this hassle. He's not coming back. You've put the fear of God into him. He was my partner, but he's disappeared now that the word's gone round.' The remaining partner, whose name was Jimmy Thompson, then told me, 'I've already had four heavies trying to muscle in on the action, and I'd appreciate it if you'd be my partner.' I didn't need to be asked twice and accepted his offer.

The club was a nice little earner, and everything was fine at weekends, but I couldn't be there on weekday nights because of the hostel scheme. Jimmy was still getting trouble midweek and was becoming a nervous wreck. He wasn't a fighting man, and it was all getting him down. One weekend, he pulled me aside and offered me a chance to buy him out. I said, 'Would £1,000 cover it?' He nodded enthusiastically. He was delighted and probably would have accepted a tenner. We shook hands, and he disappeared off the scene.

I now had to deal with the small problem of who would run the club on week nights. I only had three months left on the hostel scheme, but in the meantime I needed somebody whom I could trust. I had recently started dating a stunning dark brunette named Kathleen Brown, a beauty queen from Middlesbrough who had travelled down to London to participate in the Miss Great Britain beauty contest. Her other claim to fame was that she had dated legendary footballer Brian Clough. We moved in together, and I thought it would be a good idea to put Kathleen and my youngest sister Sylvia in charge of the bar. I then rounded up a few trusted friends to look after security and deal with any aggro. Within months, I was a free man and also a married one. Kathleen had persuaded me to put a ring on her finger, and we tied the knot at the registry office in Paddington.

However, a few months later I was single again. One night – well, it was early morning to be truthful – I came out of a Paddington gambling club potless after losing £500, which was a very large amount of money in those days, as most people were working for £10 a week. Arriving back at the house at around 8 a.m., I found Kathleen was up and about. 'Make us a cup of tea, babe.'

'We've got no milk,' she replied.

'Why? Haven't you got any money?'

'No.'

I was surprised by this, as I'd been giving her bundles. She'd been going to hairdressers, beauty parlours and all the top stores. 'What's happened to all the cash I've given you?'

'It's all gone.'

I was now losing my temper. 'But I've given you fucking hundreds.'

'It doesn't go far,' she objected. 'Wait. I think there's ten bob in the dining room. I'll go and get some milk.'

I went upstairs for a shave and spruce-up. I felt like shit. The razor blades were on top of the bathroom cabinet, and as I reached up I knocked a steam iron that was lying next to them. While I was shaving, I could have sworn that I saw the iron move ever so slightly, so I stood on the bath to be head high with the cabinet and found that the iron was sitting on a canvas bag. I opened the bag and discovered that it was crammed full of bank notes – over £1,200 in total. I finished my shave, put the money in my pockets and filled two suitcases with my clothes.

As I was walking down the garden path, Kathleen was returning with the milk. She look horrified. 'Where are you going?'

I told her, 'I've found your stash. Don't play me for a fool. Find another mug.' She started shouting and screaming and threw the loose change in my face. I walked on and hailed a cab. She was now out of my life. I soon found another flat off Westbourne Grove in Bayswater and moved in not long after.

One night, I was having a drink down in Frankie Choppin's club in Harrow Road when some of the Kray mob came in, eight-handed. The twins weren't among the crowd, but it included Willie Malone, Willie O'Dare and Benny Stewart. A few of them waved and said, 'All right, Scouse.'

'What are youse lot doing down here?' I asked.

'We've come to have a drink with Terry Kenny.'

I said, 'You'll have a job. He's in Wandsworth nick.' They contradicted me by saying that he'd won his appeal and had secured an early release. They had a few drinks and left. I rushed out. I knew I had to find Terry before they did.

I had a hunch that if he was out he might go to Billy Manning's club in Portobello Road, as I'd told him that I had a stake in it. Sure enough, Terry was there, rotten drunk. The firm would have killed him if they had found him in that state, so I dragged him home and put him to bed.

The next morning, I rang my old mate Joe Ferrugia, who was running a club in Soho. I needed two shooters. Joe did the business and that afternoon I went over to The Cue Club in Page Street, where I met Dave Barry. He told me that Ronnie Kray had rung up asking for me and that he would ring back at four o'clock. I took the call, and Ronnie gave me some bullshit: 'Scouse, I hear Terry's out. Can you two come over for a beer at Vallance Road at around ten o'clock tonight?'

I said, 'We'll be there.' An invitation to the Krays' household was like a Christian being asked over to the Colosseum by the lions.

I needed somebody to ferry us by car to Vallance Road and wait around the corner while we went in. I phoned at least four or five so-called hard men but all seemed to have prior engagements, and the one who said he was coming didn't turn up.

At 9.30 p.m., Terry and I took a cab to the East End and were met at the front door of the Krays' house by Charlie Kray, a real diamond and a completely different kind of person to his younger brothers. He said, 'All right, Scouse. Ron and Reg are in the kitchen.' With that, he shot upstairs, which made me even more wary.

As we were walking through to the kitchen, I said to Terry, 'If it all goes off, you do Reg, and I'll give it to Ron.' We were both wearing raincoats and packing loaded shooters in our right-hand pockets. Terry knew to keep his eyes fixed on Reggie. I would concentrate on Ronnie. We both had our right hands in our pockets.

As we entered, Ronnie Kray greeted us. 'Good to see you, Scouse. And you, Terry.' Reggie was to his side but remained silent. Ronnie offered his hand to shake, and I gave him my left, so the twins could see that we were tooled up. The situation was now on a different footing, and the Krays were at a disadvantage. Ron said, 'It's no good having rows. Only the police win when that happens. If you ever need a hand, we can work together and help each other.'

I knew that was all bollocks but agreed with Ron and said, 'OK. Is that all then? We've got to be elsewhere.' Ron and Reg said goodbye, and we walked over to Whitechapel Road, where we caught a cab home.

What we didn't know at the time was that there were ten heavies all tooled up in their front room who were under instructions to pile out and give it us as soon as they heard it all go off. But the fight never happened; our shooters had ensured that. As they watched us leave, they must have thought, 'What the fuck's going on?' This was confirmed to me the next day by a certain John Francis, who had been in the front room. I had known John for a while, and he had fingers in many pies. He was to have a massive influence on my life later on, but for now the striking red-haired man told me, 'You took a chance coming over there last night. You've got some bottle.' I didn't hold any grudges against John, as I knew he was using the Krays more than they were using him, and he came over as a very shrewd and intelligent guy – a latter-day Machiavelli.

The news of this episode spread over London like wildfire, and even though I wasn't concerned about having a reputation, this incident didn't do me any harm. I kept close to Terry for 24 hours in case of a reprisal, but nothing happened. After that, I began to see less and less of him, as he and his missus moved into a more family-orientated lifestyle. Terry had been a very good mate, and I couldn't blame him for wanting a quieter life. As he faded into suburbia, a new acquaintance would influence me over the next few years.

8

•••••••

Set Up and Sent Down

Rat-a-tat-tat. 'Who the fuck's that at four in the morning?' I went to answer the front door. It didn't sound like a policeman's knock. It turned out to be Niven Craig, whom I'd met while I was coming to the end of my sentence at Wormwood Scrubs. He was currently on the hostel scheme and would sometimes come down with a few mates to The Rainbow Club for a drink at weekends.

Niven's claim to fame was that he was the older brother of Chris Craig, who was involved in the 'Let him have it' murder case with Derek Bentley. They were both on the roof of a confectionery warehouse intent on robbery when they were spotted by a member of the public, who phoned the police. Bentley was quickly apprehended, but Niven's younger brother Chris was letting off rounds from a pistol. When Bentley shouted to him, 'Let him have it, Chris,' Craig fired a shot that hit PC Sidney Miles over the left eye, killing him instantly. It was also reported that after Chris ran out of ammunition, he jumped off the 30-foot-high roof to escape and landed on a greenhouse, breaking his back, but I had it on good authority from Niven that PC Miles's enraged colleagues threw his horrified brother off the roof. In court, Bentley, who had shown no resistance to the police, was sentenced to death, whilst the underage Chris Craig, who had done the shooting, received a prison sentence.

Niven and Chris were brought up in a respectable family – their father was a bank manager from Caterham – but both boys served plenty of time in prison. Niven was just finishing a 12-year stretch for battering a taxi driver to within an inch of his life whilst serving in the forces abroad. The charge was robbery with violence, and he was currently finishing off his sentence in the Scrubs.

'Sorry to wake you up, Scouse, but have you got any electrical wire for a detonator?' Niven said.

'Are you fucking mental?' I asked. 'You're just coming off a 12.'

'No,' he replied. 'There's bundles in this shop safe. I've had the word. Do you want to make one with me?'

I don't know if it was because I wanted to look after him, or if I couldn't resist the buzz of a job, but I got my hat and coat and joined him. I got in the front of the car; his girlfriend and another geezer were in the back. We pulled up at the end of a street, 20 yards away from the shop. As I stood at the back of the car as lookout, Niven and his mate broke in the front door and entered. There was no alarm. I then heard a muffled boom. They had blown the safe. I looked round to see two Old Bill running towards us, but they must have been a good four hundred yards away, so I shouted for Niven to get out, and we sped away at warp-factor six.

'Was it a good amount?' I asked.

'The safe was empty,' he replied.

I went ballistic. 'I must be fucking cracking up, getting involved with you. Drop me off in Paddington. I'm going for a drink. Keep out of my sight for a good while.'

The two beat bobbies got no closer than a hundred yards to us, and while they would have had a good butchers at the car, which was a white VW Beetle, they would have only seen the back of four heads. However, Niven Craig had borrowed the car from a mate, who dropped him right in it when the police came round. As a result, my name was mentioned by one of the three people in the car, which prompted another visit from CID to my flat. The main detective was a certain Nipper Read, who went on to become famous as the man who broke the Krays' hold on London. He buttered me up. 'Norman, can you just help us with some enquiries? It won't take long. Thanks a lot.'

At the police station, Nipper again spoke to me in pleasant tones. 'Norman, something's just cropped up. Er, can you wait ten minutes in a cell? Would that be OK?' I nodded and sat in the cell. The spyhole kept opening every couple of minutes. Unbeknown to me, it was the two beat bobbies who had chased the Beetle down the street. They were going to be on my ID parade!

I was taken out of the cell, and Nipper was still fawning all over me. 'Can you go on an ID parade, Norman, just so we can eliminate you?' I took my place in a line of 12 people. Both of the flatfeet walked along and pointed me straight out. I immediately suspected a set-up. I shouted over to Read, 'You dirty fucking cunt. They've both clocked me in the cell.'

I was then put under lock and key, and Read said to me, 'You're a first-division criminal. You've been around, Norman. The Yard want you put away. Since you've been out and about, there's been a lot of aggravation, and the bottom line is that I want you off my manor.'

I was remanded to Brixton Prison for a nine-month period, which passed uneventfully. What a great start to the swinging '60s. I was 27 and looking at another long one.

The case went to the Crown court at the Inner London Sessions, and I pleaded not guilty to all charges. Niven Craig's girlfriend got a total acquittal, but I felt sorry for the other guy in the dock, as he wasn't even the guy in the back seat that night. I still don't know who the fuck he was. He cried every day, and getting a two-year sentence didn't cheer him up any. As an alibi, I produced two witnesses to say that I'd been in my club that night, but the two beat bobbies attested that they recognised me from the robbery scene. They probably could have if they'd have had the eyes of a bloody osprey.

I knew the pitfalls of the sort of life I led, but I also expected a fair trial with corroborating evidence when I was on such a serious charge. However, all the evidence was à la Hans Christian Andersen. It was another proud moment for the British legal system. The whole trial was a whitewash, and the CID had achieved their aim.

His Honour Judge Reginald Seaton dished out a pair of fives to me and Niven. I would have to take it on the chin, but it didn't help when Read went into the witness box after the verdict and told the court, 'Norman Johnson has never worked in his life. He's been connected to illegal gaming and drinking clubs. The jury has come to a just decision.' Talk about kicking a man when he's down. I was sure that I'd been fitted up, and now I'd been disparaged, too. Read was to later go on record as saying, 'Norman Johnson is one of the six most dangerous men in London.' I took that to be a back-handed compliment.

As a footnote to the case, I have always wanted to know why I was never mentioned in Nipper Read's book, *The Man Who Nicked the Twins*. He mentions Niven Craig, who got a five, but there is no reference to me even being in court.

It was back to sunny Wandsworth for a four-month stint. Again, I knew an awful lot of faces, and the time passed quietly and quickly until I was transferred to Hull Prison. It housed longer-term cons and was regarded as the place you went en route to Dartmoor, the most feared lock-up on the circuit. The regime at Hull was very severe. It was very strict, and I didn't relish my time there. After six weeks, I was put on the cleaners (cleaning duties) and became friends with the 'Mad Axeman' Frankie Mitchell, who was later shot on orders from the Krays. He was a smashing bloke, but sometimes not all the lights were on upstairs. He really was a gentle giant and, like me, wouldn't tolerate any injustice.

One day, I had an unexpected visit from my estranged wife, Kathleen Brown. She told me that while I'd been inside a big lump called Peter Perry, who was a professional heavyweight boxer, had taken my youngest sister Sylvia to a party. Perry had tried it on, but Sylvia had rejected his advances and had returned with her blouse ripped. I was furious. Kath had told Perry, 'Norman won't be happy with your behaviour.' He'd replied, 'I don't give a fuck about Norman.'

Two months later, I heard through the prison grapevine that Perry had received six years for a serious crime. I was made up, because there was now a real chance of confronting him in prison.

Another three months passed when, out of the blue, guess who turned up at Hull? It was fated to be. I just had to bide my time and wait for an opportunity to strike. On Perry's second day in the prison, I met him on the wing. He looked a trifle nervous but brightened up when I passed him some tobacco and told him that I was sorry he'd been sent down. 'Thanks, Scouse. It's good to see you.' Perry was now on a relaxed footing, and I could wait for the right moment.

It came one Sunday morning, two weeks after Perry's arrival at Hull, when he'd gone to chapel for morning prayers. Frankie Mitchell and I were cleaning the Ones (the ground floor) when we heard a key in the chapel door. A screw came out followed by six cons, including Perry. The screw shouted up to another warder who was on the Twos, 'Six on,' and went away. The screw on the second landing shouted, 'Bang your cells shut,' to the six prisoners now under his control.

Perry acknowledged me and Frank with a wave and went to the toilets, which were down some steps. I said to Frankie, 'Go up and keep that screw busy. I'm going to sort out Perry.' I rushed down to the toilet area, where Perry was pointing 'Percy' to the porcelain. Tapping him on the shoulder, I said, 'Have this for now.' He began to turn, and I cracked him on the right jaw bone with all the hate, frustration and power I could muster. It was like a juggernaut hitting a car. Perry's flesh burst open all around the broken bone, and he crashed to the ground, his head thudding against the tiled floor. The impact of the punch had damaged my right hand, so I leaned down and grabbed his throat with my left. I said, 'This is just the start. I'll finish you down the moor.' He didn't hear a word. I realised by the white of his eyes that he was unconscious and seriously hurt.

Running upstairs, I shouted to Frank that I'd finished the cleaning and was banging my door. Frank relayed this to the screw. In the cell, my fist had ballooned grotesquely to an unnatural size and some of the bones were out of their sockets. I gingerly pushed them back in again. The pain was unbearable. It was the hardest punch I'd ever thrown, but I was well satisfied with my day's work.

Fifteen minutes later, the alarm bells went off. Perry had been discovered in the toilets, still unconscious. A short while later, all the cells were opened up for dinner. I picked up my tray with my left hand, got my grub and returned to my cell. Within an hour, four screws burst in. 'Get your kit. You're going down to the punishment block.' I'd been grassed up or somebody had put two and two together.

I was taken to see the head warder, who said, 'We know you've done him, Jonno. He's been taken to an outside hospital. It could be a murder charge. He's in a bad way.'

I said, 'I don't know what you're talking about!'

That night at two in the morning, the light went on in my cell and a screw kicked my door. 'He's dead. You're bang in trouble.' That sort of provocation went on for three months. I was treated really badly and was given no furniture or access to books. I was just provided with a board and a mattress at 10 p.m. each night, and these were taken out again at 7 a.m. each morning. I spent torturous hours pacing my cell and sitting on the concrete floor. It was a very low time in my life.

In the meantime, Perry had undergone an emergency operation on his brain, and although his life was no longer in danger he left hospital paralysed down one side, invalided to a wheelchair, a bit like the ginger-haired gay predator in the film *The Shawshank Redemption* after he'd been visited by the prison guards. No charge was ever brought against me, because of a lack of evidence, and Perry was seen a year later in Wormwood Scrubs, still confined to a wheelchair having gone from sixteen stone to about nine. How he'd got into that condition was common knowledge in the Scrubs. The inmates knew that he'd incurred my wrath and come off worse. I had no compassion for him – he'd upset my family – and I never saw him again.

My time at Hull came to an end. I think they'd had enough of me. I was taken down country in a prison van, this time to the dreaded Dartmoor. On the approach to the prison, the countryside looked bleak and forboding. My long journey ended at Princetown. The prison itself was situated 1,400 feet above sea level on the open moor, so it was exposed to all the elements. It had been built during the Napoleonic wars to house French prisoners and had been breaking cons of all nationalities ever since.

On arrival, I was booked in and taken to my cell, which was cold and dank. There was a light encased in the wall, and the furniture was spartan. I'd been in better. The next day, two cons who I knew came over to say hello and mark my card. 'Scouse, the food's absolutely crap. We're gonna have a food strike tomorrow.' I was just pleased to be talking to people again after four months of being on my own.

The following day, the vast majority of prisoners refused to eat dinner. As a consequence, everyone was locked in their cells. The governor and chief officers then set up a table on the ground floor with a view to questioning the cons one by one to establish who was leading the revolt. Some time later, I was brought in front of the committee. The governor said, 'You've only been here two days, Johnson. Who's given you orders not to eat?'

Not meaning to be flash, I said to him, 'Nobody tells me what or what not to do.'

'Oh,' said the governor. 'Then you must be one of the ringleaders. Seven days' punishment in the block.' I was off to a flyer!

When I got out of the block, I had my first experience of the legendary Dartmoor quarry. I was placed in a working party of about 100 men, and we were taken to the worksite less than a mile from the prison, where I was passed a 14-pound lump hammer and instructed to 'turn them big rocks into little rocks'.

I thought, 'This is the life – fresh air and fitness. I'll come out of this really toned.' The reality was that after an hour I had blisters on both hands and was blowing like a dray horse. I was flagging badly when the duty screw screamed out, 'Come on, Johnson. More effort with that hammer.'

'Fuck you and the quarry,' I shouted back, and then I slung the hammer 30 yards. 'I'm not doing this. Take me back to the prison.'

The screw replied, 'Right, for refusing an order, go to the work shed and wait there for an escort.'

At the shed, another duty screw said to me, 'What are you doing here?'

I said, 'I'm not swinging that hammer any more. I'm waiting here to be sent back to the nick.' Behind the screw was a large pile of wooden beams and debris that had been left lying about after the demolition of disused prison-officer accommodation.

'How would you like the job of burning all that instead of going back?' the screw asked.

I said, 'No hammers?' He shook his head, so I set to work and even got one of my mates on request to help out as well.

A fortnight later, a new con came into the quarry, a large dark-haired, swarthy-looking fellow. Three cons came over to me. One of them said, 'That bastard's in for molesting kids.'

I said, 'He doesn't look like a pervert to me.'

'What does one look like?'

I decided I'd have to remove him from the quarry party. The next morning, I decided I would take him out as we passed under a bridge on the way to the quarry while the three cons kept the screws busy. As the child molester walked into the dark shadows of the bridge, I saw my chance and picked up a large rock and threw it at him. Bullseye. It clumped him right on the back of the head. He went down quicker than Monica Lewinsky and was trampled underfoot as the other cons passed.

He was eventually spotted by the duty screw at the back of the party and stretchered back to the prison hospital for treatment. When he reappeared on the exercise yard a week later, he approached me. His head was swathed in a large bandage. 'Norman, can I have a word in your ear?'

'Go away, you dirty fucking ponce,' I said.

'No, no, you don't understand. I'm in for armed robbery. Just ask the chief screw to confirm it.' I ignored him but later received confirmation that he was telling the truth. He was indeed an armed robber – *que sera, sera*!

I carried on burning the debris for another three months. The pile didn't seem to go down a great deal, but nobody was on my back, so I went at my own pace until I was transferred to another working party. This new group maintained the gardens inside and out of the prison, and the work was regarded as the cushiest number available. This is where I stayed until the end of my custodial sentence. I'd come up covered in clover.

Dartmoor didn't break me, but many others weren't as lucky. I saw real hard men in there get a Dear John letter and break down and cry like a baby. It was a tough existence, and you had to keep on top of all your emotions, but I got through it.

When I still had nine months of my sentence to serve, I was transferred to the hostel scheme. I was glad to see the back of Princetown; however, in their wisdom, the authorities decided not to send me back to London with all its temptations but to Stafford in the Midlands, a place I'd never heard of. I was driven to Exeter Station and from there proceeded to Stafford Prison. It was 1963, and my 30th birthday was approaching. A young president would be struck down that year; the world was still as unstable and as unpredictable as ever.

I was billeted in the hostel section of Stafford Prison and given day release to work at the English Electric Company, a very large Stafford factory, later to become GEC under Lord Weinstocks. My first job was 'chipping and grinding', which entailed cleaning welders' joints. It was the only employment I've ever undertaken,

SET UP AND SENT DOWN

and a week was more than enough! I found out that the foreman, Joe Brindley, was a horse-racing fanatic, so I rang Charlie Mitchell, a friend from Fulham, who was known in the racing world for straightening trainers and jockeys. He was also not averse to having horses doped. Charlie would later be found guilty of misdemeanours concerning horse racing in a very well-publicised court case.

The day I telephoned him, Charlie gave me an inside tip on a horse that was a cert, and I passed this information on to Joe Brindley, saying, 'Here's a tenner. Don't spend your own money.' In those days, a tenner was a decent amount of money, so I presumed that Joe would be affable to any of my future suggestions. The next day, I asked him to arrange for me to go on nights. My plan was to travel to London at weekends, so working the night shift would give me an extra day and night in the Smoke. Joe wrote an official letter to Stafford Prison stating that I was doing well and that I would be a great asset on the night shift, as they were short staffed. He was very persuasive, and the prison authorities gave the go ahead, even though they were sceptical.

Once on the night shift, I paid the five other workers a score to cover my work, and they happily obliged. I then collected a load of overalls and threw them in a massive deburring drum. This was a large cylinder set on its side, and it served as my sleeping quarters for the night. I would clock on, climb into the deburring drum and settle down to sleep. One of the others would always wake me at 7.30 a.m. to clock off. Back at the prison, I'd shower, change and then go into town. The days were now all mine.

On my first free weekend, I decided to head north and visit my gran in Liverpool. She had lived all her life in the south end of the city in Toxteth. The area had now become badly run down, and she and her immediate family had moved to a new estate in Speke, which would be near to the John Lennon Airport today. She was my gran on my mother's side and was affectionately known as Ma Evans. She loved a tipple and was always partial to half a Guinness. Even though Speke was miles from Toxteth, she would catch the bus to the docks and drink in the quaintly named Rat House. Another of her favourite drinking places was The Walker House, which faced King's Gardens in Mill Street, where she was brought up. After five or six glasses of the black stuff, she would catch the bus home. When I arrived, I said, 'Come on, Ma. Where's your local? We'll go for a drink.' I should have kept my mouth shut, because I had to drive her all the way over to Toxteth.

While I was up on Merseyside, I met a pretty young redhead in The Walker House by the name of Joan Walker. She wasn't the landlord's daughter, which was a pity, as there was no free booze, but she would flit in and out of my life for the next four decades.

After a few weeks or so, I was finding my feet in Stafford. I hardly knew anyone to begin with, but I started to socialise in a few local pubs, and although it wasn't the liveliest of towns I began to feel comfortable. I always wore well-tailored clothes and liked to look smart, so when I noticed that two buttons on a handmade suit I wanted to wear had come loose I went to the Co-op in town to buy needles and thread. The striking blonde-haired girl behind the counter was very polite, almost to the point of flirting. It struck me that she could well be interested. I bought a few other items, apart from the needles and thread, which came to ten shillings. I pulled out a £5 note and said, 'Bring me the change tonight. I'll be in The Chains public house. If not, keep it.' I left it with her and walked out of the store.

Entering The Chains that night, I spotted a very smartly dressed 19 year old by the name of Diane Challinor – the same girl who had served me that day. We got on really well, and within weeks we were seriously dating. I saw Diane on most weekdays but still went to London or Liverpool at weekends. She lived with her parents, who both went out to work at nine-thirty every morning. On Diane's days off from work, I'd turn up for breakfast as soon as her parents had left, enabling us to spend lots of time together. Eventually, the inevitable happened: Diane fell pregnant. It was just as well I was finishing at the hostel, as a month later a healthy baby girl, whom we christened Teresa, was born.

When I came off the hostel scheme, I wasn't tied to Stafford any more, so we decided to move to London, where I acquired a flat in Victoria. I had a fair amount of money set aside, and there were quite a few people in debt to me, but I had to start earning again to live in the style to which I'd been accustomed previously. While I was serving my sentence in Hull Prison, The Rainbow Club had been forced to shut down. I didn't blame anybody, as I wasn't around to oversee the operation, and I now had to take steps to earn a similar income.

A cracking Polish fellow by the name of Serge Polinski approached me one night in London. He was well known for previously handling the property affairs of Peter Rachman, the legendary slum landlord. Serge told me that a Polish friend of his called Hoppy had spent a lot of money on a club in Hartington Road, Knightsbridge, but had run out of cash. The friend, a one-legged Second World War hero, who had lost his limb in battle, had taken on another Pole as a partner to refinance his affairs but, as with many partnerships, arguments had developed. It culminated with the Johnny-come-lately Pole telling Hoppy, 'Fuck off or you'll get hurt. I'll see that you get a few quid.' Hoppy was not a violent man and contacted Serge, who was now telling me the story.

I met Hoppy, and he offered me £500 to get him back in the club. I told him, 'Meet me there at eight o'clock tonight.' We went in, and the other Pole was in the lobby. I grabbed him roughly and told him that he was the one who was out on his ear. I gave Hoppy my number in case of an emergency. 'What if the heavies come back?' he moaned.

'I don't think you'll have any more bother, but ring me straight away if you do.' The next morning, the phone rang. The person on the other end had a Polish accent. 'Norman, four big men come in and throw me back out.' I went back to the club a couple more times after that and reversed the situation. The club had a different owner every day that week. After I threw the other guy out on the street for the third time, he yelled, 'I'm going to get my friends to sort you out.'

'Go and get them,' I said. 'I'll be here for the next two hours.' I took the light bulb out of the fitting in the corridor, so that if anybody came in, I could see them immediately, but they could not focus on me. Sure enough, half an hour later the front doorbell rang impatiently. I knew it wasn't Jehovah's Witnesses. I opened the door to three gentlemen. I didn't know two of them, but the other was the bespectacled Dave Barry, an old friend and well-known face who could certainly look after himself. He put his head in his hands and sighed, 'Oh no. I didn't know you were here, Scouse. We've come to put our bloke back in.'

'Not today, I'm afraid, Dave,' I retorted.

He suggested a walk and a talk, and the other two guys got back in their motor. 'We can make a few bob here, Scouse. Each time we put our bloke in, we both get paid.'

I nodded in agreement, and we made another grand each before I decided to bring a halt to the proceedings. 'When my man goes in tonight, that's it,' I said. 'He's staying in.' Barry begrudgingly accepted the situation and went on his way. Hoppy now wanted me to be his partner. He didn't like all the aggro, so I accepted his offer. The only trouble was that Hoppy was potless, and I wasn't going to put any of my own money in.

The solution wasn't a long time in coming. One day, Ginger Randall popped in. He was into gaming machines, and we had two in the club that had been installed by the vanquished Pole. 'Do you want to sell your machines, Scouse?' he asked. 'I'll give you 400.' I didn't need to be asked twice. We now had money for stock. Ginger took the machines away, and we kicked in that evening.

The next morning, four men paid us a visit: Albert Dimes, Bobby Warren and two others. One of the no-marks shouted out, 'Let's burn the club down.'

I was good friends with Albert and Bobby, but it didn't stop me from confronting them. 'Nobody's burning anything,' I said.

'We've just come down to see if anybody knows where the two machines are,' Albert replied.

I cut him short. 'I don't know anything about your machines.'

'If they've walked, just tell us who has them,' Bobby said.

'Bob, I've no interest in the machines,' I replied.

Before they left, Albert said, 'If you hear anything Scouse, let us know.'

I wasn't going to drop Ginger Randall in it, but unfortunately somebody must have planted a word into an ear. Randall's garage was broken into, and the two machines went along with ten more belonging to Ginger. What goes around comes around.

In the afternoons, a young lady frequently drank in the bar. One day, she asked me, 'Would you like a drink, Norman?'

'No thanks, babe, but let me buy you one.' I bought her quite a few after that. No one ever told me who she was, but I later found out her name was Alma Cogan. The famous singer of the 1950s and

'60s would tragically die young of ovarian cancer at the tender age
of 34.

I was drinking in a spieler one night when I was approached by
Harry Smithson (no relation to Tommy), who'd been asked to clear
up a bugbear for Sarah Macmillan, the prime minister's daughter.
She was living in a house with a guy whose relatives were part of
the Tetley tea dynasty. Harry asked me for assistance, and we made
our way over to quite a decent address. The problem was that a
load of hangers-on were poncing off the couple's generosity, and
it didn't take me and Harry long to throw out half a dozen long-
haired bohemians from the Chelsea set. As they left, I gave them
some firm words of wisdom: 'Do not come back.' Sarah thanked
us both profusely and asked if I would pop around every couple of
weeks, which was no trouble to me, as most of my business was only
five minutes away from her house.

They were a real odd couple. Personal hygiene was not on their
agenda; in fact, they went to bed in their day clothes. The house
was full of empty bottles, and they had a real alcohol problem – the
problem being that there weren't enough hours in the day to drink it
all. It was a good job that they had a cleaner in once a week, as they
would never have got round to picking up a duster. They were both
from wealthy families and each was given £100 a week, which was
deposited at Harrods for clothing and food, but a large percentage
came back home in bottles.

Once a month, Sarah had to visit her father at his official
residence. Harold Macmillan would not tolerate overindulgence, so
Sarah would abstain for 24 hours before her meetings. Afterwards,
she would shake terribly from delirium tremens.

I occasionally had to throw out the odd sponger or freewheeler,
but after a while the parasites realised that their host was no longer
welcoming. They were both vulnerable personalities, so I didn't mind
helping them out, and it was with dismay that I heard a few years
later that Sarah had died aged 40, having suffered from emotional
problems. Money and power doesn't always bring happiness.

9

......

In Tune with Bloom

Not long after the episode with the fruit machines, Serge Polinski contacted me again and asked me to go into partnership with him. We opened up an illegal spieler in Earls Court. In reality, the club was just a room with a large circular table and chairs, where up to eight punters played cards around the clock. All our drinks and sandwiches were supplied free, but the house took half a crown commission on every pound staked, and on some nights, if it was a big game, we could make hundreds of pounds. We progressed to running three of these clubs simultaneously, and the money started rolling in.

Serge was then offered another fantastic moneymaking opportunity running a gambling club inside a quality venue: The Crazy Horse, close to Madame Tussauds in Baker Street. The establishment was owned by the infamous businessman John Bloom. Serge had to take his chance, and we parted on good terms. I carried on alone with the spielers but then teamed up again with Maltese Joe Ferrugia to run a strip joint in Windmill Street, Soho, facing Raymond's world-famous revue bar. This was a real moneymaker, even though there were many other striptease joints in the area.

Joe went round to the other clubs to negotiate a set hourly rate for all the girls. In this way, no venue could be taken advantage of by the strippers, and once this was achieved I charged punters £1 admission fee. They poured in. It was a time of sexual awakening and liberation. With touts working the streets, it wasn't unusual to clear four figures a week.

Things were going very well when one day Serge came to see me at the club with a problem. That morning, he had gone to The Crazy Horse as normal but had been refused entry. Apparently, John Bloom had flown to the USA on business but before leaving had instructed his personal bodyguard, Pat Stapleton, an ex-heavyweight boxing champion of Ireland, to bar Serge from The Crazy Horse. Serge couldn't argue with Stapleton, as he was built like a brick outhouse. The upshot was that Bloom had been expecting Serge's punters to consume more alcohol in the club than they actually had and had decided that gambling was more trouble than it was worth. When he returned from the States, he was going to close and refurbish the gaming room.

Serge told me that he was owed £10,000 in gambling credits and was also building up a very lucrative clientele, so he needed to get back in, as it would be madness to walk away. 'Bloom has taken a liberty,' he added. 'If you get me back in, I'll share the profits with you.' I knew that Serge wasn't a fighting man, so I escorted him back to The Crazy Horse, where we encountered Pat Stapleton sitting at a desk in the lobby with two men standing behind him. One was Peter Rand, the other a Russian by the name of Yuri Borienko – both were top professional wrestlers, and Yuri was also a film stuntman and actor, later to appear in such films as *On Her Majesty's Secret Service* and *Superman IV*.

I told Serge to go downstairs while I sorted out Stapleton. The big Irishman didn't know who I was, but Yuri and Rand certainly did. They both said hello, and one of them must have kicked Stapleton's leg under the table, because he was speechless. I eyeballed him for a few seconds and then followed Serge downstairs.

Peter Rand later told me that upstairs Stapleton had said to him in a thick Irish brogue, 'Who the fuck's dat?'

Peter replied, 'It's not the best idea to get involved.'

Stapleton then looked up to his right to see Borienko nodding in agreement. He puffed his cheeks and picked up the phone to phone Bloom in New York. 'Jaysus, John. I've got the fooking Mafia down here. I don't like it!' With that he got up and left the club, never to be seen again. The strange thing was that Stapleton and I hadn't said one word to each other.

When John Bloom returned from America a fortnight later, he had Amber Dean Smith, a gorgeous, tall, leggy beauty and Penthouse

Pet of the Year, on his arm. He soon looked me up, as nobody knew where Stapleton had gone, and arranged to meet me in The Crazy Horse. Bloom introduced himself then told me all about his new plans and ambitions for the club, which involved sexual titillation and a high class of clientele – no gangsters or troublemakers would be welcome. In fact, his ideas were ahead of their time. Bloom wanted topless barmaids and quality erotic dancing – essentially an early front-runner of today's lap-dancing clubs. He had seen the format succeed in Paris and New York and wanted to emulate it in London.

After our discussion, Bloom said, 'Norman, would you spend some time in The Crazy Horse while you are minding the gaming area for Serge? I'll put you on a good percentage.' My star was rising towards the heavens. In a short space of time, I was running three gambling spielers and a strip club, partners with Serge in the gaming venue and minding a high-quality men's club. Life was good. I was happy at home with my wife and child, and work was getting better and better.

John Bloom was one of the most infamous men of the 1950s and '60s. A year older than me, he was a fascinating character. He came to prominence when he bought out the ailing firm Rolls Razor Ltd and started selling Dutch washing machines to the public at rock-bottom prices. He quickly took a huge share of the market through aggressive marketing, generous instalment plans and nationwide door-to-door selling. His motto was 'no sin to make a profit', and he was certainly not modest, buying a top of the range yacht and black Rolls-Royce.

He acquired a £20-million loan from merchant Sir Isaac Wolfson, who amongst others caught a cold when the market became overcrowded and spares for the washers became unavailable. Wolfson withdrew his support, hastening the downfall of the company. Many people had lost a fortune, and Bloom, pleading poverty, made out that he was one of them, although he had secretly stashed a large amount of money away.

My new partner then advertised in the *London Evening News* for topless barmaids and asked me to sit in on the auditions. I thought, 'There's worse jobs than that,' so agreed to help out. What neither of us could have foreseen was that hundreds of young ladies would apply, and we were auditioning at The Crazy Horse every day for two weeks. We saw breasts of every conceivable shape and size, and we gave names to the ones that stuck out in our minds, such as 'Pear Drops' and 'Droopy'. To tell you the truth, the great majority of girls should not have come. They must have seen something different in the mirror than what we were faced with. We narrowed it down to a short list of twenty girls and eventually employed four. These were the crème de la crème of a starting field of 400 and were absolute crackers.

I had just moved my family to a new flat in Lorry Park Road, Sydenham, near Crystal Palace. Diane mentioned that there was a nightclub near the station called The Studio, so I decided to take a look one night before I went to work at The Crazy Horse. It was upstairs above some shops and had apparently been a dance studio previously. Even though it was a well-furnished and decorated club, there weren't many bums on seats or people on the dance floor. I found out that the owner only admitted singles or couples – no groups of men were allowed in, as he thought that they were trouble. It didn't look to be taking a lot of money, but I could see it had a lot of potential, so I asked the owner if he would be willing to sell.

The owner's name was Ted Pearce, and he said that he'd think about it and ring me the next day. He phoned me after dinner and said he would accept £3,000, which I bartered down to £2,500. That night at The Crazy Horse I told John I'd bought a local club. Bloom said, 'Don't pay a penny till I've had a good look.' John was soon to demonstrate what a cunning man he was!

The next afternoon, we visited The Studio. Before we went in, John said, 'Say nothing. Let me do all the talking.' I'm sure Ted recognised Bloom straight away, as he had a high profile in the media at the time. John walked around the club, and Ted said to me, 'That's John Bloom, isn't it?' I confirmed with a nod. Bloom was now in his element: 'A roulette table can go there, the poker tables over there. Now, we'll need a new fire escape. We'll knock that wall down for a larger kitchen,' and so on. He turned to me, still blanking Ted, and said, 'This will do very nicely for a gambling club. We'll have no trouble with the planning.' At last, he turned to Ted and said, 'We don't want to buy the club, but we will give you 25 per cent of all the gambling profits. Get your solicitors to contact mine.'

Ted couldn't believe his luck. He was going to be a partner with the multimillionaire John Bloom.

I went back the next day, and Ted had all the legal paperwork ready. He was now a partner in a gambling club and handed the keys over to me. The hard truth of the matter was that there was never any chance of it becoming a gambling venue, and I had secured myself a nightclub for nothing, saving myself a bundle of money. Ted was on 25 per cent of profits that were never going to materialise.

I applied for and got a one o'clock licence, and the club started swinging, full of all the people Ted would never have dreamed of letting in. A fortnight later, Ted popped in and asked how the planning situation was going. I told him that John Bloom was on top of it. He came in again about four or five times until it dawned on him that he had 25 per cent of nothing, and he eventually stopped. It showed John Bloom's true colours; he could charm the birds out of the trees.

I was now commuting between The Crazy Horse and The Studio, while my other business affairs were being well run by trusted associates. The clubs were going through a trouble-free period, but, like anything in life, things never run smoothly all the time. One night before I'd got to The Crazy Horse, five men had been admitted who were a little bit worse for wear. I was standing in the club, unaware that they were in the gaming room, when I heard a commotion and ran through just in time to see a 30-year-old, dark-haired man smash a glass into somebody's face. I went straight for him but was held back by his four mates. I calmed down and, pointing to an alcove, said to him, 'Come round here.' He was still being verbal, so once I got him round the corner I said to him, 'Do you think you're a tough guy?' When he came back with more lip, I head-butted him onto a leather settee, but his mates reappeared and held onto me just as I was leaning over to grab him.

The guy was half groggy but picked up a glass jug from a nearby table and smashed it right on top of my head. Blood spurted out like an artesian well from lots of small cuts as the glass shattered against my skull. In the melee, he fled, leaving his four mates still holding onto me. I'd lost it by then, and the brave foursome decided that the best course of action was to run for the exit. I gave chase and managed to dive onto the last one, wrestling him to the floor. 'You're going nowhere, soppy bollocks,' I said. 'I want to know who he is and where he drinks.' Just to give him some incentive, I gave him a backhander in the face. 'If you don't tell me, you're going to get hurt.'

The information was immediately forthcoming. The bloke in question was from Walthamstow and was a nephew of the boxing promoter Benny Huntman. At the time, my cousin 'Big' Sid Murphy was minding a casino in Earls Court with another friend of mine from Birmingham, ex-professional middleweight Teddy Hayes. I asked Sid if he could hold the fort at The Crazy Horse while I went looking for the young Huntman. He said it would be no trouble, and I went on my travels. However, nobody had seen him – he'd disappeared off the map. Three days after the incident, Huntman's father approached the Krays and asked them to straighten things out. They said, 'Thanks, but no thanks.' He then went to the Nashes, who also declined. He was getting desperate, as he knew I meant business, and eventually approached Bobby Ramsey, who took up the gauntlet. All Ramsey had to go on was the name Norman and the name of the club. He didn't realise that it was the same Norman who had previously hung him over the banister; otherwise, I don't think he would have got involved.

That night, he came into The Crazy Horse reception, strode up to Sid and said, 'Who's this Norman?'

'What do you want him for?' Sid replied. 'He's not here.'

With that, Ramsey feigned to turn, caught Sid off guard, hit him with an uppercut and then ran out of the club. A stunned Sid took a few moments to recover and give chase, but Ramsey was too far up the road, and as he jumped into a motor he screamed back, 'You're all dead.' Sid relayed all that had happened to me, so I now had two scores to settle.

I thought I'd get Ramsey out of the way first. I knew he had worked with the twins on and off for years, so Sid and I turned up at the Krays' residence in Vallance Road and knocked on the door. Charlie Kray, the twins' father, answered and told us that Ronnie was in the pub around the corner. It was 6 p.m. when we walked into the empty boozer. Apart from the barman, Ronnie was the only person in there. He was in the corner reading his newspaper, and I got straight to the point: 'Where can I get hold of Ramsey?'

'Have you got a problem with him?' Ronnie replied.

'Yeah, he's making himself busy again.'

Ronnie said, 'I hit that cunt myself last week! Leave me a contact number, and I'll set it up.' It struck me that there wasn't much loyalty between these thieves. Ronnie then added, 'Do you want a drink?' I declined, and Sid and I decided to carry on the search.

Nothing came of the meeting with Ronnie, and I never saw Ramsey again – he had disappeared off the radar. It must have got back to him that it was me who was looking for him. He was brighter than he looked. But Huntman was still on my agenda, and his uncle popped up at The Studio one night. Benny came over and introduced himself. He had just returned from Wembley, where one of his boxers had been fighting for a title. He offered me a pair of boxing gloves, saying, 'These are from the title fight. I know you've an interest in boxing.'

I said, 'I don't want your boxing gloves. Give them to someone else.'

'Would you do me a favour?' Benny then asked. 'Could you leave it out with my nephew? He was right out of order and made a mistake. I'd appreciate it if you could let it drop.'

He seemed like a decent man, so I said to him, 'I won't go looking, but if I bump into him, I can't promise anything.'

Benny replied, 'I've sent him away as a croupier in the Bahamas for the time being, so he'll be out of your way.' That suited me, and, like Ramsey, he wasn't seen in the area again.

Everything else was running smoothly, and I had been partners with Bloom for a good long period, but his Uncle Alfred was beginning to get on my nerves. John and I had an agreement that if we ordered any drinks or meals for ourselves or guests, we would sign a docket slip. Alf was always fretting about this, as I was quite liberal with my generosity. It must have been his Jewish temperament. He'd shuffle up to me and whisper in my ear, 'Norman, you've signed a lot of slips this week. You're too good natured.' Then he'd sigh and say, 'It's not a charity you know.' I couldn't see why Alf was grumbling, but he was obviously one of life's natural worriers. He was also the club's treasurer and accountant, and he loved to see a profit.

John Bloom was very strict with his staff. If a bill wasn't paid, the girl who was looking after the customer would be asked to pay it herself or be dismissed, but they soon cottoned on that if they came to me, I'd sign the docket. This would prevent the girl getting into trouble and keep the till straight. The number of dockets were sending Alf crazy, and he was continually breaking my balls with his incessant pestering. I decided that I'd had enough of it and hatched a little scheme for a quiet life.

Every afternoon, Alf audited the club's accounts religiously at 2 p.m., so I arranged for an old Iranian friend by the name of Kouris, a big swarthy type who looked the part, to come into the club and demand money with menaces. The intrusion would all be a pretence – the idea was to put the fear of God into Alf. At 2.15 p.m., Kouris and an Iranian pal of his burst into the accounts office. Alf was at his desk, and I was standing in the corner. Kouris snarled at Alf, 'We've heard this is a busy club. We want £2,000 a week protection money.' Alf nearly disappeared up his backside and frantically looked to me for support and intervention.

I said, 'You'll get fuck all from this club.' Kouris feigned to go for me, and I produced a starting pistol from my pocket. It was all part of the plan, as was the hidden sachet of blood that Kouris was holding in his hand. As I fired three shots into his torso, Kouris smeared the blood over his chest and stomach away from Alf's eyeline. He then whipped round sharply, and Alf nearly fainted, exclaiming, 'Oh my God.' The other Iranian grabbed the door and bundled Kouris through it, and I followed after them. In the corridor, I shot another blank into the air then met with them upstairs in the lobby. Out of earshot, we all laughed hysterically. It had been worth it just to see Alf's expression.

I thanked my friends and went back down to console Alf. He was a nervous wreck and was shaking like a jelly. I thought I'd push it a bit more: 'I've got him in the car boot. He's dead. Don't say a word.' Alf turned a whiter shade of pale, especially when I added, 'I'll be back tonight. Don't forget, you're an accessory.' That evening at about ten o'clock, I returned to The Crazy Horse. Alf clocked me, then quickly looked down. I eventually caught his eye and put my finger to my lips, and he meekly nodded. Alf didn't seem to bother me much after that, particularly with minor things like dockets! I think his mind must have been on 'dead' Iranians.

John Bloom's wife Anne worked with top celebrity agent Eve

Taylor, and subsequently lots of popstars, MPs and film actors visited The Crazy Horse on a frequent basis. You'd see people such as Sandy Shaw, Roy Orbison, Sean Connery and Lionel Blair, who would unintentionally embarrass me in the company of London hard men by mincing across to say hello, but I didn't really mind, as he was a good guy.

The same couldn't be said for Patrick Wymark, who was one of the stars of the film *Where Eagles Dare*. He used to come in about three times a week, and at that time every drink in the club was a pound. You got a double spirit for a pound, with soft drinks thrown in, or two half lagers. Wymark had a reputation for being mean. He squeaked when he walked, and most of the girls in the club knew that it was impossible to get a drink out of him. He would buy a drink for a pound and write out a cheque for 20, asking for £19 change in cash. This went on for a while, until a barmaid complained to me. I said, 'Next time he tries it on, call me over.' The following evening, out came the cheque book. I told him, 'Make the cheque out for a pound. You're taking the piss at the wrong place.' He got up to go, and I said, 'If you want to argue about it tomorrow, bring Clint Eastwood with you.' He never came in the club again.

One night, the Welsh singer Tom Jones came in with his wife and entourage. They were enjoying a drink and I remarked to Tom, 'We've got a good card school in the back. Do you fancy playing a few hands of poker?'

'No, I don't gamble,' he replied in his Rhondda valley accent. 'Me dad gambled, and me ma and us kids went short.'

'You miserable git,' I thought.

Tom's eyes then lit up when he saw a pretty waitress by the card table. 'You can introduce me to her if you like,' he said, so I took him through to the gaming room, where the waitress stood starry-eyed and besotted. I returned to the bar, where the small band was playing some uptempo music. Out of the blue, a small woman grabbed my wrist and said, 'Come and have a dance.'

'Sorry, babe,' I replied. 'I don't dance.' But she was insistent and tried to grab my other arm. As I looked beyond her, I noticed Tom was standing in the doorway. He was not a happy man. My new potential dancing partner was his wife, but I didn't know that at the time. Anyway, nothing had happened. I spent the rest of the night drinking with him, and he seemed civil enough and didn't mention the incident.

A week later, I loaned my Mercedes to a friend, saying, 'Be back at 1 a.m. I've got to get over to Earls Court. It's very important.' At 1.15 a.m., there was no sign of the car. I was bloody fuming and decided to hail a cab. I waited outside the club, and a taxi soon came along, but it was occupied. As it sped past, somebody stuck their head out of the window and shouted, 'You Scouse bastard.'

I thought, 'You're a brave man,' and waited for another cab. As chance would have it, the same taxi came back a few minutes later. It had been to some flats in Marylebone. The cabbie said to me, 'Do you know who that fellow was who screamed at you five minutes ago?' I shrugged. 'It was Tom Jones, the singer. Do you often get abuse like that?'

I told him, 'It's not unusual.'

The Merc eventually resurfaced, and a couple of days later I took it to Kent for its regular service at a friend's garage. The mechanic said, 'You'll have to leave it. You're losing water, and you'll need a new pump.'

I asked him when it would be ready and was informed that it would be the next day. 'I'll need some wheels to get back,' I said.

He pointed over to an old Mini. 'Take that,' he said. 'I think it's reliable.'

'Cheers. If that's all you've got, that will have to do.'

I drove off, and just as I was approaching the club, it started raining. It was lucky I was close, because the windscreen wipers didn't work. I met Bloom in the club, and he said, 'Can I borrow your Merc, Norm? The wife's got mine.' John was too tight to catch a cab. He was renowned for never carrying any money, and if something had to be paid for, it wasn't him doing it.

'I've only got a Mini, John, and the wipers don't work.'

Undeterred, he said, 'I'll take that. It'll be OK.'

It was absolutely teeming down outside, and Bloom couldn't see a thing out of the windscreen, so he stuck his head out of the side window, which was a sliding glass one in those days. John was bald on top but, like many men in the 1960s, had long hair on the side to comb over the bald patch, à la Bobby Charlton. He looked a right sight tearing up Park Lane in a monsoon, his head out of the side window with his hair cleaning the pavement. He got back to The Crazy Horse and fell through the doors of the club looking like a bedraggled tramp. He said, 'Norman, every car that's gone past has hooted me. I'll never forget that journey.' With that, he ordered a treble whisky and downed it in one, which was rare, as he was usually teetotal.

He got changed and cleaned up and said he fancied going to The Playboy Club to cheer himself up. I threw him the keys to the Mini. I'd had one too many to get behind the wheel, so John drove to the club (it had stopped raining). At that time, John was in all of the daily papers, pleading poverty after the collapse of his business empire, and he was one of the most famous faces in Britain. We drew up in the crappy old Mini, and the door commissionaire, resplendent in all his livery, looked down his nose at us as we stopped at the entrance. I said, 'You don't want to buy a Mini, do you, mate?'

'No thank you, sir,' he replied. He was a great doorman, because as Bloom emerged from the car he recognised him immediately. With a straight face, he said dryly, 'I now truly believe, Mr Bloom, you have no money.' Bloom stormed off, leaving me standing with the doorman. I was in stitches.

The Crazy Horse and The Studio were going from strength to strength, and I wasn't experiencing too many problems at night – it was just the lull before the storm. One morning, Serge Polinski rang me up. 'It's urgent, Norman,' he said. 'Can you meet me later at Dorothy's nightclub in Knightsbridge?' Dorothy's was the club where Ruth Ellis had met David Blakely, whom she later murdered, becoming the last woman to be hanged in the UK.

I met Serge there, and we discussed his problem. He told me that a young aristocrat with a penchant for the gambling tables had started frequenting 45 Cromwell Road, an Earls Court gambling club. This club was owned by Henry Werner and his minder Yuri Borienko. The young lord was being taken to the cleaners in crooked games favouring the house. He was dropping £1,000 a night until he was stony broke. Werner knew he was from an affluent family and encouraged him to play on credit, as the cards were bent. The more the young lord played, the deeper into debt he got. In a short period, he ran up a deficit of £10,000, and a friendly Werner told him, 'I know you're good for it. You have a week to pull it up.'

The aristocrat came back a week later and said, 'I'm sorry. My parents have stopped my allowance.'

Werner and Borienko's attitude immediately changed. 'If you don't get the ten grand by next week, we'll break your legs and disfigure you,' Werner warned him.

This terrified the young lord, and he came out of Werner's office at his wit's end. He contacted Serge, who he had played cards with many times, and arranged to meet him in a pub. 'Do you know anyone who does robberies?' he asked.

Serge replied, 'Not my scene, I'm afraid, but those three at the end of the bar might be able to assist.'

The men were two Aussie shoplifters and a Scottish bank robber. The lord chatted with them for 20 minutes and then left the building. A week later, he caught up with Serge. He was sporting a badly severed lip, which had been sewn up. 'Thanks a lot, Serge,' he said. 'That unsavoury trio you pointed out have done this.' Serge was horrified and asked him what had occurred. The aristocrat told him that after leaving the pub he had gone with them to their flat around the corner, where he'd explained to them that his uncle was a duke and lived in a large stately house in the country. That weekend, there would be nobody there, as the family were staying in London. He would deal with the security arrangements and informed them to go for a locked glass cabinet in the hall, which housed a dozen or so priceless family heirlooms. The robbery duly took place, and the aristocrat went back to the robbers' flat as arranged to collect his £20,000 share. When he asked for his money, they told him that the items were so unique that it would take some time to sell them. He told them that he needed to pay a debt quickly. If they couldn't move the jewelled gold caskets post haste, he'd find somebody who could. The Scot lost his temper and told him that the goods weren't going anywhere – he would have to wait. With that, the young lord went to pick up the case that contained the caskets and was smashed straight in the mouth and told to fuck off and not come back. He then went to the hospital to get stitched up.

After listening to the lord's account, Serge said, 'Don't worry. I'll help you to sort this mess out.' That's when Serge got in touch with me.

I now knew the whole situation but wanted to hear it from the horse's mouth, so Serge took me to meet his friend. I was dismayed by the young man's injury and asked to hear his story again. Having satisfied myself that I had all the facts, I decided that the first stop was to be 45 Cromwell Road, as the young man was more worried about the threats against him than the jewelled caskets. I went straight over to the club, knowing that it would be quiet at that time. I entered Werner's office, where Henry and Yuri were both sitting down. I said to Borienko, 'Get out. I want to speak to Henry.' The minder left as instructed. Henry wouldn't meet my gaze and looked down at his desk. I said, 'I know the SP about the crooked card games. You've had enough money out of the kid. I'll take his marker. The debts are down to me, OK?' Werner reluctantly nodded in agreement. That was the first problem sorted.

I got back to Serge and the lord and told them, 'Don't worry about the money you owe Werner. It's been written off.' The kid was so relieved; it was like he'd won the pools. 'Right, now take me to the flat where these jokers are.' We drove to the premises, and the kid was so scared that he wouldn't get out of the car. I knocked on the door and was greeted by a balding Scotsman, who eyed me suspiciously. 'Does Fred Jones live here?' I asked. Before he could answer, I smashed him across the right eye with a cosh that sent him down, moaning and groaning. I entered the flat and found the two Aussies sitting on a double bed. Jock staggered in and sat on a chair. I shouted, 'You three are right liberty takers. Now, this is what's gonna happen. I'm not a thieving ponce. These items will be sold, and you'll get your whack, but the kid's not gonna be ripped off.' With that, I grabbed the case and walked out. Back in the car, I said to the aristocrat, 'Leave these with me. I'll get the best price I can.' I think he was just relieved to have Werner off his back.

I now had a case of expensive artefacts to move and move quickly. If I got copped with the haul, I'd be done for possession and for the robbery. I phoned a local Jewish fence from Hatton Garden, but as luck would have it he'd just gone on holiday to Israel. I thought long and hard. There was only one man for a consignment of such quality.

John Francis, an associate of the Krays, had many connections. I had known him for ten years and trusted him implicitly. John came over and couldn't believe the craftsmanship of the pieces. 'Scouse,' he said, 'it would be impossible to move these in Great Britain. It would be like trying to shift a Van Gogh.' I suggested melting the gold down and selling the stones. I could tell by his reaction that this idea horrified him. He said, 'That would be sacrilege. They must stay intact. Listen, I've got a top jeweller. Give me one item, and I'll get him to assay it and price it up, then I'll have a good idea of what it all comes to.'

I handed him a bejewelled tobacco casket, but instead of taking it to the jeweller, he took it to show the Kray twins at Vallance Road. He told them, 'This is priceless. If you can pull up ten grand, I can get ten more, but I've got to have the money by Sunday night. If you can do it, I'll get you forty grand back by Wednesday [in those days, you could buy a house in London for five grand]. If not, I'll try somewhere else.'

'No, no, we'll pull it up,' Reggie replied. 'Don't worry about it.'

Charlie, Ronnie and Reg then went out begging, borrowing and cajoling, because for all their fame they were never awash with decent money. They made frantic phone calls and late-night visits to friends and associates and just about scraped together nine and a half grand.

The following Sunday evening, Ronnie handed John Francis the bundle. John then brought it over to me and said, 'I've seen the jeweller. It's a goer. It's very old and worth a lot of money. He wants to see the rest. He values this one at 30 grand if it came on the open market but, as the items are hot, would you be satisfied with a return of 80 grand for the lot?' I told John that would be fine and handed him the case. He said that he was going to Antwerp and would be flying back into Heathrow at 10 p.m. on Thursday night. Before leaving, he handed me three grand on account, courtesy of the Krays. 'I'll see you at about midnight at The Astor Club, all being well.'

I never at that moment suspected any underhand dealings, and neither did the Krays! It just goes to show that you can't trust your fellow man. That Thursday, I arrived at The Astor to be greeted by 'Sulky', the extremely popular and well-known owner of the club.

'Can you get me a private table please, Sulky?' I asked. He found me one at the far end of the club. I noticed that the Kray firm were in, about eight-handed, and when I waved they reciprocated.

After ten minutes, Ronnie came across. 'All right, Scouse. Come over and join us.'

'It's all right, Ron,' I said. 'I'm waiting here to do some business with John Francis.'

He went up like a bottle of pop. 'That fucking bastard should have dropped us off a good wedge on Wednesday. We've not seen him.'

I said, 'He owes me a few bob as well.' The penny dropped. I thought, 'That's 80 grand gone west.'

Ronnie kept repeating, 'Fucking bastard, fucking bastard.'

I tried to console him. 'He might turn up, Ron.' But at 1.30 a.m., I realised it wasn't going to happen.

In one fell swoop, John Francis had fucked over three of the most dangerous men in London. If we didn't think that he had the balls to do it, he had proved us all wrong. The Krays for their part would never forget this humiliation, but, call it fate, destiny or kismet, I would meet John years later on another continent where the 80 grand he owed me would be repaid many times over.

That was the shape of things to come, but for now the police were about to rear their ugly head again. Diane couldn't settle in London, and after the birth of our second baby girl, Victoria, decided to take the children back to Stafford, where she first stayed at her mother's and then moved to a house on Somerset Road in the Highfields estate at the south end of the county town.

About a month later, another business opportunity was offered to me. The Blue Angel club in Frith Street, Soho, was run by a guy called 'Maltese' Tony who had been impressed by my 'no nonsense' way of getting things done and wanted me to get involved. I met Tony in the Angel one night at about 8 p.m. It was moderately quiet, as it didn't usually liven up until after ten. Eric Mason, another old friend of mine, was at the bar. He later wrote *The Brutal Truth*, a graphic autobiography of his underworld exploits. The three of us were enjoying a quiet drink when I noticed three men in overcoats hovering around the doorway. 'Do you know who they are, Tony?' I asked. He thought that they looked like Old Bill and so did I. 'I don't need this,' I said. 'I'll see you another time.' I then grabbed my coat and made my way out.

As I pushed past one of the plain-clothes officers, he said, 'Norman, the governor wants to see you down West End Central. I don't know what it's about. We're just here to pick you up.' I ignored him and walked up the stairs, but there were two more Old Bill and a Jaguar police car blocking my exit. I decided to go quietly and got into the back of the big cat.

Down at the station, I was taken to the charge room, where there was a uniformed inspector behind a desk. The plain-clothes officer moved round to join the inspector and threw a flick knife down onto the table. He then said, 'Governor, we went to arrest Johnson on suspicion of assault, and he pulled a knife on me. We've got witnesses.'

I lost my rag. 'You piece of shit. That's your game, is it? Well, if that's my knife, it should have my fingerprints on it. I don't wear gloves. Send it to forensics.'

The inspector calmly opened the desk drawer and deftly brushed the knife into it, saying, 'Don't be silly, Norman.'

'That's OK, but you're the first one I'm going to subpoena,' I replied, giving him something to think about. It seemed to do the trick, as it wiped the smug look from his face.

'Right, lock him up. Court first thing in the morning.'

Before the court hearing, I was granted a phone call and rang Michael Ostwin, John Bloom's solicitor. He was a very shrewd and capable performer. He arrived at the magistrates' court at ten, and I was soon granted bail. I told him I'd been fitted up, but by his reaction I don't think he entirely believed my account, probably due to my past record. We made an appointment to meet again on Thursday, and in the meantime he said that he would check up on the accuracy of my story. He telephoned an old college friend, who was now a chief inspector in the uniformed branch, and asked him if I'd been fitted up. The inspector rang back three days later and informed Ostwin that I had been, because the police wanted me out of the West End by any means necessary. In the future, they planned to discharge a loaded gun and say that I had tried to shoot a policeman.

Ostwin and I now knew the full SP. On a visit back to Stafford to visit Diane and the kids, I decided to visit Sir Hugh Fraser, the well-known Tory MP. I explained my current dilemma to him, saying, 'I've got a wife and two young kids, and I don't want to be doing twenty years for nothing. A loaded gun being fired is right out of order.' I asked him to write down all I had told him for future reference, just in case the conspiracy came to fruition. Fraser then rang Michael Ostwin at my behest to confirm the facts. Ostwin told him about the phone call to the inspector, although he said that he couldn't divulge the officer's name. He then assured Fraser that it had been a fit-up. Fraser made more enquiries and backed West End Central into a corner. I was now a lot more confident of a favourable outcome.

At the subsequent court hearing, I was approached by two Scotland Yard officers. 'Take the knife charge, Norman,' one of them said. 'We guarantee that no gun charge will ever be thrown at you!'

I said, 'You've got some front. I'm taking no charge. I've done nothing wrong.'

As they left, one of them said, 'Forget about the gun.' It must have got too heavy for them.

Later on, the inspector who'd pushed the blade into the drawer was subpoenaed, and my solicitor questioned him. 'Did Norman Johnson ask for the knife to be sent to forensics?'

'Yes,' he replied.

'Then why didn't you send it?'

'Too many officers had handled it.' That so many policemen had touched the weapon made no sense, as it was the prosecution's main piece of evidence. The case should have been thrown out there and then, but the senior magistrate was a knighted establishmentarian, and he got riled at me calling the CID liars throughout the proceedings, even though it was patently obvious that the evidence was tainted. Amazingly, he found me guilty and gave out a 12-month prison sentence. Michael Ostwin jumped straight up and stated, 'That's not possible. Under the new statute from Lord Chief Justice Goddard, a man who's been out of prison for five years can only be given a suspended sentence at a magistrates' court for this type of offence.'

The exasperated magistrate then shouted, 'Two years suspended sentence.' Ostwin was up again like a bolt from a crossbow. 'Under the new statute, only 12 months suspended is permissible.'

The magistrate was now apoplectic. He screamed out, 'Twelve months suspended and a £200 fine.'

Ostwin was now at his mischievous best. 'Can we have time to pay?' he asked.

The red-faced judge had had enough. 'No you can't. In fact, search him.' I emptied my pockets, and the search produced £78. 'You've got a week to pay the balance, Johnson,' the judge ordered and stormed out of court, wound up like a broken clock.

Boxers Billy and George Walker, who were later to become a multimillionaires running the Brent Walker company, met up with John Bloom and me at their Piccadilly headquarters, The Can Can club. We had discussions with a view to taking over the venue, as it had a much larger floor space than The Crazy Horse. We'd recently had a few run-ins with the owners of the building where The Crazy Horse was sited and had decided that The Can Can would be a much better proposition.

During the negotiations, John proved yet again what a wily operator he was with his masterly handling of the situation. He guaranteed the Walkers a weekly rental of a grand with no deposit put down, to be paid through his holding company, Pavilion Properties. In the meantime, I sold The Studio for two grand to 'Flash' Harry Haywood. (It was Flash Harry's brother Billy who was involved in the infamous incident at Mr Smith's in Catford with the Richardson gang and Frankie Fraser.) I was just about to open a casino in West End Lane, near Hampstead, called The Twenty-one Club so was able to let The Studio go. I negotiated with Harry that the £2,000 include a proviso: that he pick up any outstanding bills at the club. 'Don't worry about a few bills, Scouse,' Harry said, not knowing that I'd run up a boxful behind the bar.

A week later, I popped in with a few mates to see how Harry was getting on and to spend a few quid. Fair play to him – it was packed to the rafters. As we approached, Harry clocked me, climbed on top of the bar and laughingly shouted, 'A few bills, you cunt. I'll be here until I'm 80.' He got down, and everybody had a really good night.

Meanwhile, Nipper Read was making himself busy again. I picked up a daily paper and read that the Krays had been arrested. Ronnie, for the murder of George Cornell, a member of the Richardson gang, shot dead in The Blind Beggar pub, and Reggie for knifing Jack 'the Hat' McVitie to death, a minor villain who had been taking liberties with the twins.

A few weeks earlier, I had warned Ronnie Kray that the police were pulling in people I knew, asking questions about him and his brother. I had a feeling that the net was closing in. Ron said, 'Don't worry, Scouse. They've got nothing on us.' His confidence was misplaced. In fact, a lot of the firm's members deserted a sinking ship and gave evidence against them. They had been in custody for about a month when a Paddington nightclub owner by the name of Frankie Choppin approached me at The Astor Club. Frankie, who was later to own clubs in Cardiff, asked me, 'Would you come down to Brixton tomorrow? Ronnie Kray wants to see you.'

I met Frankie outside the prison, and we both went in to see Ronnie. Unbelievably, the first thing he said to me was, 'Scouse, that bastard Francis has been shot dead in China.'

I thought, 'That's the last thing you should be concerned about. You've got a lot more on your plate here.'

'Could you do me a favour?' he added. 'You're great friends of the Mills brothers. Would you ask them not to talk to the Old Bill?'

'You've got no worries on that account, Ron,' I replied, 'but I will speak to them.'

On the fateful night that McVitie died, Ray and Alan Mills had been drinking with him. They had been joined by Tony Lambrianou, who had ingratiated himself into the fringes of the Kray gang. Lambrianou invited them all to a party, the trio not knowing that they were walking into a trap for Jack the Hat.

The party was in a basement flat. Jack walked in followed by Lambrianou with the Millses at the rear. As soon as the door opened, Ray and Alan saw Reggie Kray point a gun at Jack's head. Ray turned round to Alan and said, 'We don't need any part of this,' and they left without entering. Reggie's gun seized up, so he had to use a kitchen knife to kill Jack the Hat.

I saw Ray a few days later, and he told me, 'I'm not getting involved. I'm going up to Brum.' Alan later got arrested and did give evidence under pressure from the police. They threatened to charge him if he didn't make a statement.

An era was coming to an end. Ron and Reggie were given sentences of 30 years. In their case, life meant life. Other gang members John Barry, Ronnie Bender, Tony and Chris Lambrianou all got life. Freddie Foreman and Charlie Kray both got tens, Connie Whitehead seven years and Albert Donaghue two years. At the time, it was one of the longest-running trials at the Old Bailey, and the judge, Melford Stevenson, set an example with his harsh sentencing. The authorities had taken a heavy-handed political decision that people like the Krays would not be tolerated by the system, and home secretary after home secretary didn't have the guts or gumption to release Ron or Reg.

As the Krays' reign was ending, so were the swinging '60s, and my relationship with John Bloom was beginning to leave a lot to be desired. We had a lot of domestic issues, and we both decided to go our separate ways. Bloom was under stress due to his upcoming court hearing into his nefarious business affairs and financial well-being. He was represented by Michael Sheridan, who took the case on against all the odds. There was a ton of incriminating paperwork against Bloom, but somehow, after a lengthy legal process, he escaped with a large fine. (Not that large for him.) British justice had been seen to be done.

Bloom eventually went to California, where he opened a string of English-style pubs and restaurants, but he soon got into trouble with the authorities. The FBI got involved, and Bloom told them that the Mafia had threatened to shoot him. This was another shrewd move. The authorities didn't want to cause themselves international embarrassment and decided just to kick Bloom out of the USA. The last I heard of him he was living on a yacht in a Majorcan marina, but, knowing Bloom, he could be anywhere in the world planning his next comeback. Be afraid, be very afraid.

10

· · · · · · ·

Son of a Gun

I sold off most of my smaller partnerships and concerns and concentrated on my new casino, The Twenty-one Club in Hampstead. I'd been advised that it was the sort of place to make big money, and I had a very astute manager running the club called Harry Josephs, who had a very well-known brother named 'One Armed' Lou. I kept a float of about £10,000 for the tables, but roulette was so volatile that this amount, even though a fortune in the late '60s, wasn't enough to counter a high roller hitting a lucky streak.

Cecil Zang, a millionaire who made his money through ballpoint pens, was a fearless gambler, and I had been warned never to accept personal cheques from him, although company ones were OK. One night, Zang had cashed £11,000 worth of company cheques, and Harry knew that this was the club's limit. I was at a club called Celebrity in Mayfair when Harry rang me to tell me the SP. He suggested enough was enough, and I agreed, as it was four in the morning, although this wasn't all that late by casino standards. I told Harry I'd be over in half an hour.

When I arrived, I was greeted outside by Cecil, who begged me to accept one more cheque for two grand, adding that he was a good customer and would leave if he lost. I told Harry to give him another two grand of chips and raise the house limit, thinking that Cecil would lose his money faster. I then went downstairs to my office. I hadn't been down there an hour when Harry came down and said, 'Give me two cheques. He's pulled five grand back.'

I said, 'He'll lose it again,' but lady luck was now with Cecil, and he played until 1 p.m. the next afternoon. Not only did he get his eleven grand back, but he won another three on top. It was a sobering experience.

I needed to change tack and employed six girls to bring in Arabs and players from the other venues. The girls would introduce themselves to the gamblers and suggest going to The Twenty-one Club, where they were on a percentage of the bets that their clients lost. In the long run, this plan backfired, as people kept winning, and I was haemorrhaging money. It seemed that I was out of my depth, having made a lot of mistakes, and I decided that the day had come to abandon ship. I sold the club to another gaming boss and went on my way to pastures new.

I now had more time to see my wife and family and was shuttling up and down the M1 and M6 three times a week to visit them in Stafford, although I hoped eventually to persuade Diane to come back to London. On one such occasion in Stafford, I decided to take a trip to Liverpool and drop in on some old faces, as I hadn't been back to the city for a good few years. I met up with Billy Grimwood, an old friend and legendary Liverpool hard man. He'd just introduced a new card-based gambling game to Merseyside from the Smoke. The game consisted of a baize cloth with a range of markings, and his plan was to spread the game all over the north-west – Manchester, Bolton, Preston, etc. – in the coming year. He figured it would take that long for the authorities to ban it. Billy asked me if I wanted to get involved. He had already recruited Eric Mason and David Chand, the infamous Scouser who wouldn't think twice about biting an ear off in a melee. There are still people walking around Merseyside with half an ear.

I told Billy I was taking the family to the Costa del Sol for a fortnight and would get stuck in once I got back, but while I was away an incident occurred. Grimwood and Chand were drinking in The Jokers Club in Liverpool when four London villains came in: Bertie Smalls (later to become a supergrass), Clive Butler, Joe Delaney and Mickey Green, a man I'd known for years. They impressed on Grimwood that the card game was theirs. 'It's our idea,' one of them told him. 'If you want to use it, it'll cost you two grand a week.'

Billy wasn't having that. 'This is Liverpool,' he replied. 'We ain't paying nothing, so don't start any trouble. Even if you're lucky enough to sort me and Dave out, I doubt if you'll get out of the door in one piece. Listen, have a bevvy, or we can get you some female company. We'll look after you, but you'll be getting no money for the cloth.'

With this, Butler chinned Dave but didn't put him away. Dave retaliated and knocked Butler to the floor, then leaned down, lifted his head up and bit his ear clean off. He spat the bloody tissue out in Butler's direction and said, 'Take that back to London instead.' While Dave had been sorting out Butler, Billy had head-butted Smalls and Green, leaving Delaney holding his hands in the air. The four cockneys left The Jokers Club with their tails between their legs.

On my return from Spain, I went up to Dave's house to meet with him and Billy, and they told me what had transpired. Dave was still getting anonymous phone calls, saying things like, 'We're going to kill you. We've dug the graves, and we're coming for you soon.'

I said, 'We don't need this bollocks. Let's go down there and sort it out once and for all.'

So, we drove down in Dave's Rover and headed straight for Delaney's club in Paddington. We walked in, and I went straight over to Delaney and said, 'What's all this malarkey?'

'I didn't know you were involved, Scouse,' he replied, 'but they've taken a liberty with the cloth.'

I said, 'Ring the others, Joe, and we'll sit down and sort it out.' We waited and drank all afternoon, but nobody turned up. Delaney shook hands with all of us, and I took that to be the end of the matter. I then suggested to the others that we should move on to The Astor Club to meet with a few more faces. Billy and Dave were in agreement, so we left, ready to begin another session.

Quite a few people came over to give us their regards, and we drank until three in the morning, at which time I asked for the bill. It came to over £300. I pulled up £80 and Billy threw more than £100 onto the table. We both looked at Dave, who said, 'I've got no money.' It was then that I realised that he hadn't bought a drink all day, which wasn't really surprising, as he was universally known to have tight pockets.

The waiter was now loitering with intent. Billy said, 'Don't hover over us. We'll pay when we're ready.'

As the waiter backed off, Joey Pyle came over. 'Everything all right, Scouse?' he asked. 'Are you off? Let me get the bill.' He had sussed that we had a problem.

'No thanks, Joe,' I replied. 'We're OK. You can pay another time.' That was the sort of man Joey Pyle was, but it wasn't his shout. I said to Dave, 'Don't mug me and Billy off. Pay your whack.' He eventually coughed up and we left The Astor.

The three of us were absolutely rat-arsed. 'I can't drive to Liverpool in this state,' I slurred. 'We'll go to the all-night billiards hall in Windmill Street. We can get some black coffees there.' The billiards hall was a regular haunt of mine, and I knew most of the clientele. As a result, we didn't have to put our hands in our pockets as black coffee after black coffee was brought to our table. After six coffees, I began to wonder why I felt no better. It turned out that well-wishers had put spirits into all of the beverages. The copious amounts of alcohol had taken their toll, and we all started arguing, mainly about Dave's meanness.

During a lull in the disagreement, an acquaintance came over and asked me if I would like to buy a gun. He produced a .38 calibre pistol and pulled the magazine out. Guns were not my bag, so I told him, 'Not really, pal.' Billy then asked for a gander and pulled the trigger. Unbeknown to him, there was a bullet in the barrel, and Dave screamed out in agony as the shot hit him in the ankle.

I shouted, 'You're a clumsy fucking idiot, Bill,' and grabbed the gun off him. The billiard hall had cleared in seconds, including the man selling the pistol. I couldn't leave the offending weapon there, so I took it with me.

Dave was now bleeding badly, so Billy ripped up some towels from the toilets and wrapped them tightly round his ankle. I said, 'We're going back to Liverpool right now.'

'I'll bleed to death,' Dave moaned. 'I need treatment now.'

We sped off, but it soon became apparent that Dave wouldn't make it back to Liverpool. As we had driven away, a lorry driver from Yorkshire who had been in the club had clocked the Rover's registration plate and phoned the police. Not knowing this, I drove to Charing Cross Hospital and dropped Dave outside. 'Get treated, and we'll be back in a couple of hours,' I said.

I intended to drive to Vauxhall Bridge to throw the gun in the

Thames. The weapon was under the driver's seat carpet and would incriminate us both if it was discovered. Billy and I were arguing incessantly while I was driving, and I missed a good chance to get rid of the gun. It proved costly, as I looked in the rear-view mirror and saw a police car behind us. As its flashing blue lights came on, I said to Billy, 'It's come on top. The Old Bill are on to us.'

All of a sudden, cars came from all directions, and two CID officers pulled me through the driver's door, another lay on the bonnet and two more pulled Billy through the passenger door. At a bus stop twenty yards away, eight charwomen ready to go on the early red-eye shift were watching the cabaret. These ladies would prove to be of vital importance in the later court case.

We were taken to West End Central, my second home, and put in custody. Two Scotland Yard CID officers came into my cell, and one of them said, 'If I'd have bumped into you first, I'd have got the gun and shot my toe off to make sure you got a 20, but you've got a nice surprise coming anyway.'

I said, 'Well, you never bumped into me, did you, so fuck off.'

The next day, we were remanded by magistrates to Brixton Prison, and two days later I was separated from Billy and moved to a high-security, category A section block, which housed fourteen top offenders. There were four IRA bombers, six armed robbers and three murderers in there at the time. It was now evident that the authorities were going for the jugular. I was to be on remand at Brixton for ten months, and in all that time I didn't see Billy again until the day of the court case.

I became really pally with all of the category A prisoners. The 14 of us really bonded, knowing that the system was trying to squeeze us into oblivion. The four IRA guys came over as genuine people, and even though I didn't agree with their methods, I felt a certain sympathy towards them. One of the armed robbers was a man called Ronnie Darke, whom I had known previously. He was in for a hold-up on a security van in Ilford during which somebody had been shot.

One day, I was called out for a visit. I wondered who it was, because I'd told Diane not to come while I was on remand, as it was too much for the kids. In walked Joan Walker, the pretty redhead who I'd met on the visit to my gran's years earlier. Joan had come down to Brixton with her friend Christine Corrigan, Billy's girlfriend. I got to know Joan very well, as the two girls stayed down for four days. They had little money, so Christine booked into a grotty local bed and breakfast and sneaked Joan into the room when the coast was clear. Each morning when the landlady brought up breakfast, Joan had to hide under the bed, cussing as Christine ate all the food whilst chatting to the host. They had even come down to London on the train with only platform tickets, bunking into the toilets when the ticket collector appeared.

After the second day's visit, I arranged for Joan to go to a couple of pubs where I knew some faces who would help with their expenses. I don't know how much they collected, but they moved to a hotel on Park Lane. She was a canny lass. I asked her how much she had been given, but she just smiled and said, 'Not much.' I never have found out how much it was. After Joan returned to Liverpool, she regularly sent me letters and tobacco until my trial. It was greatly appreciated.

Six weeks into my time at Brixton, I was committed for trial at the Old Bailey, where I received my deposition in the holding room. On page two, I read about my interview with DC Simmonds. This was remarkable, because I'd never made a statement or met the man. There were two CID officers outside the room, and I shouted through to them, 'Who's this DC Simmonds?'

The shorter one replied, 'I'm Simmonds.'

'This deposition is full of shit,' I said. 'I don't know you from Adam.'

He smirked and whispered, 'You know the score. The bottom line is: you're going down.'

I fluctuated between feeling sick and angry, but the worst was yet to come. Further on in the deposition, it stated that before I had been overpowered I'd pointed the gun at one of the arresting officers and remarked, 'This one up the spout is for you.'

My brief was a young Jewish barrister. His name escapes me, but he later went on to form part of the defence team that successfully represented the Maxwell brothers, sons of captain Bob, in a well-publicised fraud case. He told me that two of the arresting officers had been awarded Queen's Gallantry Medals: one for lying on a stationary car bonnet and the other for disarming me from the imaginary gun. This was all very worrying.

My sister Rose was communicating with the brief on my behalf and relaying the information back to me. I instructed her to contact the charladies who had witnessed the incident at the bus stop. One morning at 5 a.m., Rose and the brief headed down to see if any of them would give evidence in court. This resulted in four of the ladies making a statement and agreeing to appear on my behalf. Things were now looking a lot brighter for the forthcoming trial.

Ronnie Darke was in the next cell to me. Every morning he would receive a small dose of white liquid from the medic screw. I asked him, 'Why are you drinking that crap, Ronnie?'

'It calms me right down, Scouse,' he replied.

'Well, you ought to read my depositions,' I said. 'They'd send you right through the roof.'

'You should try it, Scouse. It's good gear.'

The trial was fast approaching – in fact, it was about three weeks away – so I asked the medic for a daily dose, which I didn't swallow. Instead, I saved it in a beaker until the morning I was scheduled to appear in the witness box, hoping that it would help to keep me calm.

My trial was held in number one court at the Old Bailey in 1970. I was nearly 37, and if I was found guilty, I wouldn't see the outside until my early 50s. The case went on for four weeks and produced one of the most colourful shouting exchanges seen at the Old Bailey for many a year.

Each morning, I was taken to court in a Black Maria with two motorbikes in front and a police car following, all sirens blazing. Billy and I were placed in separate holding cells and only brought together when we sat in the dock. Joan Walker attended every day of the case. I never asked her to come, but it showed her loyalty to me. The eight men and four women of the jury were sworn in, and the first few days were taken up by the prosecution outlining their case. They laid it on thick, suggesting that the accidental shooting of David Chand in the billiard hall was done on purpose.

The evidence given by the two bent CID officers stank the court out. They say that there's no smoke without fire, but in this case it was the police shovelling the coal on. It didn't take me and Billy long to suss out the judge, who thought that the police were evangelists and anybody who accused them of lying was a heretic. Billy's brief came to the decision that he should not call the police liars and when questioned Billy would simply answer, 'I can't remember.' This turned out to be a momentous blunder.

Altogether, five CID officers gave evidence. The one who was supposed to have been in mortal danger from the firearm and the other who had dived onto the car bonnet were up first, swanking as the prosecution informed the court that they had been awarded medals for bravery. They were followed by three other CID officers, who all reiterated the identical fictitious account.

Six uniformed officers who had been at the arrest were not called to give evidence, as the CID could not count on them to support their fabrications 100 per cent. At this stage, the case looked like a selling plater nag (a horse running in the lowest standard of race) taking on a classic winning thoroughbred, but my turn was to come, and the defence would have its day. Dave was summoned to the box. He told the jury that the shooting in the billiard hall was a complete accident and that we were all good friends. This snookered the prosecution's claim of a deliberate shooting. It was a small victory in the war. The main battle would be harder to win.

My brief now played his trump card. He grilled the two main CID men in the witness box, extracting the day and times that they had supposedly interviewed me and Billy. Simmonds told the jury that I had been interviewed between 11.15 and 12.15 p.m. and Billy had been seen between 1 and 2 p.m. The brief further cross-examined Simmonds. 'Every time you leave or enter West End Central, do you have to book in and out of the station?' he asked. Simmonds stated that this was the case.

My brief then turned to the judge and requested that the station attendance book be brought into the court. The judge looked down his nose and said, 'Is this really necessary? These are two officers of the Crown.' My brief insisted, and the judge ordered an hour's adjournment.

The station log book duly arrived, and the QC read out the comings and goings on the alleged interview day. Simmonds was back in the box, and my brief said to him, 'According to the station records, you left at 9.30 a.m. and returned at 4.30 p.m. Can you explain how you conducted two interviews when you weren't on the premises?'

Simmonds looked sheepish and said, 'I can't understand this.'

The judge's face was a picture. He had backed up the CID officers, but my brief had turned the case on its head, making a huge point to the jury. The establishment, police and judiciary were singing from the same hymn sheet, but the song was out of tune with the truth. Next up were the four charladies. My QC had questioned them and their statements had been beautifully balanced – all of them had told exactly the same story. None had seen me point the pistol at the copper, and three of them had watched a uniformed officer retrieve the gun from underneath the carpet on the driver's side, hold it up in the air and shout, 'I've found the shooter.' At the time, Billy and I had been detained in a police van. The prosecution tried to coerce the women into giving an account more favourable to the CID version, but they stood firm, telling the truth.

The judge was now extremely angry. So much for him being impartial and an upholder of law and justice. Billy was called and scored an own goal by not taking on the police lies. His brief must have been on something, as it was patently obvious that the CID officers were telling blatant untruths every time they opened their mouths. By making out that his memory was hazy, he did himself no favours.

I was due in the witness box the next morning. When I woke up, I drank all of my medication – it was going to be a long and harrowing day. My brief started by asking me all the usual questions, which he dollied up and I smashed through the covers for four. I breezed along until the Crown began their cross-examination. That's when the fireworks started. 'You had the gun, Johnson, in the billiard hall. I put it to you that it was you who pulled the trigger.'

I lost my rag – the medication couldn't have been working – and said, 'I'm not talking to you.'

The judge interceded. 'You will answer, Johnson.'

'If I'm going to be convicted on a trumped-up charge,' I shouted, 'I'm going to tell the 12 good people of the jury what really happened.'

Exasperated, the judge repeated, 'You will answer the prosecution, Johnson.'

'If I'm found guilty, you'll give me plenty.'

The beak was now on my wavelength. 'Maybe so, Johnson. Maybe so.'

I knew that if I called the police liars, they could bring my record up, so I decided to sink or swim by getting in first and putting my side to the jury. I faced the jury. I felt like Lincoln at the Gettysburg Address. 'I've seen people in prison for the attempted shooting of a police officer, serving decades. For me to get 20 years for something I haven't done would destroy me. I've got a wife and two little girls at home. Why would I want to shoot a policeman in cold blood? You've heard David Chand tell you that his injury was a complete accident. The police have made a big thing of this, even though there's no evidence to support it. Also, you've heard how the CID officers lied about an interview that never happened. The case should have been stopped there and then. They are also lying about my arrest. I never had the gun in my hand. It was always under the carpet in the car. The cleaning ladies have confirmed this. I'm being framed, and I'm fighting for my life.'

The judge interrupted me and told me to be quiet, but I'd got it all off my chest and seemed to have knocked the wind out of the prosecution's sails. 'No more questions,' said the deflated QC. The Crown's dodgy case had been slowly but surely unravelled. The CID's corrupt tissue of lies had been trampled under foot, but you never knew how a jury would react or reach a verdict, and it was now time for them to make a decision.

The jury were out for seven and a half hours in total. When they returned, the judge asked for their verdict on Norman Johnson. The foreman replied with the sweetest words in the universe: 'Not guilty.' Billy Grimwood was also returned not guilty in regard to the attempted shooting of the police officer, but his original charge of GBH against David Chand would go to a retrial, and he would unfairly get seven years. He should have stuck his head over the parapet and taken on the police.

I thanked the jury and looked at the judge. He was steaming. This case showed how rotten the system was in the 1960s and '70s, when the police could verbal up or plant evidence on innocent people and the Crown would back it up. I returned to Stafford, where Diane was waiting for me. She was so relieved when I walked into the house. 'I said I'd get a not guilty,' I told her, but who knows how close I'd come to getting some major bird.

11

·······

The Rock King

After the trial, I mulled around Stafford for a few days, but it was too quiet for me, so on a bank holiday weekend I took my youngest daughter down to Bromley in Kent to visit my sister Rose. She had married an antique dealer named Sandy, who woke me the next day at 5 a.m. 'Norman, I heard a bin go over outside and looked out the back window. There's two coppers climbing the wall.' I leaped out of bed and ran to the front window. There were two police cars parked outside and a throng of blue helmets. I then heard thumping at the front door. 'Are you in trouble, Norman?' Sandy quietly enquired.

'Not that I know of,' I replied. 'You'd better get down and open up before they have the door off its hinges.'

He opened the door, and the blue horde came steaming up the stairs. There were two top brass from Yorkshire amongst them. The taller one, who was wearing a Gannex raincoat, said, 'I am Superintendent Gordon from the Leeds Constabulary. Are you Norman Johnson?'

'Yes,' I replied, 'but that's all I'm saying.' In front of witnesses, I repeated, 'I don't intend to say anything more without a solicitor in attendance.' In those days, I wouldn't speak until my brief had turned up because of the underhand tactics that the police so commonly resorted to.

As I was being taken out, I asked Rose to get in touch with Micky Progl, who would put my sister on to a decent brief. Micky was a woman I knew who lived in nearby Penge. She'd written a book called *Queen of the Underworld*, which, among other things,

103

documented her escape from Holloway Prison – she was the only woman to have ever done so.

Down at Bromley South Police Station, I learned what it was all about. Somebody had been shot and murdered in Leeds. After being banged up in a cell for half an hour, the two Yorkies came in. 'Look, Norman, it's the holiday period. We've come all the way down from Leeds, and we want to get back.'

I just put my head down and looked at the floor. It was obviously going to be a case of good cop, bad cop, as the super's sidekick growled, 'We know all about you, Johnson. You better tell us what you know.' I raised my head and looked him straight in the eyes for a second, then looked down again. He gasped, 'You can tell it's him. He's got killer's eyes.' That statement didn't warrant the time of day, and I carried on giving them the cold shoulder.

They were bouncing off the walls by that point. They didn't know whether to threaten or coax, twist or stick. In their desperation, they started pleading with me. 'Where have you been for the last 48 hours? Just let us know. Then you can go home and so can we.' I carried on as if they both weren't there, saying nothing and looking at my feet.

The super couldn't take it any longer. He walked out, saying, 'You stubborn bastard.' They returned at four in the afternoon. They had calmed down and made out that they were looking out for me. 'Look, Norman,' the superintendent said. 'It's a very serious charge. Let's get this murder cleared up.' I kept quiet.

The brief still hadn't arrived, so I was offered a phone call. 'Rose, did you ring Micky?' I asked.

'It's the bank holiday, Norman,' she replied. 'Everybody seems to be away.'

I didn't want to distress Rose by telling her that it was a murder inquiry, so I thanked her and was escorted back to the cell. 'I'm still not speaking until I get a brief,' I said.

The police were hopping mad and pulling their hair out. They were even going out of their way to find me a solicitor. They had one last go. 'Look, Norman. We've been fair with you. Just tell us where you've been for the last 48 hours.' I responded with silence.

The next morning at 11 a.m., a portly brief turned up. He'd been filled in on the details and said to me, 'If you have done it, we answer every question with "No comment".'

I said, 'You can fuck off. I've never been to Leeds in my life.'

This surprised him. 'So you're not involved?' he asked. 'Can you account for where you've been?'

'Of course I can, but I'm not telling them that,' I confidently replied.

His face was a picture. 'Well, sir, let's get them back in then, shall we?'

Flash Gordon started the proceedings. 'Where were you from midday on Friday onwards?'

I answered immediately. 'I was in Liverpool at Brian Barrett's house. He's a friend of mine. From there, we both went over to Maghull [a district of Liverpool] at 4.30 p.m. on Friday. My Jag's exhaust was rattling, so I booked it into a garage in Mayhill, where it was fixed in an hour. In the meantime, I went to a pub, where there were lots of witnesses. I have the bill for the exhaust with the time and date on it, and after that I returned to Stafford at 8 p.m. and spent two hours in The West Way pub on the Highfields estate, with even more witnesses, before returning home. The next day, I left Stafford at 3 p.m. with my daughter and arrived in Bromley at 6 p.m.'

You didn't have to be Sherlock Holmes to realise that a trip to the Yorkshire Dales for a murder wasn't on the agenda. The sidekick was distraught. 'You've kept us here for two days for that? Why the fuck didn't you tell us all this straight away?' I ignored him again, which didn't seem to have a calming effect on him. 'We'll be in touch if your story doesn't tally,' he added. He was a drowning man, clutching at straws.

I was released, picked up my daughter back in Bromley and returned to Stafford. To this day, I still wonder why I was in the frame. Yorkshire wasn't on my road map, but my brief said, 'If they think the cap fits, they'll interview you.' Apparently, a witness to the murder had provided a description that must have sounded like me – and two million others!

Not long after, I made my way back up the motorway to Liverpool to visit Dave Chand, as Billy Grimwood needed money to pay the legal costs for his forthcoming trial. Dave was on his usual form. 'I haven't got the kind of money that's going to help Billy.' That didn't surprise me, but he said his brother had come up with something interesting.

Roy Chand had been working in Pwllheli, North Wales, and had started dating a local girl, who was the daughter of a businessman known as the 'Rock King'. He wasn't called this because he was Wales's answer to Elvis Presley but because he supplied seaside rock and owned a number of shops. His daughter confided in Roy that one of her father's hobbies was collecting half and full sovereigns. She certainly had Roy's attention, and when she told him that the Rock King didn't like banks and kept the coins and bundles of cash hidden around his house, he recognised a great opportunity for an earner.

He surreptitiously found out where her father lived, which was a luxury upstairs flat above one of his shops. I suggested to Dave that we ought to go to Wales to check out the lie of the land and hatch a plan, and we took three associates with us. Roy Chand returned to Liverpool, Dave and I were on standby, and our three associates did the job.

When the shop closed on the day of the blag, the Rock King went upstairs to his flat. He was on his own when the three men broke in and tied him up. The safe was opened and cash was retrieved from around the house. In all, there were about 1,000 sovereigns in a large bag and £7,500 in cash, which was a bit disappointing, as it had been suggested that he kept over £100,000 in the house.

Being professional, we drove back to England via the Brecon Beacons, keeping off all the main roads. This was a good ploy, as there were road blocks all over North Wales, following a spate of similar robberies. We eventually returned to Dave's house and paid the three other guys their share of the robbery money, putting aside a good amount for Billy's defence. (This came in handy, because Dave and I both got nicked soon after, and it became the money for our own defences.) The sovereigns were hidden away, and I went back to Stafford.

The next day, a Liverpool man called at my house. Brian Barrett was a Merseyside scally and a comical character. Known locally as 'Lagos Willy' after a bad experience in Nigeria, he was as dodgy as Bruce Forsyth's barnet. He told me that he had to go to London to pursue an outstanding debt, then asked if I would go with him. 'I don't need this, Brian,' I told him.

'OK, Norm,' he said. 'I'll sort it out myself.' He wanted to use my phone to call a guy called Freddie Stanley in Liverpool about the matter, but I'd made it a rule never to let people use my home phone and sent him across the road to a public phone box.

On his return, he said to me, 'Have you done the Rock King in Wales?'

I said, 'Don't be so stupid. What makes you say that?'

'Freddie told me that Dave Chand has had a high-speed car chase through the streets of Liverpool and been arrested. The word's out that you're involved.'

'Brian,' I said, 'I will come down to London after all. Let's get going.' At least if there was a scream-up I would be on familiar turf.

We stopped at a hotel in King's Cross, and I decided to wind Brian up. 'I was on the robbery, Brian. One of the guys I took with me had red hair and a flat nose. In fact, he could have been your double.'

I really got him going. He started frantically pacing up and down the room. 'I don't need this, Norm. Fifteen years' bird, and I've got no alibi. Has he got a scar on his upper lip?' I tried to look as serious as I could and gravely nodded. This went on all night. He kept coming back into my bedroom. 'How tall was he, Norm?'

'He's your absolute double. It's like looking in the mirror. You haven't got a twin, have you?' I then added, 'If you're in trouble in later life, he could be an alibi for you.'

Brian moaned, 'I'm in trouble now. I'll be too old to ever use him.'

I was having a job to keep a straight face but never did tell Brian that I was joking. I thought it might keep him on the straight and narrow. We didn't locate the guy who owed Barrett money, and after some consideration I decided I'd head north again to keep the police on their toes, as London might be a bit too hot.

Harry Hilton, the man with whom I'd had the altercation when I was on the run from the army, was now residing in Manchester. Since our fight, we had become good friends, and Manchester seemed as good a place as any to keep my head down, so I travelled up to visit him. When I arrived, I didn't have Harry's number, but he was extremely well known all over town. I popped into a nightclub and asked the owner to contact him.

I sat in the club for about half an hour. A spotlight that had been shining onto the stage was suddenly directed into my face. For a moment, I was blinded, and I then realised that I had a gun pointing to my head. Four CID officers were all over me like a plague of locusts, and I was dragged out of the club. I hadn't realised that there was a nationwide search out for me and that the forces in all the major cities were on red alert to apprehend me. I was taken to a Manchester police station and put in a cell. One of the Old Bill said, 'The North Wales Constabulary will be coming to collect you tomorrow.'

The next morning, I was put in a police car. One of the top officers in Wales was sitting in the front. As we crossed the Welsh border, he turned to me in the back and said, 'It will be many, many years before you leave this country again.'

The journey's end was the foreboding Caernarfon Castle,which at that time was used as a prison, and I was put in a cell that resembled a dungeon. Dave was in the adjoining cell. It was his first time in prison on a major charge, and I knew that the police would put a listening officer outside the cells to record anything that was said.

Dave called out, 'Norman, Norman, what are we going to do?'

I knew I had to shut him up, so I was sharp with him. 'Shut your fucking mouth. Don't talk to me.' Dave didn't know how underhand the police were and how they collected their information. On exercise, I told him the score. He said that he hadn't made a statement, and I told him to say nothing.

The following day, we were taken to an ID parade at a school gym. I knew that we wouldn't get picked out, because we weren't at the scene of the crime. If we were, it would be the set-up of the century. Four people came along the line and walked straight past us. The police went mental, and two Old Bill grabbed and handcuffed me. Then, instead of taking me back to the castle, they took me to the police station. One of them told the super, 'Johnson and Chand haven't been identified.'

The senior officer went bananas. He knew the case was over and shouted, 'Get them fucking out of here and back to the castle.'

I didn't appease his mood by singing, 'Please release me, let me go.' The superintendent was obviously not an Engelbert Humperdinck fan.

That afternoon, two Liverpool CID officers came down to interview me. Because the Rock King case had fallen through, the superintendent had alerted the Merseyside authorities, who had a backlog of similar wrap-up crimes (robberies in which the victim is tied up) to solve. They wanted me and Dave to help them with their inquiries by returning with them to Liverpool to stand on more ID parades. I said, 'You've got no chance.' There was more likelihood of them borrowing a fiver from a Scotsman, but the police were not beaten. If Muhammad would not come to the mountain, they would bring the mountain to Muhammad.

They commandeered an old charabanc and brought down 35 to 40 people to Wales, all of whom had witnessed the Merseyside wrap-ups. A uniformed policeman came into my cell and said, 'You're going into the magistrates' court this afternoon. You can sit where you want. There's a coach party coming in to ID you.'

I smelled alcohol on the officer's breath. He must have had a sneaky pint at dinnertime. I couldn't resist a barbed retort. 'Get away from me. You're pissed. I'm not talking to a drunkard.'

Later on, Dave and I were taken to the court room. It was full of Liverpool CID officers, so I took the copper at his word and sat next to a policewoman, putting my arm around her. In came the cavalry and picked out four Liverpool CID officers. It was comical. They even pointed out Larson, who was the head cop on Merseyside. I'm sure they had better alibis than me. The police were gutted.

The Welsh and Merseyside forces combined hadn't been able to put the finger on either of us, but they had one more ace in the hole. The police produced a female teller from a Pwllheli bank who said that money from my pocket corresponded numerically with notes she had issued to the Rock King. It was total bollocks, but why let the truth get in the way of a good story? On top of that, the Rock King's daughter belatedly told her father that she was going out with Roy Chand, the brother of one of the accused. He was promptly arrested in Liverpool. Add a little bit of verbal for good measure, and the police had a case of sorts, although most of the evidence was circumstantial.

Roy, Dave and I were all put on category A at Risley Prison for six months. In the meantime, we were committed to Chester assizes. I secured a top QC, a retired judge who had taken up practising law again, which he preferred. The money that had been put aside for poor old Billy Grimwood was now used by Dave to secure ace barrister Monty Doverner. Dave handed him over three grand, but I knew this was money well spent, because if Dave got off, Roy and I would also walk.

Monty, a large, imposing man, was on mega money in Liverpool, such was his ability to turn hopeless cases into victory. He made policemen speechless and policewomen cry in the witness box, saying that they were mistaken. He was the absolute dog's bollocks, a man with a loud stentorian voice that boomed across the court room.

The trial at Chester was in court number one, which had recently been vacated by the Moors murder case featuring Ian Brady and Myra Hindley. Our trial would last the best part of two weeks, with numerous ups and downs. The police had a good prosecutor who told the jury that Roy Chand had been dating the Rock King's daughter. He argued that Roy had learned about the lax security surrounding the father's finances and hadn't wasted any time informing his brother, a well-known Liverpool hard man, of the potential of the situation. The brief continued that Dave had in turn involved me, a top national criminal. In this way, he maintained, the plan had been hatched.

The prosecuting brief was very persuasive, but he hadn't reckoned on the brilliance of Monty Doverner. Monty had the jury in the palm of his hand. He ripped every bit of police evidence to pieces. The equivalent of a Siberian tiger, he really put the cat amongst the pigeons, overturning the odds and making a not-guilty verdict the favoured outcome. Even so, the jury was out for seven hours. It was the day before Christmas Eve, and they returned to court at 7 p.m.

I had just beaten one charge of twenty years, and, although not quite as serious, this one needed to be put to bed. Altogether, I had been on remand for nearly 18 months, apart from a small interlude of freedom between cases. Was I feeling lucky? The pressure was unbearable. The jury came back in – this was it. The judge asked the foreman, a middle-aged gentleman, 'How do you find the first defendant, David Chand? Guilty or not guilty?'

Christmas had come a day early. 'Not guilty, your honour,' he replied. With Chand getting an acquittal, I knew that Roy and I would also get a not-guilty verdict.

The Welsh and Merseyside police alliance were there in force and looked like they'd all been to a funeral. Larson in particular was a picture of misery. I couldn't resist smiling and waving over to them. Outside the court, Joan Walker gave me a kiss on the cheek and handed me a bottle of whisky. It tasted great. It was Christmas, and I was a free man.

On the journey home, I reminisced about better times with Billy and Dave. I told them about the time years before when I had been drinking in The Astor Club in Mayfair and had felt a hand on my shoulder. It was Joey Pyle. 'Scouse, here's one of your very own.' I turned around and clocked Freddie Starr. I'd never met him before, and he was even smaller than he looked on TV. He joined me for a drink, but after ten minutes he began to get on my nerves. He was putting cutlery in people's pockets and generally messing about, so I said my goodbyes and didn't see him again for a few years.

The next time I saw him was at The Jacaranda, an all-night drinking club in Liverpool. He was with my mate Brian Barrett but couldn't keep still and was winding everybody up again. It was OK for a short period, but he was outstaying his welcome. Before I left, he invited me, Dave Chand and Billy Grimwood to see him in cabaret at Terry Phillips's club in Garston.

On the night, we arrived just as Freddie was getting into his act. He saw us walking down the aisle. 'Look out, the heavy mob's just come in. There's Billy Grimwood – don't mess about with him. And Scouse Norman – watch out for the head-butts. And Dave Chand – don't let him near your ears or you might go deaf.'

Even worse, the spotlight followed us right down to the front table. I had the right hump and whispered to Grimwood, 'Tell that prick he's going to get hurt.'

Billy crouched down and moved up to the stage. Freddie leaned down, and Billy told him, 'Shut up, you cunt. You're bang in trouble.'

But Freddie didn't know when to stop. He told the audience, 'If I'm not about tomorrow, you know what's happened.' He finished his act and left the stage.

A few minutes later, Terry Phillips brought a large bottle of champers to the table. 'Compliments of Fred,' he said.

'Fuck his champagne,' I replied. 'I want to see him. He's taken a liberty and insulted us.' I liked a joke as much as the next person, but Freddie, as usual, had gone too far.

Two minutes later, Terry came back. 'He's gone, Norm. He's slipped out of the back door.' Freddie was like the guy you see in a pub, playing pool one-handed. He didn't do anything wrong in particular, yet he was the odds-on favourite to get clumped before last orders.

Billy Grimwood tells a great, perhaps apocryphal, story about Freddie Starr. They were having a meal in a restaurant on the riverbank of the Thames. Near the end of the meal, Fred noticed the waiter admiring his Rolex watch. Unbeknown to the waiter, Freddie had just completed a tour of the Far East, where he had purchased half a dozen fake Rolexes for a fiver each. 'Do you like the watch?' he asked the waiter.

'Very much, Mr Starr,' he replied.

'It's yours if you want it.' Fred then lobbed the watch into the Thames. The waiter dived in after it and emerged dripping in filthy water, holding the watch triumphantly in the air. Billy and Fred were rolling about the table.

On another night, we were in a Liverpool club called The Wookey Hollow, and Billy, Dave and I were introduced to that night's star act. It was the tremendous Irish singer Josef Locke, a man not averse to a drink. We were buying him large brandies, which he despatched with great aplomb, and he was mullahed by the time he was due on stage. We kept him going by sending him up more brandies via the waitress. His tie and jacket were on the floor, and Joe was staggering about, but he still belted out song after song. He should only have been on for half an hour but stayed on for an hour and a half. We all had a fantastic night, and as I drove home from the court case I hoped for more of the same in the future.

Young Norman starting
a pugilistic life at
13 years of age

Kicking off at approved school
with Chalky White v.
Fulham Reserves

Me, standing, with two mates after
winning the Middlesex Darts Cup

Me and sister Minnie celebrating
the day I turned pro

Mother May Johnson
and brother Len

Sisters Rose and Sylvia
in Park Lane

Christine Keeler's party,
including me and Reggie Kray

Me with wife Diane in the Canary Isles

Happy times with the family in Puerto Banús

At Wargrave on a visit. Back row: eldest daughter Teresa,
wife Diane and Queen Mother's bodyguard Abdul; front row:
middle daughter Victoria and youngest Rachel

The only known photo of
Princess Umaima, pictured
here at Wargrave Manor

Me on duty with intercom
at Wargrave Manor

Me, Liverpool hard man Billy
Grimwood and Johnny Oates

Back row: cousin Sid Murphy and ex-middleweight Terry Coombs; front row: me and ex-middleweight Teddy Hayes

Terry Coombs, prize-fighter Roy Shaw, comedian Jimmy Jones and me

Relaxing in New York

Me with Rocky Graziano (left)
and Jake LaMotta

My sisters' offspring
from Kansas City

Me and Spencer Morton taking
bets at Chester racecourse

My girlfriend Joan Walker
with a friend in New York

12

•••••••

Kentish Man

In the New Year, my third and youngest daughter Rachel was born. The family was now complete. We were a happy quintet. I was still hitting the tarmacadam to London on a regular basis, but my life was to take another unforeseen turn when I took a phone call from the ex-wrestler Tony Buck, who was now a club proprietor in Liverpool. He said that he had some legitimate business for me regarding a club and asked whether I would be interested. I asked him if the pope was a Catholic and zoomed up the M6.

As I was approaching Tony's club, which was down a one-way street in Liverpool, a car carrying four men cut me up. They were shouting threats and gesticulating, but I'd heard ducks fart before, so I parked up outside the club and locked the car. As I turned round, the four men were running across the car park screaming abuse. I waited until they were right on top of me and then reacted. I head-butted the first one full in the face and then copped the second one on the chin. They both went down, which stopped the other two dead in their tracks. They started shuffling backwards, and I told them, 'Pick those two wankers up and fuck off.'

I went into the club and met Tony Buck. I'd only drunk half my lager when two uniformed policemen came in. They said that they'd had a complaint and were arresting me for GBH. I was taken to the police station and given bail on the understanding that I would return to the magistrates' court on the following Monday. The case was eventually committed to the Crown court for four months' time, but in the meantime I had to report to Stafford Police Station every day at 7 p.m. This was a ball ache, because it stopped me from visiting my businesses in London.

The rivers of life never run smooth, and another incident occurred in Stafford. I came home one day to find a crowd of neighbours gathered outside my house. 'What's going on here?' I asked Diane.

'Somebody's tried to abduct Teresa.' I hit the roof. Teresa was only about seven at the time. It transpired that the man in question was a black guy who lived in the high-rise flats at Brooke Court around the corner. I put Teresa in the car and drove over to the flats.

At Brooke Court, I left Teresa outside with a friend of mine by the name of Taffy while I went inside. On the ground floor, I pressed the lift button, which responded straight away. The door opened and inside was a black guy. I grabbed him by the lapels and dragged him outside. 'What you doing, man?' he screamed. 'You crazy. I get the police.'

I said to Teresa, 'Is this the man?'

She shook her head and said, 'No, Dad.' Well, anybody could make a mistake. I let him go, but I could tell he wasn't happy. I then decided to knock on the caretaker's door, and he pointed me in the right direction.

What I couldn't understand was that this particular bloke was always molesting and bothering young girls, but nobody would do or say anything. I knocked on his flat door. He was a big lump. He said, 'What do you want, man?'

I had to play the situation diplomatically. 'You're wanted downstairs.' I grabbed him by the arm and pushed and coaxed him into the lift.

'What's this all about, man? What's it about?'

I got him outside and again asked Teresa, 'Is this the guy?'

She nodded and said, 'Yes, Dad.' Bing. I cracked him right on the chin, and as he went down I jumped on him. I gave him two or three back-handers and told him, 'If you so much as look at another girl, I'll come back and cut off your balls.'

A crowd had now gathered, and there was cheering, as everybody knew he was a neighbourhood menace. I took Teresa home, and a couple of hours later Taffy came round, saying, 'There's police swarming all over Brooke Court.' I thanked him and went down to Stafford Police Station. I had to report there anyway so decided to give my version of what had happened. I spoke to the duty sergeant. He said, 'Go home, Norman. I've heard nothing.'

As a matter of principle, I'd never help the police, but on this occasion I'd solved a problem for them. They knew that nobody would ever divulge that it was me who hit the guy, so everybody was happy.

Around that time, a couple of pals of mine from Liverpool decided to pay me a social visit. But as soon as Tommy Barry, Terry Corcoran and the two other faces with them reached the outskirts of Stafford, a police car pulled them over. The copper asked why they had come to Stafford and where they had come from. They replied that they'd come from Liverpool to visit a friend. The copper wanted to know who the friend was, and the name Norman Johnson prompted another police car turning up. The four Scousers were escorted down to Stafford Police Station, where they spent five hours in the cells being interrogated. They were eventually released with the instructions that they were to head straight back to Liverpool and not come back.

Tommy Barry telephoned me that night. 'It's bloody marvellous, Norm. We come down to see you, do nothing wrong and end up in the cells. We didn't like them much, so we won't be coming down again.'

'That's considerate of the Stafford Constabulary,' I thought to myself. They obviously didn't want me to be led astray.

The four months to my trial in Liverpool flew by, and I took a Legal Aid barrister, as I thought a not-guilty verdict was a mere formality, but there was a surprise to come. The trial was scheduled to last a day, and the prosecutor called the four blokes as witnesses. They all stated that they came over to me in the car park to discuss the motoring incident. Funny that: I could have sworn they came across to knock my head off!

When it was my turn in the witness box, I told the jury, 'They came over in an aggressive manner, so I acted in self-defence.' These were the days before CCTV, and it was four words against mine, but I was still flabbergasted to get a guilty verdict. What came next was even more surprising. The judge said, 'Norman Johnson, you are an ex-professional boxer. Your hands are lethal weapons. You cannot attack members of the public. You are a man of violence, and you will go to prison for 12 months.'

I couldn't believe it. I had expected to get off, or at the worst receive a suspended sentence, which would have been par for the course. I had even taken my car down to the court car park, so I had to arrange for Diane to come up and pick it up the next day.

I was sent to Walton Prison. In the reception area, the head screw said, 'Look, Jonno. You're a cat A prisoner, but I can't spare two men to follow you all day. I'm going to put you up as a cleaner in the hospital wing. It's a cushy number, but the security is tight, so it'll suit both of us. Keep your nose clean.'

I thought, 'Top banana.' I was put in a dorm with a dozen other guys, and we even had our own TV set. However, after a while, something began to annoy me. Just as I was getting into a TV programme, one of the cons would switch channels. I found out that his name was Wenton. He had been a good ABA champion boxer in the past, and his son would later go on to fight for the British title. One night, I'd had enough and snatched the remote control off him. I then said to the dorm, 'Right, who wants BBC?' I went through the rest of the channels, putting it to a democratic vote. This was a mistake on my part, as Wenton had now lost his little bit of power.

I'd been in the dorm for about two weeks when I was told I'd got a transfer to an open prison. 'Unbelievable,' I thought. 'I've got a right result here.' I was taken over to the main prison and put on the top landing, which was known as the Fours, and kept in a cell for four days. The principal officer then paid me a visit. I said, 'What's this about an open camp?'

He smiled and said, 'You know you can't go to an open prison, Jonno. They just didn't want you in the hospital wing, as you were controlling the TV.' I later found out that Wenton had been putting notes in the letter box (a comment box), saying that I was controlling and manipulative with the TV remote. 'You can clean the landing wing here,' he continued. 'Keep yourself busy. That way your cell will be open all day. Will that do?' I had no option. I suppose it could have been worse.

The rest of my sentence was uneventful, and I was eventually released. When I got home, if I was ever watching TV, I would always pass the remote to Diane and say, 'Here, you have this. It can get you into trouble.'

Stafford seemed like the far reaches of the universe, and I needed to be at the centre, so I spoke to Diane about moving. 'Look, this travelling is getting me down. I want all the family with me down south. I know you don't like central London, but what would you say to Kent?' Diane was up for it. She thought it would be good for the children, so I went house hunting and rented a place off the A2 near Gravesend, which I eventually bought.

The whole family was happy, and my business was going well. I had opened another spieler in Earls Court, and people were approaching me to collect debts and do favours. It was like I had never been away. The money was flowing in again and life was good. Living in Kent, I soon realised what a beautiful county it was, so I started looking for an opportunity to swerve London and set up something in the garden of England. That way I could be even closer to the wife and kids.

I started frequenting and drinking in a large nightclub near Brands Hatch called The King's Lodge, which attracted a large number of south London faces and characters. One night I was drinking at the bar with the owner, a Turkish guy called Oscar, when his brother Paul, who was the manager, came across looking agitated. 'Oscar, I'm having trouble with table 11. I've been over twice, and they don't want to pay. They don't seem like gentlemen.'

I said to Oscar, 'I'll sort this out.' I knew a few faces at the table and walked over. I was warmly greeted and said, 'Look, sort your bill out. Don't take liberties. These are good people here.'

'No worries, Scouse,' one of them replied, and I returned to Oscar and Paul.

'You won't have any problems with the bill now,' I said. Paul returned to the table, and the bill was settled on the spot.

Oscar was impressed. 'Norman, would you like to look after the club?' he asked.

'No, but I'd be interested in buying it or becoming a partner.'

Oscar nodded. 'Maybe we can come to some arrangement. Let's meet at my house tomorrow over dinner.'

The next day, I went over to Oscar's house, which was behind another smaller drinking club he owned called Oscar's. (How did he come up with such an original name?) Again, it was a well-known drinking haunt for the south London fraternity. Oscar had mulled over my proposition, and he declared an interest in us forming a partnership for £10,000. I gave him four big ones straight away and paid the balance within the month.

The club was already doing very well without my input. It held 600 on disco nights at £5 a head admission, and on cabaret and meal nights we could cater for 400 people at £10 a throw. I decided to invest more money in the club by upgrading the decor and spent thousands on seating and upholstery, as I wanted to attract class acts for the public.

One evening, Roy Shaw, the bare-knuckle boxer and a one-man source of menace, came in with a friend. I hadn't known Roy long, as he had just finished a long stretch in prison. We had first met at Ronnie Knight's club, and I thought he was a lovely man. He became a legend when he had two fantastic fights with another cracking fellow, the late, great Lenny McLean. I knew Lenny's mother Moggy very well. She could fight as well as any man. Roy had come in with the comedian Jimmy Jones, whom I'd heard of but didn't know that well. However, Roy told me that Jimmy was the business, so I booked him to appear one Saturday night.

Well, we could have sold the place out twice over, and on the night we were turning scores of people away. Jimmy played the club many times after that and was only one of the many great comedians to appear at The King's Lodge. Legendary Liverpool comedian Jackie Hamilton was a popular entertainer, and the Scouse hall of famer had them rolling in the aisles on a number of occasions, while Bernard Manning and Faith Brown also gave show-stopping performances and brought the house down. The great nights were too numerous to mention, but a good time was always guaranteed.

Mondays were disco night. The club DJ was a guy called Pete Tong, who later went on to become very famous and have great success. Mind you, he had a fair old following in those days. Disco nights were packed and the club was always jumping. One Tuesday, the manager Paul came over to me and said, 'Pete Tong wants more money.'

I said, 'Tell him to sling his hook,' and left it at that.

The following Monday, I drove into Kent from the West End. On approaching the club, I noticed that there weren't many vehicles in the car park, which was strange, as it was normally packed. Even the road outside was often bumper to bumper, but on this night there were only about 20 cars in total on the premises. It was about as busy as a pork-pie shop in Tel Aviv.

I went in and buttonholed Paul. 'Where the fuck is everybody?'

'They've all followed Pete Tong down to The Tavern,' he replied. 'I got rid of him like you said.' I hadn't realised that even in those days DJs had a following.

Paul and I jumped in the car and drove down to The Tavern. I said to Paul, 'Go in and tell him he's got his rise. I want him back next Monday.' The following week, the car park was full again – Pete Tong was back. He was certainly a boy going places.

After a few months, I made Oscar an offer he couldn't refuse, and he succumbed to the chance of making a very handsome profit on his investment. I was now the sole proprietor. I kept on all the staff that Oscar had hired until I formed my own opinion of them. The head chef Carlo was an Italian from Bologna, and his menu wouldn't have won any Egon Ronay awards. His starters were always soup or prawn cocktail, the main courses steak or chicken and the desserts were very basic. However, Diane took a shine to him, as every time she went into the kitchen he addressed her as 'Madame'.

When I joined the partnership, Carlo's wages were £400 for three nights' work, so I asked a few friends who were au fait with the food game and was told that this was way over the top.

When I took over sole ownership, I said to Carlo, 'I'm putting your money down to £100 a night. You can leave if you want.'

Carlo declined to move and started to address Diane as 'Mrs Johnson'. She said to me, 'Have you dropped Carlo's wages?' I admitted that I had.

People were still telling me that chefs at the top London hotels weren't earning what Carlo was, so I popped in to see him again. I said, 'Carlo, I've been thinking about things. The top whack I can pay you is £200. What do you want to do?'

He looked grim and replied, 'OK, I stay, but no more droppo.'

That night Diane came to me and said, 'You've cut his wages again, haven't you?'

'How do you know?' I asked.

'Because he's now referring to me as "Hey You". Can't you put his money back up? I liked being called Madame.' Carlo never got a rise, but I had a good laugh about Diane's delusions of grandeur.

The club was firing on all cylinders, and one night Paul Moriarty, the famous doorman and occasional actor, came in. His list of credits now include *The Long Good Friday*, *Jaws III* and *Lock, Stock and Two Smoking Barrels*. He asked me if I had any door work, so I took him on. There wasn't much trouble at the club, but I'd met him many times and liked him, and he did good work.

Six months later, Terry Donnelly, an old friend of mine, came to the club for a drink. He said, 'Scouse, I've been down a few times, but you've not been here.'

'I'm only down for the last few hours, as I've interests in the West End as well,' I said.

Later that evening, I said, 'I'll tell you what, Terry. I don't trust the manager, Paul. He's good at his job, but I've heard he was robbing his brother Oscar before I came along.' I then said, 'Come and have a look at this,' and led him to my office. In the room, there was a noose hanging from a beam. I said, 'Paul will be on the end of that if I catch his fingers in the till.' Terry laughed, but he knew I meant it.

Terry told me that he was leaving the building trade and would like to get involved in the nightclub game. He said, 'You can trust me 100 per cent, and you could take a break whenever you like.'

I hadn't had a holiday for ages. 'I'll think about it,' I said. 'Leave your number and I'll get back to you.' I consulted Diane, and we agreed that it was a good idea, although it turned out later that it was far from it.

It didn't take long for the new partnership to fray at the edges. On his say so, Terry's friends were coming down at weekends from south London drinking clubs at 1 a.m. Some nights they arrived when Terry wasn't even there. If I was there when they came down late, I would give them a welcome to remember. 'You're not coming in at this time,' I'd say. 'Come at eight o'clock like everybody else. You're not using this club for your own ends.' They would turn tail and slink back into the night. If I'd let them in at one o'clock, I might have lost my licence, and then I'd have been left with an empty shell. I didn't need to give the police an excuse to close me down, as they were constantly watching me.

Terry started not turning up on the busy nights when I needed a hand, and his cronies continued to arrive late and expect to be let in. This carried on for another two weeks before I decided that the partnership wasn't working. Me and Mr Donnelly were going to have a falling-out. On the next busy Saturday, there was again no sign of Terry, and, just to rub it in, six of his buddies turned up at 12.30 a.m. I told them matter-of-factly, 'You're not coming in. Don't even try.'

A gobby one retorted, 'Terry's a partner here. It's his club, and he told us to come down.'

I said, 'I'm the governor here. I say what goes, not Donnelly, so fuck off.' They reluctantly departed, but it was the final straw for me, and the next morning I phoned my erstwhile partner. 'Terry, I want a meeting here today at one o'clock,' I said before slamming down the phone.

Terry arrived at The King's Lodge promptly at 1 p.m. 'What's up, Norm?' he asked.

I was aggressive and sarcastically asked, 'Did you have a nice weekend? You're playing me for a fool. Why are you sending every Tom, Dick and Harry down at one in the morning? The club doesn't need these people. It's not going to be a pisshole.' He made some weak excuses, and I told him, 'I'm not having this, Terry. After this meeting, there's only going to be one governor here. One of us is walking.' I was getting itchy feet at that time. I was always stuck at the club at weekends, so I gave Terry the opportunity to take over. 'You can have it all or you can walk.'

'OK, Norm. How much do you want for it?'

Terry had already paid me what I'd paid Oscar, and I'd made a good profit from the club over the period, so I played fair with him and said, 'I want £10,000. That's what I came in with, so that's the amount I want to walk with.'

He pulled up five grand that week and told me that he'd get the rest as soon as he could. I said, 'Take as long as you like, but until you've paid it all give my wife £500 extra every Monday.' That way I reckoned he wouldn't be able to use the club's profits to pay the remaining balance. Diane collected for six weeks until he gave her the last five grand, so he ended up paying £13,000.

Not long after this episode, Diane said that she felt like a break but didn't want the long haul of going abroad, so we took the kids to the Butlins in Minehead, where they had a great time, as there was so much to do in the camp. However, on the second morning, Diane and I had a blazing row. I don't remember what it was about, but it was a barnstormer. I retired to the bar, and Diane went the opposite way. Apparently, she then had a walk around the reception area, where there were notice boards listing the week's events and sporting contests. Glamorous granny, Miss Butlins and snooker ace were among the many titles to be won. The one that caught Diane's eye, however, was boxer of the week. Yours truly was duly entered for that afternoon's entertainment in the ring.

Later that day, I returned to the chalet, fully expecting another ding dong, but she was quite convivial, which surprised me. She suggested that we go to watch the boxing bouts in the main hall. She reckoned that I'd enjoy it and that it would be a chance to relax.

Well, that would do for me, although I did wonder why she was being so considerate. The kids were packed off to an event in the playground with the Redcoats, and we were free for the afternoon. I settled down to watch the pugilists, whether they be good, bad or indifferent. A guy sitting close to Diane was summoned to the ring. He looked shit scared. I laughed and said to Diane, 'I bet his missus has stuck his name up.' He got battered, bloodied and bruised. Afterwards, it was clear that his nose had seen better days, and when he leaned over the top rope to show his wife the damage, his expression seemed to say, 'This is your fault, you bitch.'

I watched three or four more bouts. There wasn't a lot of quality about. The standard ranged from swinging 16 year olds to gasping men in their early 30s. The announcer then called out the fighters for the next bout on the card. The second name seemed familiar. 'Norman Johnson.' I glanced at Diane, and she looked furtively at the floor. 'You sneaky cow,' I thought. 'That's your game, is it? Watching me get knocked around the ring.'

'Is there a Norman Johnson here?' the announcer repeated. I acknowledged the call. I was the wrong side of forty-six and two stone overweight – ten pints a night and forty fags a day weren't the best training regimes – but I still had a devastating punch in either hand. There's an old boxing saying: 'Your legs might go, but your punch never leaves you.' It was only a pity that I couldn't use my head. Then again, what would the Marquess of Queensbury have said?

The guy I was fighting was about 20 years old. I was very adept at sizing up an opponent quickly, after having been in hundreds of fights, legal and illegal. I came in with my hands down, looking to see what he had. Two crazy swings later, I knew how much boxing ability he possessed – none! I feinted to the left, and as he moved in I swung my right into his side. He went down quicker than the Wall Street Crash. I hadn't been too hard on him, though, as he was only young – he was just winded.

I won three more fights, and I had hardly had a glove laid on me, so stamina wasn't a problem. I was despatching them quickly and quietly. I was through to the final against a guy who had quite a vocal backing of about ten or twelve raucous supporters. He'd been dropping opponents with aplomb. It was obvious to me that he'd done a bit between the ropes, and I was also giving him 20 years.

The first round was even. He was a good boxer and caught me with a couple of smart shots. He took mine well, too. The problem was that when I got back to my corner, I was gasping for air. I knew I couldn't go three rounds at this pace. I'd have to finish it in the second. Thirty seconds in, he provided me with the perfect opportunity. I don't know if it was intentional, but he butted me on the left eye, causing it to swell like a golf ball. I went at him with a disciplined aggression. Bish, bosh. Two lethal body punches put him on his knees. He stayed there for a ten count. He'd made a good decision.

Later on in the week, I was presented with a little cup. My eye still wasn't pretty, but my picture was taken and the compere announced that I would represent Minehead against other holiday camps later on in the season. There was more chance of crawling under a rattle snake with a top hat on. I would retire gracefully and undefeated. I also told Diane that I would never be taking her back to Butlins again.

I still had the spieler in Earls Court, and it didn't take long for another opportunity to cross my path. An old friend by the name of Terry Coombs asked me to meet him for a drink in The Downham Tavern, a very large pub near Catford. While we were drinking, the landlord, George, came over. I hadn't seen him for the best part of five years. He had a large fresh scar on his face and forehead. 'Who have you been fighting with?' I asked.

'Oh, there was some aggro at the disco, and I went over to stop it and got glassed.' Before I left, he gave me the lowdown. 'I'm looking for someone to manage the disco. I'll give them all of the door money, because I'm sick of the trouble. There's been stabbings, gang fights and criminal damage [and that was just on ladies' night]. Could you help me, Scouse?' I told him that it wouldn't be a problem.

I went down to a billiards hall in Lewisham, as I wanted help from somebody local. I spotted two ex-boxers, whom I knew well. 'What are you two up to at the moment?' I asked.

'Not a lot,' they replied in unison. I explained to them about the disco and told them that if they ran the door, I would pay them 25 per cent of the take each. They were delighted, and we met up early on the following Friday evening. The Tavern quickly filled up, and on the first night we took over £500.

I left them to it on the Saturday. I expected the takings to be about the same and was looking to take home approximately £500 each weekend for myself. I told them, 'If it ever kicks off bad, call me and I'll come straight down. Give my share to Diane each week, and I'll look after my other concerns in the city.' Diane was made aware of the arrangement and expected to receive the money every Monday. I was happy to leave it at that.

About a month later, I said to Diane in passing, 'It's a cracking little earner, that disco.'

She pulled a face and said, 'Well, it must be dying on its feet, because I get less and less each week.' She told me the figures and explained that the last time they'd been round they'd handed her less than £100.

The pair of them must have been punch drunk from their boxing careers, as it seemed that they were unable to count above a certain figure, so I decided to put in a surprise appearance at The Downham Tavern that coming Friday evening.

I was accompanied by Johnny Crompton, who was a very useful fighter, and we walked in to find the place heaving. The two ex-boxers were larging it up at the bar with their cronies, and two of their other mates were collecting at the door. I walked straight up to them, and one of them said, 'Scouse, it's unbelievable that you've come tonight of all nights. It's been as dead as a doornail.'

'Do you think I've come down the river on a banana boat?' I asked. 'If you'd have sent the wife a decent amount, I'd have swallowed it, but you've taken the piss. This is your last night here.'

I sat down with John Crompton for a drink, and George the landlord eventually came over. 'John's going to take over the disco, George. He's a handy man, and I'll still be about if I'm needed.'

I said to John, 'Is £2,000 all right?'

'Lovely, Scouse. It won't take me long to pull that back, looking at this crowd.'

I went back over to the pair of them and reiterated that their services had been severed. If only they'd used their common sense and played honest indian, there would have been a good slice of the cake for everyone. At that time, I had to keep a continual watch on my associates in case they tried to take me for a grand or a monkey (£500), serious money in those days.

I didn't know that a momentous change in my life was just around the corner. The money that I'd spent and saved thus far was like a grain of sand in the Sahara Desert in comparison to what I was about to experience.

13
· · · · · · ·

When Worlds Collide

Oh, East is East, and West is West,
and never the twain shall meet.

RUDYARD KIPLING

It was 1979, and I was a young 46-year-old man on a mission. I was still making a good few shillings out of the spielers when out of the blue I received a phone call from my younger brother Leonard. Now, Len and I were never that close, the main reason being that I'd been in approved schools, borstals and prison from the age of 13. Len had never received so much as a parking ticket. It's sometimes hard to believe that he's my brother, as he's never seen the inside of a police station, but God works in mysterious ways, and it's amazing how frequently these family anomalies crop up.

Our paths hadn't crossed much over the years, as we'd lived completely different lifestyles. I was a night owl, and Len had built up a good career as the boss of a car-hire firm. He married a young Jewish girl called Barbara Katz at the age of 19. She was the daughter of the pianist Dick Katz and his wife Julie. Dick was a boyhood prodigy in his native Austria but escaped with his parents, who were quite wealthy, just prior to the German Nazi occupation during the 1930s when Jews were starting to come under the cosh. He later became a highly successful London theatrical agent, with such stars as Dana, Lulu and the Dave Clark Five under his wings. He also played piano in the Ray Ellington Quartet and tickled the ivories on many UK radio shows during the 1950s and '60s, such as *The Goon Show*. Dick generously gave the happy couple £3,000 as a wedding present, and they decided to try their luck in America but returned six years later.

For the previous five years, Len's luxury limousine company, named Seymour Limousines, had been doing very nicely. The fleet was comprised mainly of Daimlers, but he also had a couple of Jaguars. Len was working long hours but was attracting affluent clientele – among his many patrons were Frank Sinatra, Kirk Douglas, Dionne Warwick and Burt Lancaster. My brother became good friends with most of these superstars, and it did him no harm that his father-in-law had excellent contacts in the pop world.

Len had recently gained a contract to chauffeur the Omani royal family and all their flunkies. As a result, he had four Daimlers for the sultan and his family on permanent standby at £100 per car per day. Len also took me into his confidence that not only was he ferrying the Omani royal family around, but they had also asked him to provide the security at Wargrave Manor, Berkshire, their main base in England. The sultan had outbid Elton John for its purchase; even the Rocket Man couldn't compete with the Omani riches.

This is when I received the phone call that was going to change my life and nearly alter the relationship between Britain and the Middle East for ever! Len asked me if I'd like to take a short holiday with him in West Germany, offering to take me to Garmisch, the picturesque ski resort. I wondered what he was after but fancied a nice break away from the madding crowd. Len had been to Garmisch before, as the sultan had a large castle there. We spent two pleasurable days wining, dining, clubbing and catching up on old times. On the Sunday morning at ten o'clock, Len received a telex from his office that informed him that the Omani queen mother and princess were arriving in Blighty the next day on their private royal jet. After a frantic call home, he discovered to his horror that two of his security team were out of the country. 'We've got to leave straight away, Norm,' he said. 'Could you help me?'

'I don't open doors for anyone, Len,' I replied.

'You won't have to. You can just sit in the security room and watch on the cameras. It'll only be for three or four days. I'd appreciate it if you could help me out.' I couldn't really refuse him and reluctantly agreed to stand in. We caught a flight to Heathrow, from where we drove straight to Wargrave Manor, a large white mansion on a high hill surrounded by rambling acres. I was introduced to all of the staff as a new security man and then went upstairs to get changed.

The next morning, Len and Sid Murphy, one of our cousins who'd also worked for me in the past, went back down to Heathrow to meet the two royals. The Omani jet flew in, and the princess and queen mother were ushered into a private suite for royalty and celebrities. The room was named the Alcock and Brown Suite after the famous British aviators but was affectionately known amongst the staff as the Sammy Davis, Junior.

They arrived back at Wargrave Manor without incident. I was in the security room, which was situated near to the back door. The day was dragging, and the clock hands seemed to be moving in slow motion. Len, Sid and another big lump by the name of Wally Groves joined me in the control room. Suddenly the princess flounced in unannounced. The three other guys leaped to their feet and nearly butted the floor with overelaborate bows. I didn't move a muscle and remained stationary in my seat.

Len said, 'Would you like to inspect the new horses, your majesty?' She totally ignored him and turned on her heel, but not before giving me the look of Beelzebub. Apparently, she had an awful reputation and temper, and the staff were petrified of her, but I didn't work for her and couldn't have cared less.

The next day, the same thing happened again. This time, though, it was only me and big Wally in the security room. In she waltzed and up went Wal like Nat Lofthouse, nearly giving himself a hernia. I nonchalantly carried on watching the security screens, refusing to defer to her. She gave me the evil eye again. If looks could've killed, I'd have been a dead man. Silence was the order of the day, and she went on her way. On the fourth day, which was supposed to be my final one, she walked in on me, Len and Sid. Up they went like bottles of pop and kowtowed to the princess. I still wasn't having any of it.

'Would you like a walk in the grounds, your highness?' She didn't reply. Instead, she stood stationary for a moment then pointed to me and departed. Len said to me, 'Quick, Norm. She wants you to escort her.'

I said, 'Fuck me, Len. I don't need this,' and slowly trudged after her. We walked side by side and seemed to be heading in the direction of the stables. These were lavish, with living quarters above the stalls for the Omani staff, who were all ladies. I followed her into the state-of-the-art stables, which housed two new thoroughbreds. Inside, there was a large steel drum full of oats and a silver scoop lying by it. The princess gestured for me to scoop up the oats and said in broken English, 'You give to horse.' I filled the scoop and passed it to her. 'No, no. You, you,' she insisted.

I wearily went towards one of the horses to tip the oats into his door trough. As I got near his face, he whinnied and tossed his head back and forth as horses do, but he must have been really hungry, because he covered my face and jacket in thick slobber. 'You dirty bastard,' I exclaimed and threw the scoop back into the drum. When I turned round, the princess was laughing hysterically. I was amazed by this, as she hadn't shown any emotion at all over the previous four days. 'Maybe the cold fish is swimming into warmer currents,' I thought.

I had half a gallon of horse flob on my face and jacket and was trying frantically to wipe it off. The princess knew I had to get washed and changed, and we walked back to the house in silence. Nothing more was said, and it was back to normal again.

The next morning, I met Len downstairs. 'Have your security guys turned up yet?' I asked.

Len gave me the bad news. 'They can't get here until the weekend. Can you stay a tad longer?' I wasn't happy, but I couldn't let Len down.

That day, the personal doctor to the Omani royal family, who was on 24-hour call, asked Len to get one of the Daimlers ready. The princess wanted to go on a shopping expedition. Her favourite port of call was Harrods, where she spent the Omani millions at will. The chauffeur was a very large Scotsman called Mark, and he pulled the Daimler up in front of the manor. The princess got in the back, and the car sped up towards the gatehouse and was just going through when the princess uttered something to the doctor in Arabic. The doc then said to Mark, 'Turn around now. Princess Umaima wants to go back.' The car shot back to the house, and the doctor said, 'Umaima wanted the other man.'

Len was gutted – he always enjoyed the London shopping sprees – and went to fetch Sid. On seeing Sid, the princess said, 'No, no, no,' so Len went back to fetch big Wally, who was made up. However, his arrival was met with the same response. Apparently, she wanted me, but, again, I could have done without it. To tell you the truth, I was having trouble with peptic ulcers. On top of that, an old ankle injury was giving me a lot of gyp. I squeezed into the front seat, and the doctor passed me a large bundle of bank notes. 'There's £5,000 there, Norman. Get a receipt for everything.' The procedure went as follows: the princess would buy something, I would pay for it and the chauffeur would take it to the motor. Well, that was what was supposed to happen.

We pulled up in front of Harrods. I don't care if you are the king of kings or God Almighty, you cannot park in front of the department store. So, I placed a foot stool by the back door of the car for the princess and, once she had alighted, said to Mark, 'Find a parking space and get back double quick.'

The princess was off like Shergar, and I hurried to catch her up. She headed straight for the perfume counter. The assistant handed her the latest fragrance, and she sprayed it onto her wrist to take in the aroma. 'I like. Ten,' she said. Then she was gone, up and away to the next counter. I had to pay for the ten perfumes and still not let the princess out of my sight. There was no sign of the flying Scotsman, and I began to panic. I needed eyes in the back of my head to take in everything that was happening. She had now reached the handbag counter. 'I like. Six.' She ordered six of the the same leather handbag, one in each available colour. My ulcers were starting to irritate me, and I was sweating like a dray horse. Big Mark had now returned. 'Where have you parked it?' I asked. 'Birmingham? Take that bag of perfumes and grab those handbags.'

I paid for the handbags and caught the princess by the wrist. 'No more. We're going home. Shopping's over.'

'Don't talk to me like that. I say what to do.' She then kicked me right on my dodgy ankle. I was hot, flustered and irate. My ulcers were murder, and now my ankle was throbbing. 'No, I say enough. We're going back to the car.'

The doctor decided to stick his oar in. 'You're a very bad man. You cannot talk to the princess like that.'

'Shut your mouth. You stay if you like. We're going.'

A distinctly unhappy band of warriors returned to the Daimler. The princess was shooting me daggers, while the doctor was muttering under his breath and Mark was looking at me incredulously. The journey back to Wargrave was tense and silent, and I decided there and then that I was going back to my wife and kids and the nightclubs. This life was alien to me, and I was never going to be a lackey.

Len was at the front door. I walked straight past him and went upstairs to start packing my clothes. He came into my room and said, 'I need you to stay, Norm,' but I told him that I couldn't put up with all this horse shit. 'Think about it,' he replied. 'I really need you to hang about a while longer.' And with that, he left the room.

Len had given me a dilemma. I wanted to help him out, but the call of London was tugging me the other way. Just then, I felt another presence in the room and wheeled around. The princess was standing in the middle of the room. 'What are you doing?' she enquired.

'I'm packing my clothes and going home.'

She looked troubled and said, 'You're a good soldier. I want you to stay. I don't want you to go.'

This got me to thinking. I'd been distinctly unfriendly and uncommunicative, so why would she want me to stay? I was extremely curious to find out, and my loyalty to Len meant that I decided to stay around for a short while. 'OK, I'll stay, but just for a few days.' The princess's face lit up. She seemed pleased and bounced out of the room. Things would become a lot clearer in the near future.

I settled into my security work again. My call name was 'Whisky One', Len was 'Whisky Two', Sid 'Whisky Three' and Wally 'Whisky Four'. There were also two men in each of the rear and front gatehouses, making eight security men in total. The estate manager was a fellow called Major Rose, who had served in the British Army in Oman. His glittering career in the forces had unfortunately come to an abrupt end when he'd trod on a land mine and had both his legs blown off. After a lengthy convalescence and recuperation, he'd been sent from Oman to Wargrave to look after the estate by a Colonel Harcourt, the top military man there. He was also under orders to keep his eyes on the comings and goings of the Omani royal family. The British empire and army were politically and strategically intertwined with the Omani royal house, a situation which suited both their needs.

Rose was a disciplinarian and tried to run the estate like an army battalion. The stable and gardening staff especially resented his regime. He was always throwing his weight about with the kitchen staff and even the chauffeurs, which culminated in Rose and Len falling out. Len told the half soldier, 'Keep out of the house. It's not your jurisdiction. I'm in charge inside. You look after the estate like you're supposed to and keep well away from my drivers.' Of course, this caused friction and ill will, and Major Rose was never slow to report back to Harcourt in Oman about the disrespectful civilians in the Wargrave household. I was later to have my own exchanges with Rose, but that was another matter entirely.

14

·······

Dangerous Liaisons

It looked like I was in for the long haul, as I was now settling into the job and quite enjoying it. Len was paying me a good whack, and my clubs were in good hands.

About three weeks later, I was in the security room one night. It had just turned midnight when the phone rang. Sid, Len and Wally usually worked until around about that time, but I would stay on until 1 a.m. in case of any late calls. I answered the phone. It was the princess. 'You bring me a cup of tea,' she said.

'The butler has gone to bed,' I told her.

'No, you bring,' she replied.

I thought, 'I'm back to menial work again,' and went to the kitchen, which contained the finest Royal Doulton porcelain laid out on silver salvers. I brewed up and poured the tea into a workman's mug. I always think tea tastes better in a mug, especially in one that says 'I Love London' on the side. I knocked on her door and entered to find Umaima sitting on a huge white leather settee. She clocked the mug and smiled. I think it was because she saw that I had no pretensions that she found me interesting. I put the mug down on the table next to her, but she didn't seem interested in the rosy lee. Instead, she patted the other end of the sofa and said, 'Sit. You like movies, Meesta Norman?' Being a man of few words, I nodded and sat down.

She put on a home movie of her half-brother Qaboos, the new sultan of Oman, visiting the shah of Iran in Teheran. She added, 'Shah is a very good man. My brother is weak. I am strong.' I was getting a history lesson on the Middle East. Umaima then proceeded to tell me about her father, who had been deposed by his son, her half-brother Qaboos. Her father adored her, and she explained how Qaboos had interacted with the British to overthrow him.

The truth of the matter was that her father, Sultan Said bin Taimur, had been a despot who had ruled his people with an iron rod. The country had never been modernised and was barely out of the dark ages. Despite having huge oil reserves, the sultan refused to use the money to benefit his people. It was forbidden to build a house or install a lavatory or gas stove, and people couldn't wear spectacles, go to movies or smoke in the street. Stringent travel restrictions were in place, and personal permission from the sultan was needed to purchase a car. The sultan had a saying: 'Keep the dogs hungry, and they will follow you.'

Qaboos, Taimur's only son, was born in 1940, and at the age of 20 entered Sandhurst Military Academy. Afterwards, he joined the Scottish Rifles, with whom he served out his military career in the British Army. On returning home, he studied Islam and his country's history. Relations with his father soon deteriorated, as they had conflicting notions as to which direction Oman should head, culminating in Qaboos being placed under house arrest. With the help of the British military, Qaboos successfully plotted and overthrew his father in 1970. Said bin Taimur was shot in the uprising but survived and was exiled to England, where he stayed at The Dorchester Hotel, living like a virtual recluse until his death in 1972. He was buried in Woking.

After the film finished, Umaima said, 'You're a good soldier. I watch you.' It hadn't gone unnoticed by me that Umaima's six ladies' maids were always around the house at all hours, checking up on everything. They were her eyes and ears; in fact, they were the security who watched the security. Having been in prison, I was very security minded, and being a criminal meant that I knew better than most how a breach might occur. I would go round the manor checking locks and roller shutters, and when Sid and Len were drinking and playing cards in the staff room, I would be manning the screens and phones. I liked a drink but never on duty and made it a rule to only partake when I was socialising. When I was on my rounds, I would often see a pair of eyes looking out of the darkness from a secluded corner of a room. The maids were ubiquitous; it didn't matter which way you turned, they were there. What they saw must have all been reported back to the princess, which must have stood me in good stead.

She again repeated, 'You're a very good soldier,' and looked at me deeply with her large, dark almond-coloured eyes. As she arched herself forward, closing the distance between us, I was sure she was coming on to me. If I was reading the situation wrongly, what was the worst that could happen? In Oman, I would probably have had a part of me amputated, but this was Great Britain – we didn't go in for that sort of thing. We kissed passionately, for what seemed like for ever, and afterwards sat and gazed at each other for a fleeting moment.

I got up and left. We both knew in which direction this affair was heading. A relationship between a Muslim Omani princess and a notorious London gangster would make one of the most remarkable romantic liaisons in world history. But at that moment, neither of us knew how complicated this amorous tryst would become.

From then on, I was summoned to the princess's room most nights. The other security men were unaware of my movements, as I was always last to finish. Our rendezvous were becoming more passionate, and eventually the inevitable happened when we shared the royal bed. I'm too much of a gentleman to disclose our most intimate moments, but we didn't bother watching any home movies after that.

I always left in the early morning for a few hours' kip in my own bed. Before long, Len commented, 'You're working too hard, Norm. You always look knackered.' Little did he know that on top of my long working hours I was emulating Casanova with the insatiable princess in the early hours. Len had put my money up to £1,000 a week, and I was sleeping with a beautiful Arabian princess every night. At that moment, I couldn't see much wrong with the world.

I spent many hours with Umaima, and I always insisted that she spoke to me in English. This greatly improved her vocabulary and pronunciation, and we started to discuss Western values and culture. One day, Umaima asked, 'Are you married, Norman?'

I solemnly nodded. 'A wife, Diane, and three daughters, princess.' I was still managing to see Diane and the girls a couple of times a month.

'You tell them to come down tomorrow. I'd like to see them.' I phoned Diane and arranged for her to bring the kids down the next day at around noon. They arrived at midday, and I showed them into the lounge. The princess said that she would be down soon, and half an hour later I introduced Umaima to my family. Diane and the kids were lined up as if they were backstage at a Royal Variety Performance. The princess approached Diane, handed her a box of gold jewellery and said, 'Nice to see you.' This gesture was repeated three more times with Rachel, Vicky and Teresa. Once this was done, Umaima spun round, looked at me and said, 'We go shopping now.' She then left the room. This surprised me, as I thought Umaima would want to spend time with my family, getting to know them, but it seemed she just wanted to clock Diane and weigh up the competition. I shrugged my shoulders and said to Diane, 'I'm sorry. I've got to go to London.'

I escorted the princess around Harrods until 6 p.m. 'You think they've gone now?' she suddenly enquired.

'I should think so, princess,' I answered, with a wry smile on my face.

She seemed relieved. 'OK, we go back now.' To this day, I still haven't been able to fathom out how a woman's mind works, whatever nationality she happens to be.

Bibi, the Omani queen mother, also had six hand maids and her own personal bodyguard called Abdul. She was Umaima's stepmother, as the old sultan had married his first wife, Umaima's mother, and then decided he wanted another. Whether Bibi was her name or nickname, I never found out, but that's what she was universally known as.

The sultan had married Bibi when she was slim, but over the years, with the help of a sweet tooth, the queen mother had ballooned. She was a lovely woman, and I got on very well with her. Umaima loved her to bits and treated her like her own mother. She would rarely come out of her living quarters and was always working her way through a large box of chocolates.

Her maids all slept in her large chamber on the floor, wrapped in blankets and cushions, and they never left her side. Stepmother and daughter would regularly lie on the bed for hours on end, the queen mother stroking and teasing her stepdaughter's hair. Occasionally, she did venture out, and I would escort her into the gardens and locate a seat for her in a sun trap.

A few months later, Qaboos came over to Britain from Oman. He swerved Wargrave and went straight to his luxury apartments in Park Lane, the entrance to which was on Upper Brook Street. Sid and Len met him at Heathrow. He trusted them implicitly and used them as his official bodyguards. This left me and Wally to run the security at Wargrave.

The queen mother got wind that her son was over and asked me to find out when Qaboos would be visiting Wargrave. I told her that I'd make some enquiries and telephoned Len at Park Lane. I asked Len to let me know when the sultan was coming over, as Bibi wanted to see him. I was currently spending more and more time with the princess and was sending Wally home at 8 p.m. each night. He lived locally and returned each morning at 8 a.m.

After he left each evening, I would change into T-shirt, slacks and slippers – not really security garb, I know, but I always carried my gun and holster. I was very relaxed, as I knew the princess and I had the run of the house, with all the domestic staff finishing around the same time as Wally.

At 9.30 p.m., two days after Qaboos had arrived in Britain, my walkie-talkie crackled into life. 'Whisky Five to Whisky One. Blue Mercedes arriving at the front gate. Len and Sid with a passenger.'

'Fuck me rigid,' I thought. Len hadn't given me a call, and I looked a right state. I rushed to the front door. Sure enough, Qaboos was pulling up in his privately made armour-plated Merc. Sid and Len jumped out and ushered the sultan in. He didn't look me up and down – he just looked me down. I was given a curt 'Good evening', and he brushed straight past me. I hadn't made a good first impression, because he hadn't seen me suited and booted.

Qaboos went up to the queen mother's quarters. Umaima was in there with her, and they must have chinwagged for about two hours. I don't know what was said, but a different man came down the stairs. I was standing by the front door and opened it as Qaboos approached. He paused, looked me square in the face and said, 'I'd like to thank you for what you're doing for my mother and half-sister.'

I thought, 'If you only knew the half of it.'

I could tell from this brief meeting that he was a man of culture and education, as he spoke perfect English. A product of the British university system, Qaboos was a thoroughly modern and Western-orientated Arab leader.

Not long after this, we had an unwelcome visitor at the manor: the queen mother's eldest brother. Although a fabulously wealthy sheikh, he preferred to live in a tent and move around the desert when he was in Oman. He was from the old school and couldn't adapt to modern living. When he first arrived at Wargrave, he pointed to the telephone, lifted one finger and said, 'Phone one.' I took this to mean that there was a phone call expected at 1 a.m. from Oman. I manned the phone and alerted the sheikh when the call came through.

This went on all week until one afternoon he said to me, 'Phone two and three,' and gesticulated with his fingers.

I thought, 'You're a right comedian.' What with my security work, dalliances with the princess and now these late phone calls, I was getting no sleep.

When I made my feelings known to Umaima, she said, 'I'll sort it out.' And later that day, she told me, 'No more calls.'

'Thank God for that,' I thought, because I was practically dead on my feet.

Umaima must have really read him the riot act, as every time I saw him he sneered down his nose at me. And I had one more surprise before he left. One of the cleaners came to me one day and said, 'Norman, come and have a look at this.' We both went to the sheikh's room. 'He doesn't sleep in the bed or sit on a chair, you know,' she continued. 'He squats or lies on the floor.' As the door opened, I couldn't believe my eyes. The white shag-pile carpet was covered in hundreds of cigarette burns. She said, 'I've asked him time and again to use the ashtrays, but it looks like the effort's beyond him.' The sheikh was a funny old bird who didn't fit in well to the twentieth century, so I wasn't unduly distressed when he returned to his beloved sand dunes in the Middle East.

Every couple of weeks, the maids were treated to an Arabic film in the large library to stop them getting homesick. They really enjoyed the night, and the film would generally finish at around midnight. Most of the ladies lived above the stables, so I would escort them safely back to their quarters. The princess must have always ensured that they had ample amounts of money, because without fail they would try to tip me for my trouble. I always refused to take the money, but they became most offended. I told Sid about this and said that I wasn't bothered about getting the tips. He saw this as an opportunity to supplement his earnings. 'Lovely, Norm,' he said. 'That'll do for me. I'll start taking them back on film nights.' Well, he must have taken them five or six times – not a sausage, not a bent tanner, nowt. He said, 'Norman, I'm having no more of this. They can find their own bleeding way home. I must be unlucky, me.'

So, I resumed taking the ladies, and the first night back they crossed my palm again. In the morning, I couldn't wait to tell Sid. 'Is there something wrong with me, Norm? I can't get a touch for love nor money.'

Christmas was looming large, and the queen mother had a tradition of sitting in the conservatory and dishing out presents to all the staff. Security would let them in one at a time to receive their presents, and Len would introduce them all to Bibi by name. The gardeners, stable hands and cleaners would be given jewellery from Asprey of New Bond Street. They were brilliant presents, as the queen mother was a very generous person.

After all the staff had been weighed in, she also had presents for the security staff. Len was up first. She gave him a red box, which contained a gold Rolex and a pair of diamond earrings for his wife. Sid whispered in my ear, 'Brilliant, I could just do with a Rolex.' Wally, Sid and I went up and were given blue boxes. Inside were lovely expensive watches but not Rolexes. Sid said to Len, 'Bloody marvellous, Len. You already own three Rolexes. What about a swap?'

Len was the master of the witty retort. 'Go fuck yourself, Sid.'

That evening, the princess asked me how many staff worked at the house, so I found the rota board and gave her the number. She passed me a handful of envelopes, each containing £1,000. The gardeners and cleaners must have thought that they'd won the pools. As I took the gifts, Umaima noticed my new watch and said, 'Queen mother give you that?' I nodded and she added, 'I have something for you, too.' She went to a cabinet and returned with a red box. I guessed that it was red for Rolex.

The next morning, I placed it on the table in the security room. It was for Sid's eyes only. 'Whose is that?' he asked when he walked in.

'Mine,' I replied, with a smile bigger than a Cheshire cat's. 'The princess gave it to me yesterday.'

Sid said, 'Maybe she'll give me one.' As each day passed, Sid became resigned to the fact that he wasn't going to get a Rolex. Len and I would tease him, and he'd reply, 'What have you two got that I haven't? I don't even get to go on the shopping trips now.' He had a new daily mantra: 'Anything else you've got that I ain't getting?' There was no malice intended, but Sid always had the same pained expression on his face. It wasn't as if the Omanis would have missed the odd Rolex, but Sid was destined never to receive one.

15

·······

Brighton Breezy

John Asprey, the royal jeweller, was a frequent visitor to the manor. He would bring a suitcase full of very expensive jewellery for the princess and queen mother to peruse. They were both prodigious buyers of bling, and the queen mother once bought thirty Rolexes from him at one sitting. The Omani petro-millions certainly funded a lifestyle that most could only dream about.

Umaima had a large personal chest full of jewellery, and one day when she was wearing a green outfit she asked me to look through it to find her emerald necklace and earrings. Well, it was like Aladdin's cave. Talk about pirate's treasure. Captain Kidd would have walked the plank himself if he'd ever discovered a trove like this. I went through handful after handful of gold and exotic stones. The chest was crammed full of rings, necklaces and bracelets. There must have been several million pounds' worth of gems and precious metals. I delved deep and eventually found the emerald set. The princess was totally blasé about having the equivalent of a third-world economy in her bedroom.

Asprey seemed friendly enough and one day greeted me at the front door. 'Morning, Norman. Is the princess about? I've got the tiara she designed.' Umaima had sketched a tiara she wanted to wear to a large function and had commissioned John Asprey to make the head piece. It was unbelievable: layer after layer of brilliant drop diamonds, tapering up to a larger diamond. God knows what John Asprey made from the Omani royal family, but I wouldn't have minded being a pound behind him.

Qaboos was very busy with his official duties and business affairs, dividing his time between Oman and England. Two months after Asprey's visit, the sultan returned to his luxury apartments in Park Lane, which were spread over two floors, with Len and Sid again by his side.

A week later, his wife, Queen Kamila, arrived at Wargrave, and the atmosphere changed completely. Kamila and Umaima just didn't get on. In fact, it's fair to say that the princess disliked the young queen intensely. Kamila was like her husband: very well spoken with perfect English and a penchant for Western clothes. On her second morning at Wargrave, Kamila approached me. 'Is the princess in the lounge?' she asked. I confirmed to her that she was, and she strode off in the opposite direction. I got the message very quickly and did my best to keep the kittens apart whenever possible.

Kamila had essentially come over to accompany her husband to a large banquet hosted by Princess Michael of Kent. On the evening of the event, I left Wally in charge at Wargrave, and I accompanied the queen as her bodyguard as far as Park Lane. Big Mark was driving the Daimler, and we arrived at Qaboos's residence at 8 p.m. I looked up to see Len at the upstairs window and Sid waiting in the hallway. Qaboos kept everyone waiting for a further 15 minutes, and when at last he emerged from the building he totally blanked me and the queen and strode briskly to his waiting Mercedes. I opened the Daimler door for Kamila and escorted her over to Qaboos's motor.

Len and Sid were on bodyguard duty for the rest of the evening. Mark and I sat in the Daimler in Park Lane for about three hours, waiting for the royals to return. Just after midnight, I heard the purring of the Mercedes. It parked up and Qaboos jumped out. He walked straight past me without so much as a by-your-leave. I assisted the queen back to the Daimler and sensed that all had not gone well.

On the journey home, I noticed in the rear-view mirror that the queen was sobbing softly. We arrived at Wargrave, where Wally greeted us. I told him, 'You can knock off now, Wal.' The queen had walked through to the lounge, and I asked her if there was anything she needed, such as a hot drink. She nodded, and I brought her a hot mug of tea. Old habits die hard. Unlike the princess, she started sipping the tea, and as I motioned to go she blurted out, 'Could you please stay for a while?' I chatted to her for about 20 minutes; it was mainly small talk.

She seemed to have calmed down, so I made my excuses, saying that I had to do a security check, but she immediately became very tearful again. I said, 'Is there anything I can do?' She stepped forward and put her hands on my shoulders. With her head on my chest, she sobbed uncontrollably for about two minutes. I gently patted her on the back. Qaboos had obviously disrespected her and hurt her feelings earlier that night. She said, 'I want to thank you for being so thoughtful,' and with that retired to her bedroom. Until now, I have never related to anyone what happened that night – not even to Len, and especially not to the princess.

The next morning, three boxes arrived from Harrods with the words 'Queen Kamila' written on them. They were taken and left outside the security room, where Umaima spotted them. 'Who wrote on the boxes?' she asked me.

'I couldn't tell you,' I replied.

'She is no queen. It is Sayid Kamila.'

I took it that she didn't rate Kamila as a monarch. I got Wally to change the word 'Queen' to 'Sayid', and the princess strode away content. Kamila stayed on another week and then flew back to Oman.

A short while after the queen left, Umaima told me that a special guest was arriving that night.

'Who's that then?' I asked.

'King Hussein of Jordan,' she replied. I'd read reams about him and had watched him on TV. His visit to Wargrave would mean cranking up security. I told Wally that he'd have to stay on till late and make sure that the gate security were on the ball.

At 7 p.m., the gatehouse called in. 'Whisky Five to Whisky One. King Hussein in limo, fronted by a Rover. Eight Special Branch accompanying.' It was all systems go. I opened the front door, and the Rover drove past, while the limo braked right outside the entrance. I was concentrating on the rear door of the limo, waiting for King Hussein to alight, when I felt a tug on my right arm. 'Good evening. How are you?' It was Hussein. He'd been in the Rover, and the guy in the limo was a double. If there was an assassination attempt, he'd be the one to cop it. I thought, 'Very cunning,' and welcomed the king to Wargrave. 'Sir, the princess and queen mother are in the lounge. Would you follow me?'

I introduced King Hussein to the ladies and returned to the main hallway. In the meantime, Wally had admitted four Special Branch detectives through the back entrance. I wasn't having that. 'What are you four doing in here? I'm in charge of the house. I don't need any of you. The back and outside are your concern. You belong out there.' There were a few mumbles of complaint, but they must have thought that I was a top security man, not having a clue that I was a moonlighting criminal from London.

I was now treating them like the authorities had treated me for years. The butler came in and said, 'I've got to make all this lot tea and sandwiches.'

I told him, 'Don't make anything. Make out that you're too busy.' I was a right bastard where the police were concerned.

King Hussein stayed for three hours. When he was ready to leave, I told Wally to inform Special Branch that he was on his way out, and they all assembled at the front door. Before he left, Hussein politely thanked me for my trouble. He was a real gent and full of class. I bade him farewell, and he sped off into the night.

We were normally given good warning that a VIP was going to visit, and this was the case the day that Umaima was visited by King Hussein's wife, Queen Noor. A tall, leggy blonde, she had been born Lisa Halaby to Arab-American parents.

On the day of the visit, the guys at the back gate informed me that Queen Noor had arrived, so I went to the door to meet her. She was accompanied by her two children, and I ushered her into the manor. I found her to be charming and polite but not so the Special Branch officers who were with her. One of the big bruisers tried to follow her in, but I halted him with a palm to the chest. 'What do you think you're doing?' He remonstrated with me, but I told him, 'You can patrol the grounds. You're not wanted in here.' I wasn't being flash; it was just how it was.

Again, I wasn't popular with the authorities. At that time, they still didn't realise who I was. But they had long memories, and when they twigged the floodgates would open and their true colours would come out.

Another regular visitor to Wargrave was Dr Zawawi, an affluent Omani who lived in Mayfair. His business was import and export to and from the Middle East. He was always telephoning or calling on the princess, and I think he fancied her to death. Every time he called at the manor, his drivers had to sit in the car the whole time, and he expected them to be available at a minute's notice. I would often ask them in for a cup of tea and some nosebag but would always be rebuffed, as they were under strict orders. Zawawi would arrive for dinner or tea – any excuse would do – and at one stage was coming to the manor about eight times a month.

I had no love for him, but we had a good system in place: he ignored me, and I totally blanked him. He had a bad attitude, and I wasn't going to suck up to him. However, I got a surprise one night. He'd never spoken to me before, but as he was leaving he said, 'You're Norman, aren't you?' Well, for one of the few times in my life I was tongue-tied. He said, 'I'd like to thank you. The princess tells me you are a very good soldier.' I was beginning to think that I was Audie Murphy. He added, 'She thinks a lot of you.' I just nodded. The princess had a habit of talking me up to everyone she met, and I was getting rave reviews through the Arab grapevine. Even Dr Zawawi was civil to me from that moment on and always said good evening and goodnight.

One Friday night, the family doctor came over to me and said, 'The princess and queen mother would like to go for a picnic on the Brighton seafront.'

'Which idiot with a warped sense of humour has come up with that one?' I wondered. I had the raging hump. It had disaster written all over it, and I tried to dissuade the princess, but she was adamant. So, the next morning at eleven o'clock, three Daimlers set off to the seaside: the doc, the chauffeur, the queen mother, the princess and I were in the front Daimler; the butler and the servants were in the second; and all the picnic food and paraphernalia were in the third.

My plan was to disembark at a quiet spot just outside Brighton, away from prying eyes and potential trouble. But this plan evaporated. As we were travelling through the centre of Brighton, the queen mother said something in Arabic to the doctor, who turned to me and said, 'We stop here.'

I thought, 'You've got to be kidding.' It couldn't have been a worse spot. The promenade was heaving with passing holidaymakers. My head was thumping, and my ulcers were reminding me that they were still about.

The convoy came to a halt close to a shelter on the seafront, and I escorted the queen mother and the princess towards it. We were then followed by a procession of the staff, two leather chairs, a table, silver cutlery, tureens, crockery, a large chicken and half a tonne of side dishes and sweetmeats. It was a surreal scene: two royal Omani women in Eastern dress, surrounded by maids, servants and a butler, setting up a picnic in what could be likened to a bus shelter. It got better. You can never find one when you need one, but two plods on the beat strolled up. 'You can't set up here, sir,' said the bigger flatfoot.

I flashed him my Oman security badge and tried to bluff my way out of the situation. 'Special Branch. Everything's in hand.'

He looked at me suspiciously and muttered, 'OK, I'll buy it, but move them three motors.'

I told the chauffeurs to park the cars up a side road, and the Old Bill departed. For the rest of the afternoon, I had to deal with drunks and hecklers. I met the odd comment of 'Give us a piece of chicken, Mrs' with a polite reply: 'Keep walking, you dozy cunt.' After what seemed like an eternity – although in reality it was only a few hours – we all packed up and headed back to Wargrave.

I'll never know how we managed to avoid a major international incident, and when we got back I laid it on the line to the princess. 'If we ever have another episode like that, I'll walk.' She knew I wasn't kidding, and even though I can laugh about it now, at the time I realised that it could have been a real disaster.

16

·······

Inseparable

One of the queen mother's maids knocked on the security room door one morning. As usual, Wally and I were at the controls. The girl came in with two kaftan-type gowns, which were presents from Bibi. I immediately saw an opportunity for some comic mischief. We thanked the maid for the gowns, and I said, 'Wally, the queen mum will expect us to wear these kaftans, but I've got an official appointment with the princess today, so you put yours on and I'll wear mine tomorrow. Go and get changed. And remember, the Arabs are au naturel underneath, so no vest or pants.'

He took it all in and popped off to get changed. In the meantime, I rushed around the house and told everybody not to laugh when they saw him. I even told the security and gardening staff outside. Now, Wally was a big man – at least 18 stone – and the kaftan, which was sheer cotton, wasn't sized much above medium. In the right light, he wasn't hiding many secrets. When he came waddling down the corridor, the kaftan was so tight that he couldn't stride out more than nine inches at a time. He looked like a gay cheerleader mincing along, and you could see his wedding tackle.

'I don't believe this,' I thought and did everything I could to suppress a bout of laughter. Keeping a straight face, I said, 'Wally, go and thank the queen mother.' Off he went, his huge arse kneading the cotton like two giant basketballs. It was priceless. He entered the queen mother's chamber to find the princess and six maids in attendance. Eight mouths dropped open simultaneously, and the room fell silent. Wally broke the ice. 'Thank you, your highness, for the gown. It is superb.'

The chamber had a dozen large windows and was well illuminated, so Wally was standing there in all his glory. When he returned to the security room, I told him that the walkie-talkie was playing up and asked him to go to the front security lodge to inform them. On his way, he passed the gardeners. 'Morning, Wal. Nice gown,' one of them said with the countenance of Buster Keaton.

A hundred yards further down the driveway, Wally met the oncoming Major Rose, the only man on the estate not in on the joke. 'Morning, major,' said a cheerful Wally. Rose was speechless and carried on walking, shaking his head.

The two guys in the gate lodge didn't bat an eyelid when Wally shuffled in looking like a demented Danny La Rue. He still hadn't caught on that he looked a right plonker in his Arab gear.

While he was outside, Umaima came over to me. She was wagging her finger and laughing uproariously. 'You naughty man. The queen mother is still holding her sides laughing.' Wally kept the gown on all day until he knocked off at 8 p.m. He didn't have a clue.

The next morning, he said, 'Your turn today, Norm.'

'You must be joking,' I replied. 'You did enough for the both of us yesterday.'

'But you've got to,' he complained.

'No chance. It ain't going to happen.' Wally was extremely put out, but the biggest swinger in Berkshire had brightened up everybody's day.

A few days afterwards, Wally approached me. 'Norm, I haven't had a holiday for a year, and I could do with a break.' He'd been a good sport with the kaftan, so I told him that I'd see what I could do and have a word with Len. I called my brother and explained the situation. He said that he'd get back to me. That night, he phoned back and said that his wife Barbara had a friend whose husband worked for the Wembley Police Force but was currently on sick leave, so he'd send him over on Monday morning.

I put the phone down. 'Just what I need,' I thought. 'A copper on the premises.' Wally travelled to warmer climes, and the flatfoot turned up at Wargrave. He was typical Old Bill: nosy, bolshie and overbearing. On his first day, he was asking too many questions and giving me severe grief, so I determined to put him in his place. I have never liked policemen, although some of them have been all right, and I didn't have to wait long for my moment. At 6 p.m., he said to me, 'I hear the princess likes the run of the house after seven o'clock.'

'You've heard right,' I replied.

'I'm going to watch *Coronation Street* in the restroom, then retire to my quarters. I don't think the princess will mind, as I'm security.'

I replied, 'No you won't. I'm in charge of security, and you'll go with the rest of them.'

He looked aghast. 'I've not missed an episode of *Coronation Street* for six years.'

'Well, you have now.'

Maybe it was my inherent dislike of the police, but I had a magnificent feeling of contentment running through my body. He trudged away, a sorrowful and broken man. He tried everything to watch *Corrie* that fortnight, but I knocked him back every time. He didn't even get to see the cat on the roof, and he must have really hated me, but I was getting perverse satisfaction from the situation because of all the years the police had mistreated me.

Not long after, the queen mother was due to return to Oman for a lengthy stay, and Umaima, who was supposed to be going back with her, made me a proposition before she left. She asked me to join her permanently in Oman – money wouldn't be a problem. I gave it careful consideration but knocked her back. Living in a foreign country, where most of the customs were alien, I could end up being treated like a servant. There was also the other little matter of my wife and kids. I couldn't leave them, even though they'd be financially secure for the rest of their lives.

On learning this, Umaima decided that she would accompany the queen mother to Oman and stay for about ten days before returning with an Indian lady, who would tutor her in English. She did want to educate herself in Western ways, but we were falling in love, and she couldn't stand to be away too long. I was smitten and couldn't wait for her to get back. I didn't know where we were both heading, but it was a fantastic journey.

Len and I escorted the royal ladies down to Heathrow and saw them off on the royal flight. With no duties at Wargrave, we both returned to Qaboos's apartment in Park Lane, where Sid was waiting. Qaboos was returning to England from Oman the next day, and Sid and Len duly picked him up. I was to learn a lot more about the sultan in the coming week: what sort of a man he was and what made him tick.

He came over with an entourage of six young man servants, which didn't discourage rumours that he swung both ways. Most nights, he invited us into his private lounge for a social drink, talking into the early hours about his ideas, plans and ambitions. His tipple was Scotch. As the whisky disappeared, the sultan would loosen up. He declared to us that he detested communism and a lot more besides. It wouldn't be fair to disclose all of what he said, but he was certainly a man who wanted to change the world.

Another night, he told us, 'I could give you all millions. Every few minutes, I earn a fortune through oil, but if I gave you money, I'd lose three good friends.' He later explained that his country had spent colossal time and expense drilling for fresh water, but they kept striking oil instead. How unlucky can you get?

In the middle of my second week at Park Lane, Qaboos informed Len that Umaima was coming back on the royal flight and had requested that I be the only internal security operative at Wargrave on her return. This surprised me. Even though I knew what her thinking was, I hadn't realised just how much influence she had over her half-brother, the sultan.

Umaima returned, and I picked her and her staff up from the Alcock and Brown Suite at Heathrow. We carried on as before but with more privacy, as we had the run of the house at nights. I was adapting to a comfortable lifestyle, but an incident occurred later that week that demonstrated to me and Len that our relationship with the Arabs could be over at the drop of a hat.

Qaboos bought a dozen expensive cameras from Harrods to send back to Oman and asked Len to bring one of the twelve into his lounge so that he could inspect it thoroughly and get acquainted with it. A week passed, and Qaboos returned to Oman. However, he went ballistic when his palace staff informed him that only 11 cameras had arrived from England. He put two and two together and came up with five. The matter was blown up like a major diplomatic incident, and the riot act was read. Qaboos turned to his right-hand man, Brigadier Tim Landon, the 'Mystery Soldier' and one of Britain's richest and most secretive men.

A former cavalry officer, Landon was known as the 'White Sultan' and had amassed an approximate £500-million fortune in oil-rich Oman, where he was sometimes thought to be the power behind the throne. Qaboos had been a Sandhurst friend of Landon's, and together they had seized power in the coup. Landon, who later owned a Hampshire village and married Katerina Esterházy, a Hungarian princess, died of lung cancer in 2007.

After speaking to Qaboos, Landon in turn pressed Colonel Harcourt into action, summoning him to the royal residence. Frantic communications were made to England regarding the missing camera, and Len was woken up and quizzed about it. Len had a hunch and rushed over to Park Lane. Sure enough, the camera was sitting on the table in Qaboos's room. It was a crazy, over-the-top reaction to a minor incident. Qaboos had it in his head that the camera had been stolen and went berserk. This was typical nouveau riche behaviour: pennywise, pound foolish. If one of the Omani staff had taken it, they would have probably lost a hand for their trouble. I was amazed at Qaboos's paranoia, but it showed the megalomania of the people who surrounded me and that I had made the right decision to stay in England.

I spent most nights sharing Umaima's bed but still left in the early hours before the first staff came on shift. As usual, she was praising me to all and sundry and showing absolute loyalty, something that came to the fore on a couple of shopping trips. (Everything was more relaxed by then and a little retail therapy was no longer a problem.) One day, we visited a well-established woollen shop opposite Harrods. The princess took a shine to some cashmere dress and cardigan sets and ordered six outfits, which I clocked at £150 each. She picked out some more woollens, and as the staff were boxing and parcelling up the knitwear I was presented with the bill. In total it came to £3,500. I don't know if London shops think that the Arabs have more money than sense, but I checked the bill carefully, and the twinsets were down at £200 each. I queried the price with the main man, a plummy-voiced Hooray Henry, and was given a load of old flannel. The princess saw that I had the hump and said, 'You're not happy, Norman?'

I shook my head and said, 'No, princess.'

She responded by saying, 'OK, we'll go then,' and we left the parcelled-up clothes where they stood.

On another shopping expedition, again in the vicinity of Harrods, the princess took a shine to a blue parrot in a large gilded cage in an exclusive pet shop. We went in to inspect the bird, and I noticed a small price tag at the foot of the cage, marked at £900. The princess told the salesman, 'We like.'

'We'll come back in half an hour and pick the bird and cage up,' I added. As we were leaving, I noticed the salesman removing the price tag. On our return, he presented me with a bill for £1,050, so I told him that he was trying it on. He insisted that the previous price hadn't included the cage, but I wasn't having that. Again, the princess saw my discomfort and said, 'We don't want it,' and turned on her heel. She'd backed me 100 per cent again. These were strange and complicated times, but I was falling deeply in love.

Early one evening, one of the chauffeurs told me that it was his wife's birthday, so I told him to go home and celebrate. He asked me what would happen if the princess needed him, but I told him to let me worry about that and make sure that his wife had a good night. After he had driven off the manor, I told the princess that I was going to take her out and show her how the English lived. I suggested that she wear Western-style attire and told her that I'd call for her in about two hours. I didn't have a motor on the grounds, so I went round to the head gardener's quarters and asked to borrow his car, not mentioning that it was to be the royal carriage for the night.

I pulled up at the front doors of the manor in the motor, which was a two-tone Mini van. It ran OK but had seen better days. The princess came out and gave me a look that said, 'I'm not getting into that thing.' I proceeded to open the door for her. Inside, you could see the springs poking through the passenger seat. 'Where's the chauffeur?' she enquired. I told her that I'd given him the night off, as I fancied a drive.

We drove past the security lodge at the front, and the disbelieving faces of the guards were a picture. They must have thought that the Omani royal family had gone bust. We hit the highway, and I told the princess to remove her diamond earrings and ring, which I kept safe in my jacket pocket. We didn't travel a great distance, and I headed for a pub I knew in Henley on Thames, where she quietly sat in a corner while I went up to the bar to order the drinks – an orange juice for her and a pint for me.

People were moving about the pub and some were entering Umaima's comfort zone. A couple even sat next to her, and she seemed extremely nervous, as she had never been in this situation before with so many strangers. As we began to make these trips to the pub a regular occurrence, Umaima gradually became more confident in her new surroundings. We went out many times after that, and I'd always try to show her something new.

One night, I went into a fish and chip shop and came back to the car with the food wrapped in newspaper. I showed her how to eat the fish and chips with her fingers, but she didn't seem too impressed. Another night, we went to McDonald's. Little did the young staff know that they were serving a princess. We started frequenting a famous pub in Henley called The Bell, which attracted stars and celebrities. One night when we were there, Mickey Rooney, the Hollywood film star, was at the next table to us. We were certainly mixing with commoners and kings. Umaima and I were sharing everything. She was becoming increasingly Westernised without losing sight of her Eastern upbringing, and I loved her all the more for it.

John Asprey was forever pestering me with invitations for the princess to dine at his new residence. I told him, 'John, I'm only security. I can't ask her.'

'No, she's always talking about you, Norman,' he replied. 'You're a big influence on her.' I told him to leave it with me and I'd get back to him.

I had a word in Umaima's ear, telling her about Asprey's offers. She said, 'What do you think?' I told her that I thought that it would make a nice change, and she agreed. I rang Asprey up and told him the news. He was delighted, and we arranged the meal for the following Saturday afternoon.

I followed Asprey's directions to his new country cottage. Just past Henley, it was a modestly sized traditional building, set in two acres of countryside. Asprey greeted us at the door and said, 'Norman, I've set you aside some food and drink in the kitchen.'

He thought that he was following protocol and meant no harm by it, but the princess immediately exclaimed, 'No, no, no. Mr Norman sits with me.' Asprey, slightly taken aback, concurred with the princess's wishes and another place was set at the table. He introduced the princess to his parents, his wife and two ginger-haired children (you can't have everything in this life). Asprey then showed Umaima the seating arrangements. The princess was to be seated next to Mrs Asprey. I saw it coming before it happened. No she wasn't. She was going to be by Scouse Norman! The seating was changed round, and the dinner was a remarkable success, enjoyed by all.

The evening had increased Asprey's social standing in the local community. Not only did he do business with royalty, but he could now claim that they were his friends and came round for a bite to eat. We both knew that he owed me one after that, and, fair play to him, he said to me that if I ever needed work I could accompany him on his jewellery buying trips around the world as his personal minder. I thanked him, but I wasn't thinking of leaving the princess for the time being.

Living at Wargrave, I was losing all track of time. This couldn't have been demonstrated more clearly than the night I was sitting with the princess in her lounge and we heard loud bangs coming from outside. 'Jesus, what's that?' I thought. It sounded like automatic gunfire. I leaped off the sofa and shouted sternly to Umaima, 'Get to your room now.' I pulled the gun from my holster and ran towards the back door. My mind was racing. The firing was coming from the direction of the rear gate. Were the outside security guys coming under fire? I reached the back door and was just unlocking it when I sensed somebody behind me. It was the princess. I shouted louder and more sternly, 'Get to safety. Go!' She didn't budge an inch, but I didn't have time to argue with her. 'I'm going out,' I said. 'Lock the door behind me.' I ventured out and looked round. She was standing in the doorway. I could have killed her.

At that moment, the sky above the manor lit up. The heavens were full of fireworks. I'd been so engrossed in my job that I hadn't realised the date: 5 November. Embarrassed, I told the princess, 'Emergency over. It's bonfire night.' Back in the lounge, I explained to Umaima the tradition of Guy Fawkes and the gunpowder plot.

In some ways, living at Wargrave was like living on a desert island away from the real world, but it was all worth it, and the Guy Fawkes incident showed that the princess didn't want to leave my side, even in times of danger.

17
· · · · · ·

Endgame

Major Rose began to rear his ugly head again now that Len was spending more time at Park Lane. He started coming back into the house, giving orders to the staff. I had to confront him and reiterated what Len had previously told him. 'Stay out of the house unless the princess requests to see you. I won't tell you again.'

He wasn't a happy soldier, and unbeknown to me he was in constant contact with Colonel Harcourt in Oman, spewing his venom and disdain to him. Harcourt, being the big military cheese, had no option other than to investigate the claims personally. Meanwhile, it had got back to me that Rose was telling the Wargrave staff that our outfit was finished as the security detail.

Three days after my spat with the major, a military car arrived at the back gate. Security informed me that it contained a driver and three soldiers, one of them being Colonel Harcourt. They proceeded through security and parked up outside Rose's tied cottage. They touched base with the major, then the three of them marched up to the back door of the manor. I opened up to the posse and stood square on, face to face with Harcourt, who was flanked by the two military policemen, both over six feet tall. 'Colonel Harcourt, here to see the princess,' he said.

'Certainly, sir,' I replied. 'Would you come over to the library.' He entered, and I slammed the door shut on the two chinless wonders.

Harcourt sat down in the library, and I went to inform the princess. I found her in the lounge. 'Harcourt's here,' I told her. 'I have to tell you something. I had an argument with Rose last week, because he'd been intruding into the house. Since then, he's been spouting to the staff that the present security is finished. I presume that the colonel's visit has something to do with that.'

Umaima thought for a minute and then said, 'I will see Harcourt in an hour, but don't tell him that.' I returned to the colonel and informed him that the princess would see him presently. The little minx then kept him waiting for over an hour.

After about ten minutes of their meeting, they both came out of the library. The princess returned to the lounge, and Harcourt came over towards me. 'Norman, I must thank you for your sterling effort with the princess. She has high regard for your work and resolve.' He shook my hand and left Wargrave Manor. Everyone the princess talked to had me on a pedestal. When the news got back to Rose, he was livid. He realised that he was out in the cold, both literally and metaphorically.

When all the staff had gone that night and I had settled down with the princess, she related to me what had earlier transpired in the library. Harcourt had come with the intention of replacing the present security set-up with the two large military policemen who had travelled with him. Umaima had immediately baulked at this, telling Harcourt, 'No, no, I'm happy with security. Mr Norman is a fine soldier. Don't change.' Harcourt reluctantly accepted the princess's wishes but had made it clear that he would be looking into the situation further.

I realised that the pressure was on, and it was only a matter of time before Special Branch was brought in to oversee the security operation. In that scenario, the game would be over. The princess forcefully suggested to me that now would be the time to run away and start a new life. Over the months, I'd been slowly coming round to this way of thinking. My kids were growing up, and I'd not been missing my Diane as much as I should have. But it was no good leaving on a whim. It would take meticulous planning and secrecy.

Umaima needed to return to Oman one last time, later on in the week, to tie up certain matters, and I told her to say nothing and return with as little baggage as possible. 'When you get back, do not return to Wargrave,' I said. 'Go to your private suite at Claridge's.' Before that, I would get us two hookey passports so that we could go incognito anywhere in the world. The next morning, we both went to Woolworths and had passport photos taken in a sit-down booth. The great-escape plot was under way.

Two days, later Umaima flew back to Oman. She would be away for ten days, and in the meantime I returned to see Diane and the kids. My intuition had been correct. Diane and I had drifted apart. We were like strangers, and in my heart the only woman I wanted to be with was Umaima. Whilst I was back home, I heard some sad news. A good friend of mine called Richard Sullivan had passed away. He had been living in Swansea, so I drove over to Wales to pay my condolences to his wife Margaret. She asked me how I was doing, and I told her without explaining my position that I needed to get hold of two passports. I said, 'Margaret, could I borrow yours and Dickie's birth and marriage certificates?' She was a bonny lass and handed them over without much contemplation. I gave her £1,000 for her trouble. Margaret and Dickie were about the same ages as me and Umaima, so there weren't going to be any problems on that score.

I returned to London and went down to the passport office, where I had two passports made up in the names of Richard and Margaret Sullivan, carrying my and Umaima's photos. Now all I could do was sit and wait for the princess to return. She flew back the following Monday on the royal flight into Heathrow. Len was instructed to meet her at the airport. Special Branch were there, too. It looked like Qaboos and Harcourt were already exerting their influence. The princess was as good as her word with the baggage. She had only brought four maids back instead of six.

'Would you like Norman as security at Claridge's?' Len asked her.

'No, no, no,' she replied.

This took Len aback. 'Me and Sid then?' he suggested.

'No. No security!'

He thought this was a bit strange but dropped her and her entourage off at Claridge's. After helping them up to their suite, he rang me. 'Norman, the princess is back. What have you done? She doesn't want you as security.'

I feigned surprise and hurt and said, 'I don't know, Len.'

Half an hour later, I received another phone call. This time it was a female voice on the other end. 'Hello, I'm back. Come to Claridge's.'

I set off from Kent and arrived about an hour later. We talked for over two hours, finalising our plans. When I showed her the two passports, she was over the moon and said excitedly, 'Do we go tonight?' I had to curb her enthusiasm. There was no way we could leave so soon. The staff would have raised the alarm if they had found the princess missing the next morning. We needed to time our escape properly.

Umaima calmed down and pointed to a large suitcase. When I tried to lift it, I nearly got a hernia. I dragged it over to the bed and hauled it up onto the mattress. It was jam-packed full of high-denomination bank notes. 'Do you like?' she asked.

'No, I don't like,' I replied. 'Take it back to the embassy tomorrow.' I had my own cash – about £100,000 at the last count – and I wasn't running off with the princess for her money. I was in love and didn't want anything to go wrong in our quest for a new life. Umaima didn't realise that Joe Bloggs wouldn't take cases full of money to the airport. We would have been apprehended straight away. You could hardly lift it off the ground. Can you imagine it? Dickie and Margaret Sullivan carrying a suitcase containing more than £1 million? Customs would be interested, not to say Interpol and Special Branch. It had to go, but not with us.

We decided that the USA was the place to head for. I would open a restaurant-bar, and we'd keep our heads down for a couple of years. Then, when the furore had died down, we would come back.

The next day, a problem cropped up. The princess intimated to me that she was experiencing a sharp pain in her right side. She had her own private doctor in Harley Street, and I advised her to make an appointment to see him forthwith. She telephoned me the following lunchtime and told me that she was being admitted to a private hospital for a very minor operation. She expected to be up and about in two days' time. I therefore made up my mind that we would definitely leave at the weekend.

I received an unexpected phone call at 10.30 p.m. on the Friday night before the exodus. The caller was a man I'd met quite a few times at Wargrave, the queen mother's younger bother, Sheikh Mustahail. 'Mr Norman, can we talk?'

'Yes, talk.' I wasn't playing any more.

The sheikh replied, 'No, sir. Not over the phone. Can we meet at your place or mine?'

'I'll come over to you. Where are you staying?'

He was at a hotel near Harrods, and I got over there in less than an hour. I went up to his suite, and he greeted me with the words, 'I do not believe what I'm hearing. This cannot happen.'

'What can't?' I shouted back aggressively.

'You and the princess running away,' he replied.

I put him straight. 'It's going to happen, and nobody can stop it. We are going whether you like it or not.'

'The princess cannot leave. I don't believe you are doing this.'

I thrust the passports under his nose. 'Well, believe this.'

He examined them, frowned, dropped his head and quietened down. I snatched the passports back and wheeled round to leave the room. 'Please sit down and have a drink,' he begged me. 'We can sort this mess out.' I returned and sat down but refused his offer of a drink. Mustahail continued, 'You can stay at Wargrave and look after the princess, but she must stay.'

I knew that this was a no-goer. I didn't like to be told what I could or couldn't do. 'Are Qaboos and the British military behind all this?' I asked the sheikh. Mustahail didn't reply, which gave me my answer. 'What right has he got to prevent her happiness?' I continued. 'He's the last man to be moralising. I know more about Qaboos than you could ever realise.' And with that I walked out of the room.

By then, it was the early hours of the morning, so I didn't disturb the princess, deciding to ring her the next day. As soon as I heard her voice, I knew that something was wrong. She seemed down in the mouth and said, 'Norman, you must come to me now.' I sped over to Claridge's. In the lobby, I received a hostile greeting, as Special Branch were there in force. I approached the desk and two of them came over. 'Norman, you can't see the princess,' one of them said. I ignored this remark and asked the manager to ring the princess's suite to inform her that I had arrived. He told me to go up, as she was expecting me, so I entered the lift with the two Special Branch officers in tow.

A maid let me into Umaima's quarters, and the two detectives waited in the corridor. The princess was standing in the middle of the room. She gestured for the maid to leave and said, 'They know about our plans at the palace in Muscat.' Then she burst into tears.

'How did they find out?' I asked.

'I've said nothing,' she replied. 'Well, I've mentioned a little to the queen mother. I'm waiting for a phone call from her at the moment.' I realised that Bibi must have been concerned enough to mention it to Qaboos. Umaima started sobbing again. 'I'm sorry, I'm sorry, but we must wait a while for everything to calm down.' I knew in my head and heart that this was the end. I would never be allowed to get close to her again. Qaboos, Special Branch and the British military would see to that.

We embraced, and I tried to console her, telling her that everything would be all right, although I knew that things wouldn't be the same ever again. I handed her passport to her. 'Take this for the moment. You have my phone number.'

It was like being hit by a juggernaut. My insides were churning, and as I went to leave the room she flung her arms around me and was crying hysterically. As much as it hurt me, I had to prise myself gently away. I walked out of Claridge's, totally blanking Special Branch, and went home. I'm sure they tailed me, but I was too upset to care. I was absolutely devastated.

I conceded that I would never see Umaima again. As much as it hurt me, there was nothing more I could do for her. The security around her would be extremely tight from then on, and with Special Branch to the fore it wouldn't be long before my background would reveal itself.

Two evenings after my last meeting with Umaima, I received a phone call at home. It was obviously someone from Special Branch. 'We're onto you, Johnson. You should have never worked for the royal family. With your record, you shouldn't have got within 1,000 miles of the princess. Our time will come. Don't make yourself busy.' Before I could respond, he'd slammed the phone down. If they thought they could intimidate me, they were very wrong.

Three days later, just after midnight, the phone rang again. I knew who it was phoning at that unearthly hour. Someone with a Scottish accent growled, 'I want to see you, Johnson.'

'Who the fuck are you?' I shouted.

'Never mind who I am,' he replied. 'I want a meeting.'

He was challenging me, so I told him, 'Whenever and wherever you want.'

'Hatton Garden at midday tomorrow. Come down from the Holborn end, and there's an alleyway on your right. There's a pub down there. That's where I'll be.'

'What do you look like, big man?'

'Don't worry what I look like. I'll recognise you. I know you. Just be there.'

Before I could say, 'Make sure you turn up,' he'd put the phone down.

The next morning, I rang my brief and told him about my late-night exchanges. He advised me not to go, but I was in the mood for a confrontation and my instincts told me that I must meet the challenge head on.

I arrived at the pub early to suss out the situation. At first, I waited in the pub, then went outside and stood around for half an hour, but there was no sign of anybody – nothing. I had a last look inside, but it was futile. It was now 12.45 p.m., and Rob Roy MacGregor hadn't shown his face. I returned home and phoned my brief again. He said, 'Norman, you've been set up. I've been making enquiries. I phoned a friend of mine from The *Sunday People* newspaper. He told me that the alley you went down contains offices belonging to the Special Branch. They've had you under surveillance, taking photographs of you for their files.'

I thanked him for his work and thought to myself, 'Cunning bastards.' By threatening me on the phone, they knew that I wouldn't be able to let it go and would go exactly where they wanted me to.

As the weeks passed, I was getting more and more wound up by the part Qaboos had played in my break-up from the princess. It was a well-known fact that Qaboos hated publicity and always tried to live his life below the radar. An opportunity presented itself to bring him to the public's attention.

My brief rang me again and said, 'Would you like to meet my reporter friend? He wants to know all about your time with the Omani royal family. It could lead to an exclusive story.' I realised that this might be my only chance to get back at Qaboos and agreed to meet the hack in a pub. I explained that I was trying to help the princess to escape from her overbearing half-brother and her gilded-cage existence. I didn't mention our full-blown affair. He listened intently and seemed to think that it was definitely a newsworthy story.

It appeared as a scoop in the centre pages of the *Sunday People* in December 1980, complete with a picture of the princess with me and Diane. Afterwards, I did regret publicising the account, as I should have just put it behind me and carried on with my life.

A few weeks later, I received more news, none of it good. A court summons fell through my letter box. I was being charged with the possession of forged documents: namely, the fake passports. It was more aggro that I could have done without, but once the authorities get their claws into you they never let go. I turned up at Bow Street magistrates' court at 9 a.m. to be met by a throng of media and paparazzi. I strolled through the clicking and flashing and went into the courthouse, where I was immediately met by two lumps from Special Branch. They introduced themselves, and one of them said, 'Norman, we want this wrapped up as soon as possible. This has been an embarrassment. Plead guilty, and I guarantee that you will only receive a small fine. There definitely will not be a custodial sentence, but you must not on any account mention the princess.'

I was pensive, but I knew I was on a serious charge. Could I trust the police? The authorities knew that I could dish the dirt and create a diplomatic and political scandal of international proportions. They had too much to lose by lying. It went against the grain, but I said, 'OK, I'll take you on your word. But if there's any double cross, I'll say my piece.'

The detective seemed satisfied with that and even offered to pay my fine if I was short of money. In court, I pleaded guilty, and the magistrate gave me a £100 fine. It was all over in two minutes. It was a joke, a total whitewash by the authorities. The conspiracy theorists would have had a field day. When I left the court with my brief, the circus was still in town. There were cameramen, reporters and bystanders everywhere, but I ignored them and jumped into a waiting car. The next morning, the papers didn't include a single picture or paragraph about the case. The cover-up was complete.

It was a remarkable period in my life that has now been assigned to the annals of history. Although it sounds extreme, I was in a position, if I had been so inclined, that I could have assassinated the sultan of Oman or King Hussein of Jordan, or have given information to a group opposed to the Arab states. The British secret service must have had a bad day in the office, because in reality a man with my criminal record and reputation should never have been that close to the Omani royal family, especially with a firearm. I bet that heads rolled behind the scenes at Special Branch, but I take credit that security would never be so lax again.

I wasn't a political animal, and international intrigue wasn't my barrow. Enough was enough, and it was time to return to my old ways.

18

·······

Go West

I was emotionally shot, so I decided to take Di and the girls to
Florida for a fortnight. I thought that my relationship with Diane
might be able to be resurrected, and I needed to recharge my
batteries, as I'd been working solidly for the Omanis for two years
and was desperate for a break. It was fantastic to relax again. The
family thoroughly enjoyed their time in the sun, and I came back a
new man.

I was determined to go forward with a vengeance, and a chance
meeting was to thrust me back in the right direction. I would never
forget Umaima, but the fates were conspiring to take me further
away from her Eastern homeland.

I'd arranged to meet a couple of business associates at London's
Hilton Hotel, and when I arrived I found that they had been joined
by two American businessmen, who were connected superficially to
the New York crime families. Talk about being in the right place at
the right time. At first, my conversation with the Yanks was cordial
and run of the mill. Then, out of the blue, one of them blurted out,
'Norman, do you know John Francis?'

On hearing that name, I reacted like a professional poker player,
giving nothing away. Did I know him? He'd only disappeared with
thousands of pounds' worth of jewellery belonging to me. I didn't
divulge this to the Americans and nonchalantly told them, 'Yes, he's
an old pal of mine. How's he doing?'

The bigger of the two Yanks said, 'He's doing great, Norman. He's
a big name in New York. Russell Bufalino has him as his right-hand

man.' (Bufalino was the acting boss of one of the five biggest New York crime families.)

I said, 'Does he still hit the clubs?'

'Sure, Norman. He lives in them at weekends. Dangerfield's, Jimmy Weston's and Giacomino's are his favourites.'

This was very interesting. I'd heard all I needed to know and changed the subject. As we were leaving, the Yanks offered me the chance to go over to New York. I thanked them but said that now just wasn't the right time. The smaller one said, 'No problems, Norman. What's your surname? We'll give John your regards.'

'Peterson,' I replied and wished them a safe journey home. I was going to New York, but it would be in my own time and when John Francis wasn't expecting it.

Less than a month later, I booked a flight to the Big Apple. I was going to kill two birds with one stone. My sisters Sylvia and Minnie had both married Americans and emigrated to the USA. In the intervening years, I had seen them only once, and that was when I sent them tickets to come over to England. Sylvia lived in Norfolk, Virginia, with her navy diver husband. She had two boys and three girls. Minnie was in Kansas city, Missouri. Her husband had just died at the age of just forty from a massive heart attack, leaving her to bring up five boys and a girl alone.

I told Diane I was going to America to visit my sisters. I didn't mention anything about John Francis and New York. I flew into JFK Airport and caught a cab to the Lexington Hotel in Manhattan. This was the area John operated in, and I was hot on his trail. I decided to visit Dangerfield's that night. Arriving at 9 p.m., I said to the manager, 'Do you know John Francis? I'm a friend of his, just over from England.'

'Sure, I know John well, but he only comes in at weekends,' he replied.

'You couldn't do me a favour, could you, and give him a bell telling him Norman Johnson's in town?'

He went to use a nearby wall-mounted phone and relayed my message. I could hear him saying, 'Yes, John. Yes, John. OK, John.' He came back over, 'Norman, John will be here in an hour. In the meantime, come over to John's table and take in the show.'

He led me to a table that fronted the stage, and champagne quickly followed, but I declined the bubbly and asked for a beer. After a while, I spotted John coming towards me. I hadn't seen him for more than a decade, but he didn't look any different. He sat down and immediately revisited our last days together. I let him speak, listening intently. 'Norman, it's great to see you,' he said. 'I couldn't return to England from Antwerp, as the Jewish jeweller took the money and disappeared. That motherfucker left me roasting in Belgium. With you and the Krays waiting for me over the water, there was no way I could come back without the money or the jewellery. I had no choice but to make myself scarce, and I decided that the USA was my best alternative. Hey, I'm doing really well here. This is the land of opportunity, and now that you're here I'd like you to stay and work with me.' He then passed me a large manilla envelope, 'This will help with your expenses.' It contained $80,000, and it certainly sweetened my mood. I didn't know if his version of what happened in Belgium was the truth or bullshit, but I didn't really care any more, as he had gone a long way to putting his past misdemeanours right with his cash offering. I was now ready to listen to his proposals, and he proceeded to tell me all about his time in America.

He told me that he had arrived in Miami practically broke and did all sorts of menial jobs. He soon realised that if he was going to make it big, he'd have to learn Yiddish and Italian, so he went to night school and passed his exams with flying colours. He then made the journey to New York, where he made some profitable connections. John Francis was one of the cleverest men I'd ever met, not to mention an extremely shrewd businessman. He started mixing with the New York underworld, and some of the shadowy figures at the top came to realise what a smart operator he was. He quickly came to the attention of premier mobster Russell Bufalino, who had been accused of ordering the murder of Teamsters boss Jimmy Hoffa, amongst other things.

John had a massive house and grounds with a swimming pool in Connecticut, where he lived with his gorgeous wife Kathy, an Irish-American beauty. He was doing very well himself. Their house was full of quality antiques and bespoke furniture. John wanted me to come and stay at his place that night, but I told him I was still booked into the Lexington, so we agreed that he'd pick me up at 9 a.m. to show me around town. Bang on nine, John turned up at the front of the hotel in his gold Mercedes saloon. I jumped in, and we headed for his offices on Park Avenue.

He had acquired the whole second floor of a skyscraper, from where he ran his computer company. We entered the offices, and a dozen young people were sitting at their terminals. At the other end of the room was a spacious lounge and boardroom, with the obligatory long table and chairs. John was expecting visitors, so his secretary made me a coffee. As I sat sipping my drink, various businessmen dressed in overcoats, suits, homburgs and trilbys arrived for the meeting.

John beckoned me into the boardroom to meet his associates, who all seemed to be of Italian and Sicilian descent. I could tell by their demeanour that it was a serious gathering. I was introduced to the group, and they all kissed me on the cheeks. I wasn't really into all this male bonding and went to leave, but John stopped me and said to the ensemble, 'The deal that's going down today involves me and Norman.' The assembled all concurred that my participation was not a problem.

I left them to it and sat in the lounge while they got on with business. After an hour, John came out and said, 'We've finished, Norman. I'll take you over to meet Russell.' This was good of him, because Bufalino was a very important man in New York.

We were dropped off at an Italian restaurant near Broadway. Four men were sitting at the far end: Bufalino, getting on in years but immaculately dressed and coiffeured, his solicitor and two other associates. John introduced me to Russell, who said, 'Norman, I'm very pleased to meet you. I've heard a lot of good things.' John must have talked me up, and I shook hands with the other three.

John kept referring to me as 'My very good friend Norman'. I later found out that this was part of the protocol: if you said 'friend', it meant you were all right; 'good friend' meant that you were more than all right; and 'very good friend' meant that you were one of us and could be trusted implicitly.

We all ordered dinner and spent an enjoyable afternoon socialising. I found Bufalino to be a most polite and generous person. John wanted me to meet a lot more of his contacts, so the rest of the day was spent frequenting his favourite watering holes, including Paddy Quinn's on Third Avenue at Fiftieth Street. I met a lot of characters that night, and they all seemed to accept me straight away, as John kept giving me blinding introductions. As the evening drew to a close, he said, 'I'm going to Chicago tomorrow on business, Norman. I'd like you to accompany me.'

I knocked John back, as I realised that this would be a good opportunity to visit my sisters. I said, 'I've got a bit of business in the Midwest myself, John. I'll see you again in two weeks.'

'Phone me when you're back, Norman. I'll pick you up from the airport. There's a lot more we can do together.'

After all the backslapping, kissing and handshaking, I was glad to get back to my own hotel room. The British don't seem to be as tactile as the Italians. It must be something in the Chianti.

I booked out of the Lexington early the next morning and headed for JFK Airport, where I boarded a plane to Kansas City. When I arrived at Minnie's house, I could see that life hadn't been kind to her. Her kids, Mark, Sam, Dave, Steve, Chris and Lisa, knew what it was to go without. I hadn't realised that Minnie had been through the mill, but I was in a good position to help, and I was only too happy to do so.

With Minnie back on an even keel, it was time for me to visit my other sister. Minnie pleaded with me not to go, but I had to see Sylvia. I had a brainwave. I suggested to Minnie that she accompany me to visit our sister, as they hadn't seen much of each other over the years. She jumped at the chance, and we both headed north.

Sylvia's house was larger than Minnie's, but, if anything, her family seemed to have even less. I later discovered that her husband, Des Desotell, was a deadbeat who hardly contributed anything to the family, even when he was in full-time work. On subsequent visits, he would keep well out of my way, which was a good decision on his part, as I disliked him intensely, but on this first visit Sylvia and the five kids, Theresa, Desmond, Tina, Tracey and Danny, had a fantastic time.

Like Minnie, Sylvia's life hadn't been a bed of roses, and I was there at the right time to make a difference. Sylvia told me that a few years earlier she had won $15,000 at bingo and had put it all down as a deposit on their current house. Before that, they had been struggling for a better life. This made me really angry, as her husband was hardly contributing anything towards the bills and was content to see his family slip behind. I wanted to give him a slap, but Sylvia pleaded with me not to, so I let it lie.

Two years after I first met him, Des really showed his true colours. Sylvia was out when her eldest daughter started to have terrible headaches. She asked her dad to take her to the hospital, but he informed her, whilst watching baseball on TV, that he had no fuel. Theresa started pleading, but he just told her to lie down on the sofa and put a wet towel on her forehead. Half an hour later, she was dead from a massive brain haemorrhage. This crushed Sylvia, and she was never the same again. She bitterly resented Des's treatment of their daughter and kicked him out of the house. He stayed in an old banger on the drive for a fortnight. The situation was upsetting the other children, so Sylvia reluctantly let him back in the house. It is commonly said that America is the land of opportunity and that the streets are paved with gold, but my two sisters walked down a very different road.

Minnie and Sylvia were distraught when it was time for me to fly back, but I explained to them that now that I had business interests in New York, I'd be able to visit them more often. Knowing that I was just a short plane journey away seemed to quell their anxiety.

I flew back to JFK, and, as promised, John was waiting to collect me at the airport, insisting that I stay with him and Kathy in Connecticut instead of at a hotel. The next morning, we did the same tiresome rounds of backslapping and handshakes, but I did meet a fascinating character at Paddy Quinn's. His name was Louis Rush, and he was of Jewish–Russian extraction. He was getting on – possibly in his mid-70s – but was still a very feared and revered man. He was a small pit-bull of a man, who had a ruthless reputation as a hit man. From his early 20s, he had worked for all the renowned crime families. He had a cast-iron pedigree for getting the job done and had been at the top of his profession for decades. Louis would become a very good friend of mine over the next ten years.

At that first meeting, I'd been drinking with him for about two hours when a couple of FBI men approached the table. 'Hey, Louis,' one of them said. 'At the last count we had you down for 35.'

Louis came back with, 'You motherfuckers never could count.' They laughed and left. Louis Rush was certainly a one-off.

Later that evening, I told John, 'I've got a few things to sort out in England. I'll get off tomorrow and return as soon as possible.' John had involved me in numerous business deals, so I was going to be criss-crossing the Atlantic on a regular basis. Another new chapter in my life was just beginning.

19

·······

Tails of the Unexpected

B ack in England, I told Diane that I would be working in the States for long periods. This gave her an opportunity to ask me if she and the kids could move back to Stafford, as she wanted to be close to her parents again. I had no objections, as I had already run down my business connections in the south, so we put the house in Kent up for sale, and I headed for Stafford to purchase a new property.

I booked into Tillington Hall, a hotel at the north end of Stafford, with a view to going house hunting the next morning. After leaving the hotel, I hadn't gone two hundred yards when I spotted a very nice property for sale: a four-bedroom detached house in Holmcroft Road. A middle-aged guy was mowing the lawn around the new for-sale sign. It transpired that the house had only recently been put on the market. 'How much are you looking for, pal?' I asked. He came back with a figure of £48,000. I added, 'I'm looking for a quick deal,' and the owner stated that he could leave yesterday. That suited me. I never quibbled on the price, and we went down to his solicitors in town.

Once I'd deposited my cheque, the deal went through in a few weeks. Diane and the kids moved back to Stafford immediately, first staying with her parents before moving into the newly acquired house in Holmcroft Road. It had been quite a month all in all. I'd finalised all my business matters down south, the family were safely nested and I was ready to return to the USA.

Whilst in England, I was in constant communication with John Francis, and I told him when I'd be returning so that he could book me into the New York Hilton, as it was close to his offices. On my arrival, he picked me up at JFK Airport, and the adventure was back on.

I soon settled into the American way of life. One day, we visited Gallagher's, the world-famous steak restaurant. It was a sight to behold. Extensive glass partitions surrounded the cloakroom, behind which large carcasses of beef were hung – you could see what you were about to eat before you'd sat down. There were a dozen chefs, and the waiters and waitresses needed muscles like Popeye just to carry in the large platters. The steaks were about two inches thick, and there were little old ladies attacking the beef with gusto. Some of the steaks seemed almost as big as they were. Amazingly, most of the platters were wiped clean. The meat was really tender and melted in your mouth. The reputation of Gallagher's as a great steakhouse was well justified.

The head waiter and a few other attendants were all Scousers. I thought I was back in Liverpool when I heard all the accents. You can't keep good men down. I got talking to one of them. His name was Jim, and he was from Garston, a suburb on Merseyside. 'What part of Liverpool are you from, Norman?' he asked.

'The south end. Toxteth.'

'Do you know Sonny Newcombe, then?'

'As it happens, I know him very well.'

'I bet you didn't know that he runs an Irish bar on Seventh Avenue.'

This took me by surprise, and I asked Jim if he had Sonny's number. He wrote down the details on a scrap of paper, and the next morning I gave Sonny a bell. He seemed pleased to hear from me and said, 'Norman, I work seven days a week, but when can we meet? I'll find the time.' I told Sonny that I'd pop over to him in order to save him from changing his schedule, so I visited him at his bar, and we spent a good few hours reminiscing about old times.

Before I left, Sonny asked for my number, and I gave him my hotel line – big mistake. I think all the Scousers in North America had access to it. After that, a Liverpudlian by the name of Frank Oats was always ringing. 'Norman, my wife's made you Scouse [northern stew]. Come over for a meal.' Eventually, I went over, and although

I was used to eating the finest cuisine in New York, I really enjoyed the gesture.

On another of my visits to Sonny's bar, I had a chance meeting with another Liverpudlian that could have turned out to be very profitable. I noticed the guy in question because he stood out from all the others in the bar, with his expensive suit, Rolex watch and Gucci shoes. I said to Sonny, 'What line's he in? He must be making a few bob.'

Sonny's reply was not what I expected. 'That's Brian James. He's doing fantastic. You won't believe this, but all he does is sell saucepans!'

'Get the fuck out of here.' I was picking up the New York patois.

'I ain't kidding. Brian's got a franchise back in England for a new type of non-stick pan. They don't need any fat or oil. He has a container load sent over from a factory in Warrington every now and then.'

I was even more interested when I found out that the pans sold like hotcakes as soon as Brian demonstrated their uniqueness. Apparently, there wasn't anything of that quality or calibre on the market in the States at that time. I wasn't slow on the uptake and could see massive potential if the product was developed correctly. But before doing anything, I wanted to pick John Francis's brain. If he also thought that it was a sure-fire winner, it was time to act. I told John what Sonny had told me about Brian's product, and he responded enthusiastically. 'This could be very good, Norm. Organise a meeting, and we'll take it from there.'

I rang Sonny and got him to arrange for Brian to meet me, John and two other money men at Gallagher's. After the meal, John read the literature on the product and quizzed Brian on the salient points. Then he announced to the table, 'This could be huge. We can go nationwide with this product.'

Brian added, 'The factory in Warrington is only scratching the surface at the moment. It could manufacture substantially more.'

'The way to go with this is TV advertising,' John said. 'I know the head producer on the advertising channel. I can get us a premium slot.'

Everything was sorted that afternoon, and we left Brian at Gallagher's in a very happy mood. Sure enough, John's influence paid dividends, and we were ready to appear on prime-time TV in a fortnight's time. I rang Sonny again to relay the good news to Brian, but Sonny hit me with a bombshell. 'He's gone back to England, Norm.'

'What do you mean he's gone back to England? We're on telly in two weeks.'

Sonny explained that after we'd left Brian at Gallagher's, a waiter had come over and commented on him being in heavy company. When Brian asked what he meant, the waiter put him straight. 'Yeah, they're all Mafia. Very dangerous people.'

Brian's brain must have gone into overtime. 'Mafia? Once they've got the product, they won't need me. I'll end up floating in the Hudson.' The more he thought about it, the more he must have fretted. Apparently, he flew back to England on the first available flight, and he didn't return, which was a shame, because he'd have made millions and got to keep what was his. We had all missed a right touch.

A few weeks later, I took another call from Sonny. 'I've got a problem, Norm. Can you help me out?' I drove round to his bar, and he told me that a couple of his pals from Liverpool had been having trouble with two wise guys who had been making themselves busy. (The term 'wise guy' always made me laugh. Most of the wise guys I knew were skint, dead or in prison.) The Scouse duo had opened a spieler over some shops on Third Avenue. It consisted of a room for dice and a separate room for cards. They'd been up and running for about two months and had just started to make a living when a couple of mobsters had started casing the joint. The New Yorkers enquired what the Brits were making and declared themselves in for a cut of the takings in return for protection. The Liverpool lads neither wanted nor could afford this so turned to Sonny for assistance. I told Sonny to leave it with me, and I'd get right back to him.

I was seeing Louis Rush most days, as we had now become firm friends, so I mentioned the predicament to him. I could have sorted it out myself, but I didn't know whose toes I would be treading on. At least Louis would know the score in that part of New York.

Louis said he'd get over there and take a look. I added that there would be some money in it for him as soon as the lads got on their feet, but he didn't want anything. He was just happy to do me a favour. The Scousers were expecting him and got him a table and some drinks. After a few hours, the wise guys arrived. As soon as they spotted Louis sitting there, their jaws dropped to the floor. Louis said firmly, 'There's nothing for youse here. I'm involved. Don't let me see you again.'

The two gangsters departed crestfallen, and Louis told the Scousers that he'd pop in now and again to check everything out. He needn't have bothered to go back. Louis's word was a very powerful persuader, and the wise guys never returned.

I'd now been grafting in the States with John for about three years. I was mostly involved in loan sharking, but I had my fingers in many pies. John's financial brilliance was providing my family and me with a very prosperous lifestyle. All was quiet on the western front, but John was always a bit slippery, and you could never read him 100 per cent. The first time he decided not to tell me the full SP of what he was up to caused massive ructions and put me face to face again with my old enemy: PC Plod.

Unbeknown to me, John had been conducting business deals with Howard Marks, the cannabis king. Two publications about Marks, *Mr Nice* and *Hunting Marco Polo*, mentioned John Francis by name. I was only mentioned as the man being covertly watched by the Regional Crime Squad team based in Stoke on Trent, led by Dave Young. This is the full version of what happened.

John was corresponding with Marks's right-hand man in Canada, John Denbigh. Neither of them knew that Denbigh was under close surveillance by the Canadian authorities, who were watching his every move. When Denbigh arranged a meeting with John in New York, he was followed to the border by the dogged drug squad, and as soon as he crossed over into America the FBI took over. The Canadian and US authorities didn't know why he was travelling to New York or who he was meeting, but it didn't take them long to find out. As soon as Denbigh hit New York, he headed straight for the famous P.J. Clarke's bar for a meeting, and the FBI agents staking out the bar couldn't believe their luck when a golden Mercedes pulled up outside. It was like Christmas, Easter and Thanksgiving all rolled into one. John was filed under 'O.C.C.' (Organised Crime Connected), and the FBI didn't waste any time in obtaining permission from a local judge to tap John's phone at his Connecticut home.

At that time, I was on one of my temporary sojourns back to Blighty. John phoned me most days to touch base, so you can imagine which phone number kept cropping up on his FBI file. This culminated, without my knowledge, in my own phone in Stafford being tapped and me being placed on 24-hour surveillance by the Regional Crime Squad, as our boys were only too happy to collaborate with their American cousins.

The day things came to light started with a phone call from Sid Murphy, who had worked with Len and me at Wargrave Manor. 'Norm, I've got the chance to buy a nightclub near Maidstone. It's close to where I live. Could you give me some advice, and would you be interested in putting some money in?' I told him that I'd come down to check it out and discuss it. Early the next morning, I jumped in my Porsche 911 Turbo and made an uneventful trip to Kent.

Sid lived in a country cottage in a little village called West Malling, which I found without too much trouble. I had a quick pint in the local and then went round to Sid's. He got a brew on, and as he brought me a cup of tea, his phone rang.

In his spare time, Sid staged illegal boxing matches to raise some money. He loved boxing, so he was profiting from something he enjoyed. One of Sid's patrons was the local bobby. They had become good friends and were frequent drinking buddies in the village pub. The plod knew that Sid was no angel, but he also knew that he wasn't a bad 'un either, and it was the copper's phone call that interrupted our tea and tiffin. 'Sid, your cottage is surrounded by police. It's swarming. I'll try and find out what it's about.'

Sid put the phone down and said to me, 'What the fuck are you involved in now, Norman?'

I was staggered. 'Nothing, Sid.'

'Well, the fucking cottage is surrounded by filth. You've dropped me right in it.'

I protested my innocence to Sid and said, 'I don't know what's going on. I'll get off and see if I'm being tailed. Phone me tonight if you hear anything.'

I jumped in the Porsche and had a good look down the lane. I could just make out two car bonnets sticking out of a driveway. I turned into the lane and booted it for about half a mile – I was absolutely flying – then I slowed right down and looked in my rear-view mirror. Sure enough, two saloons came hurtling into sight like two bats out of hell before they too slowed right down. They must have known I was onto them.

I got to the Wrotham roundabout and decided to stop at the adjacent petrol station. As I filled up, I noticed that my pursuers were both parked in the opposite lay-by. I didn't need any more confirmation, and I played cat and mouse with them all the way back to Stafford. This involved mind-numbing periods going 30 miles per hour, followed by mad chases at 120 miles per hour. They must have thought that I was a complete nutter, but I wanted to be in control of the situation.

As I parked in my drive in Holmcroft Road, I noticed both cars turn into the Tillington Hall car park. I went upstairs and watched the two cars through my binoculars, poking them between the blinds. There were three men in each motor. Five of them disembarked and entered the hotel, leaving one to watch my house.

Who the fuck were they? And why were they following me? I was as clean as a whistle in England, and even Sid didn't know that I was working in America. I didn't tell anybody anything. I racked my brains all night but couldn't come up with a reason for the surveillance, and even Sid's phone call didn't answer many questions. 'My mate's found out that the Regional Crime Squad followed you from Stafford but didn't realise that you were going to travel so far and were running out of fuel when they got to the Kent area. They contacted the Kent Constabulary to ask them to carry on tailing you while they filled up. They tailed you to my drum and kept it surrounded until the regional boys turned up. That's how my mate knew what was happening.' I thanked Sid. I now knew who was following me, but I still didn't have a clue why.

My mind was spinning, so I thought I'd try something. I came downstairs and got into my Porsche. I parked it outside on the road and then came back to the house. I grabbed my binoculars and looked towards the hotel. Five men in various states of undress were running and stumbling in their attempt to get to the two police cars.

This was very worrying. I had six heavies on my case, and the worst thing was that I didn't have a clue why they were following me.

John Francis telephoned me the next day. 'I'm coming over, Norm. Can you pick me up at Manchester Airport tomorrow?'

I told him I would and said, 'John, I'm under heavy surveillance, but I don't know why.'

John laughed it off. 'Norman, they're like that in England. If you haven't done anything wrong, what can they do? It must be who you're running about with.' He had never spoken a truer word. I was under surveillance because I was running around with him, although neither of us knew that at the time.

John touched down in Manchester, and I brought him down to Stafford. I was followed back and forth again; it was really getting on my nerves. I decided to try and relax, so I took John to Reynolds' nightclub for a drink and something to eat, but there were at least four plain-clothes policemen mooching about the club. What is it about the Old Bill that makes them stand out like a sore thumb in a crowd? Two of them came over. 'Evening, Norman,' one of them said. I returned an unenthusiastic nod. They looked at John. 'Do we know you, sir?'

'I wouldn't have thought so,' John replied. Neither of us liked being observed, so we left soon after our meal and returned home.

John had some business in London. 'It's in the early stages,' he explained. 'I'll fill you in when it's established, but I can't say much about it until then.' We drove down to Bobby McEwen's club in Chelsea, and he greeted us in the reception. I noticed another guy standing near the reception desk. He was rather scruffy, with long hair, and he was wearing a dirty mac. It looked like he didn't have a pot to piss in. John called him over and introduced him to me. 'Norman, this is Howard Marks.' We shook hands. I didn't know him from Adam, and he looked like a charity case to me. Marks didn't need any charity, though. Millions of pounds had passed through his hands, and he was on half the world's most-wanted lists. The Americans were especially eager to nail him. For years, he'd led a charmed life, running the international drug enforcement agencies ragged. They would eventually have their day, but that's another story. After a short discussion, John told Marks that he'd meet him again the following day, and the cannabis king left clutching a battered old suitcase.

I suggested to John that we have a drink, so we went into the bar, where Charlie Kray and Eddie Richardson were drinking at a table with two ladies. Charlie greeted me with a beaming smile, but his face dropped when he saw John following behind me. They gave each other a curt nod. Charlie knew that John had shafted Ronnie and Reggie on the jewellery deal, but he wasn't the sort of man to react like his younger brothers would have. I acknowledged Richardson, then Bobby McEwen suggested moving to a larger table on the balcony, where we could all have a chinwag. He moved some of the regulars to a corner, enabling us to have some privacy.

Bobby turned to me and said, 'You know that suitcase Marks had?' I nodded. 'Well, there was a million quid in it.' I glanced at John. He gave me a wry smile that said, 'Never judge a book by its cover.'

We reminisced for hours. I talked mainly to Charlie, and Richardson and John were in deep discussion, putting the world to rights. We left after an enjoyable afternoon and booked into the London Hilton Hotel to get our heads down. The next morning, John knocked on my door. I was in the middle of breakfast. 'Norman, I'm just going for a meeting with Bobby and Howard. I'll be back in a couple of hours.' After his return, we drove back up the motorway to Stafford. I still didn't know who Marks was and didn't ask, as that's not my way, but I was soon to find out.

John flew back to America, but nothing changed on the surveillance front. I was still being followed everywhere, but I gave as good as I got. I took them to cafés and shops and on thankless meandering trips just for the hell of it. I must have really wound them up, but it had a drip, drip effect on me and slowly started to take its toll, so I mentioned to Diane that I was going to Spain for a few weeks to get away from all the aggro.

I hatched a cunning plan that Baldrick would have been proud of. I arranged for a friend to park in a side street near my home in a car that the police wouldn't associate with me and bolted out of the house at four in the morning. I sprinted to the car, and we roared off. If my timing was right, the police wouldn't see us for dust. We headed for an unlit area on the outskirts of Stafford called Sandon

Bank and sat at the bottom of a hill for 15 minutes. Old habits were dying hard, and I was still very cautious, but you could never be too careful. Nothing appeared, not even a milk float, so I dropped my friend off and sped south for Heathrow, destination España. I was heading for the sun and a quiet life.

I purchased a one-way ticket to Malaga and hired a car at the other end to take me to Marbella. I settled into a holiday flat and decided to go out on the town that night to see if there were any faces about. It was like 'Little Britain'. If the devil could have cast his net, he would have had a trawler full. Ronnie Knight and Freddie Foreman were there on an enforced holiday, and the Brink's-Mat robber Tony White, amongst many others, was enjoying the good life on the so-called 'Costa del Crime'.

It was great meeting up with old friends, some of whom I hadn't seen for years, but I couldn't fully relax and enjoy myself because of the circumstances back home. Every day, Diane would ring me from a call box. For three days, she had nothing to report, but on the fourth she had news. John's wife Kathy had telephoned Diane to tell her that John had been arrested and taken to the Manhattan Correctional Center. While Kathy was visiting him, two FBI men had told John, 'Your buddy Norman Johnson has been arrested in England. We've got you both.' Kathy was under instructions from John to ask Diane why I had been arrested. Diane told her that I hadn't been apprehended and was out of the country for a while.

After Diane's phone call, I wasn't happy and took steps to get a moody passport. The man to see was Tony White, and I left it with him. If it all came on top, I would travel to France and then fly somewhere safe. I pressed Diane time and again to find out why John had been arrested, and things went from bad to worse when Kathy suddenly went AWOL and their phone in Connecticut continually rang out.

After what seemed like an eternity, Diane finally managed to make contact with Kathy again, and a lot of things fell into place. John had been arrested for money laundering, along with Denbigh and Marks. The slippery rat had dropped me in it by not disclosing to me what he was up to, but it was also a massive relief, as I was not involved and in the clear.

I immediately returned to England and was disappointed to be tailed once again, although it only lasted a week and eventually petered out. I returned to a normal life, if you could ever call what I did normal. John's brief got him bail, and he would appear in court at a later date, but for the time being he was a free man.

Account by Dave Young on his observations of the tailing of Norman Johnson

(Dave Young was a leading member of the Regional Crime Squad)

I had actually been working back in Staffordshire for two to three months when I returned to the Regional Crime Squad. I had been told on my first day back that the team was watching Norman Johnson from Stafford.

Johnson was something of an enigma in Stafford. Plenty of people knew of him, both in the police force and outside of it, but nobody seemed to know much about him. The police knew he was a 'Liverpool criminal', and it was believed that he had met his wife whilst on the hostel scheme at Stafford Prison. I knew that he had once lived in a council house on the Highfields Estate and had then been missing from Stafford for some years. He had returned and was living in a rather nice detached house in Holmcroft Road with a Porsche in the driveway. No one seemed to know of any source of legitimate income, and he was certainly not working.

On my first day back, I joined up again with my regular partner DC Wood, known as Woody. On the first day that the surveillance team took up its position at Holmcroft Road, we spent the first three to four hours bored stiff doing crosswords, etc., until there was a sudden movement mid-morning. Johnson got into his Porsche and drove to junction 14 of the M6. The police team assumed that he would be heading north, possibly to Liverpool, but they were pleasantly surprised when he turned south.

Surveillance is a 'science' of extremes. When the target is 'housed', it can be very boring, but once on the move things obviously liven up. When things get going, intuition kicks in, and various members of the team will always speculate as to where they will go next. On that Monday morning, no one would have guessed where we were heading.

We hit the M6 and travelled south towards Birmingham, carrying on to the M1 and then the M25, before coming off the motorway system in Kent. Johnson's driving was exemplary, giving the impression that he did not want to draw attention to himself, and this excited the police team even more.

Once in Kent, he visited a country pub, and the surveillance team put a footman in to follow him in the hope of seeing if he met with anybody. Unfortunately, either Johnson was known in the pub or he certainly must have met someone who was, as he was served with a drink, even though the police tail was refused service on the grounds that it was after lunch closing time, this being at a time before all-day drinking became legal in pubs. What we did know, though, was that he obviously hadn't driven 174 miles for a beer.

The lads and I were very upbeat, and after a while Johnson left the pub and drove down to Meopham, a nearby village, where he visited a residential property. After a while, Norman left Kent, and there was an uneventful drive back to Stafford.

Woody and I then decided to have a closer look at Johnson, and virtually every corner we turned excited us more. We learned where he banked, where he booked his frequent trips abroad and where he did his shopping. We learned more about his inner circle of criminal friends and visitors. And we made friends with some of Johnson's local acquaintances – not close friends with whom he would reveal any significant confidences, but people who provided snippets of information that helped to fill the ever-growing portfolio on Norman Johnson. At that time, Woody and I probably knew as much about Johnson as Norman did about himself. The big problem was that there was plenty of information and intelligence, but none of it could be turned into evidence that Johnson was currently active.

It was then that my superiors dropped a bombshell. They told me that no more time was to be spent on Johnson if results weren't forthcoming and I had to move on to other targets. I was never a quitter, and whilst I was criticised at that time for not knowing when to bring a job to an end, within months I was being praised for the tenacity and professionalism in respect of my enquiries in this case.

Johnson knew that the police were looking at him, but he didn't know why. Around that time, he was visited in Stafford by his old friend, the New York-based John Francis. One night, they went for a drink at Reynolds', one of Johnson's regular haunts. This bar was also regularly frequented by the local police, and some of them were in having a quiet drink on the night of Francis's visit. The police and Johnson knowingly nodded to each other across the room, and after a while Francis asked the police officers why they were following his friend. They knew nothing of the Regional Crime Squad operation and quite truthfully denied all knowledge. Francis was quite affable and told them that the problem was that Johnson was a 'big fish in a little country town pond', which was why the police were interested in him.

Woody and I got to look into John Francis's file and started researching him, too. We learned that Francis was a made man with the Bufalino family in New York. A new file was set up in the Regional Crime Squad office, and almost as much intelligence was accumulated on him as on Johnson, including details of his wife and family.

Around that time, the squad accidentally stumbled onto the police operation to track Howard Marks, the cannabis king. We had gone down to London to visit the then national drugs intelligence unit at Scotland Yard, where we ran some checks on the names of John Francis associates. Within a couple of days, I was contacted by Metropolitan Police detectives, who were leading the massive Operation Eclectic, the Howard Marks case. The Stafford-based investigation became tentatively linked to the worldwide investigation, albeit very much on the periphery.

Information had come to light that Norman Johnson had been staying at five-star hotels in Park Lane, so Woody and I went to the Smoke for a few days to make inquiries. We were both delighted to discover that John Francis had been staying at the same hotel as Johnson on the same dates.

We established that Francis had in fact met some of the other players in the huge investigation into Marks. We also identified a bank in Chelsea that had been visited by John Francis. Our inquiries continued but hit a brick wall when we established that there was no account at the bank in his name. Almost as a throwaway remark, I asked Woody if there was an account in Francis's wife's maiden name and we discovered that there was. It turned out that this was one of the many routes used by John Francis to launder money for the Marks empire.

The big sting eventually took place, with many arrests worldwide. Francis was caught with his finger in the pie, but Norman Johnson was never implicated, and I moved onto other things with the Regional Crime Squad.

20
· · · · · · ·

Atlantic Crossing

There were still many reasons to return to America, one being that John Francis owed me money. Our newly acquired club The Sportsman was doing well, the loan sharking was booming and three or four business deals were yielding profits. On my arrival, John handed me the $200,000 I was due. No matter how accustomed you are to money, it's always nice to take delivery of a sum like that.

I stayed a few days, then returned to England. I stashed the $100 bills, tightly wrapped in elastic bands, in my attaché case. My plane touched down just after 5 a.m., and as I sped through Customs I was apprehended by a jobsworth. 'Just a minute, sir. Can I look in your case?'

'Come on,' I replied. 'I'm in a hurry.'

But the Customs officer proceeded to open up my case, revealing bundle after bundle of green bills. 'Holy mother of God,' he exclaimed. 'How have you come across this?'

'It's got fuck all to do with you.' At that time, it wasn't against the law to bring large amounts of money into the country.

The officer requested my passport, and I knew that he was going to inform the Old Bill. He returned five minutes later. 'Have you got any security measures in place?'

'Yeah, a taxi.' He passed me my case and passport, and I headed for the taxi rank, where I jumped into the back of the first cab. 'Stafford, pal.' I leaned back and shot a glance out of the rear window. Sure enough, the ubiquitous police car was 50 yards behind. It was like being stalked by an ex-girlfriend; the police just wouldn't leave me alone.

185

The moment I arrived home, I said to Diane, 'I'm flush at the moment. Go to the estate agents and look for a larger property, one a bit more secluded. I'm fed up with a thousand eyes on me all the time.' She didn't muck about. By the end of the day, she had located Pool Cottage, a large six-bedroomed modern house situated in twenty-two rolling acres. One side faced the Staffordshire County Showground across the main road, while the other three sides were surrounded by open country and woods. It had been built by Kelly Brothers, a local construction firm, so I knew it was a quality building. It was also a quality price. I handed over a cheque for £150,000, which got you an awful lot of house in those days. I quickly extended the kitchen into a kitchen-cum-diner. A firm from Liverpool came down and fitted the area out in oak, walls were knocked down, and patio doors and panoramic windows were installed. After the conversion of the barn into stables for the horses and dogs, I must have spent the equivalent amount of money that I'd bought the house for.

I should have known better about peace and quiet, though, as within a few days of moving into Pool Cottage, the Old Bill were prowling in the woods around the house with cameras and binoculars. I was beginning to understand how Hollywood film stars felt being under scrutiny day and night. The ironic thing was that I never crapped on my own doorstep. All the dodgy stuff I was involved in was back in the USA. I never received so much as a parking ticket at home. What a total waste of police time and money.

Not long afterwards, my eldest daughter Teresa asked me to buy her a horse. Little did I know that the nag she had her eye on belonged to a member of the mounted branch of the Staffordshire Police Force. Evidently, he was unaware that Teresa was my daughter. I gave her £1,500, and she took immediate delivery of the animal.

A week later, the mountie came up to Pool Cottage to see if the horse was settling in OK. Teresa was outside, and when I heard her talking to someone I went out onto the patio and clocked the policeman. I thought, 'What the fuck does he want?'

He glanced back with a quizzical look that seemed to say, 'Do I know you?' They were laughing and joking, so I left them to it. As they walked over to the stables, two squad cars careered onto the drive. The mountie cried to Teresa, 'I shouldn't be here,' and dived into some hay.

As I came out onto the patio to see what was happening, one of the Crime Squad coppers approached me. 'You're doing well for yourself, Norman,' he said.

'Yeah, yeah. Turn around and get off my property.' They left post-haste, except for the mountie, who was obviously waiting for the coast to clear. He later told Teresa that he'd been interrogated by his seniors. They wanted to know his reasons for visiting the Johnson residence. He received a right telling off and was told to stay away. What a shame – we hadn't even been introduced!

Around that time, a top boxing event was staged at the Stafford County Showground. This was handy, because the showground was 30 yards from my front door. Top of the bill was Tony Sibson, fighting for a title, while Nigel Benn was involved in a big fight on the undercard. Diane and I, along with some married friends of ours, had ringside seats. Plenty of people I knew from London and Liverpool attended, and I spotted quite a few faces in the crowd. Most of the night went swimmingly, but it was marred when supporters of Nigel Benn clashed with Tony Sibson's fans from Leicester. A smoke bomb was let off, and there were scuffles and disturbances. It was time to return to Pool Cottage.

Back home, we were all enjoying a social drink when two limos pulled up outside. I greeted an old Liverpudlian friend of mine by the name of Jackie Hart at the door. 'Where can we get a decent drink in Stafford, Norm?' he asked. 'Are you coming out for a jar?' I was reluctant to go with them, as I was entertaining guests, but I gave Jackie directions to Reynolds' nightclub and informed him that I'd be down in half an hour.

I rang the club and spoke to the manager, an Iranian called Sharo Diba. 'Dib, there's a few of my friends coming down. Don't give them a hard time on the door and look after them.' When Jackie and his eight chums arrived, the champagne was already uncorked. Included amongst the Liverpool faces were brothers Tony and Joey Ungi of the very well-known Merseyside family.

I apologised to Diane and my guests, and added that I wouldn't be away long. Down at Reynolds', all was not well. Jackie Hart immediately approached me when I walked in. 'We're having a problem with one of the bouncers, Norm.'

Reynolds' was built on two levels, and three of the group,

including Kevin Maguire, a squat bodybuilder and martial-arts expert, had been refused entry to the basement floor, which was called The Cellar Bar. An 18-stone Wolverhampton bouncer of Caribbean extraction named Cliff had got between Maguire and the door. There had been a heated argument, but big Cliff had stood his ground. He obviously wasn't in on the welcoming committee for our friends from the north. Jackie Hart said, 'When we go back to Liverpool, he's coming with us.'

I said, 'Leave it out, Jack. That's not going to happen.'

Hart was very agitated. 'We've got the right hump with him. He's going up the M6.' I put my foot down and told him that the people who ran the club were good friends of mine. I didn't want anyone playing up, and I eventually calmed the situation down. Cliff never did know how close he was to going on a mystery tour to Liverpool that evening. I thought it best not to mention it! A few years later, the aforementioned Kevin Maguire was shot dead outside a gym on Merseyside in broad daylight.

After the fight night, I read in the *Staffordshire Newsletter* that there wouldn't be any more big boxing events at the showground, because of the chronic dearth of decent hotels in Stafford. This put a notion in my head. I phoned George, a friend of mine who ran the local estate agents Clothier and Day, suggesting my rolling acres might just alleviate the hotel shortage. George was enthusiastic about the proposal and recommended I submit a planning application for a 42-room motel, restaurant and bar, as the council was more likely to give permission for the construction of a motel than a hotel. He added, 'I could probably get you a million if we get full planning permission.' I told him to get on with it, as I was heading back to the good old US of A.

I returned to Britain two months later. I figured that George must have been on holiday, as I hadn't heard from him since I'd returned, but Diane's father soon phoned me with some good news. 'Have you read the *Newsletter*, Norm? You've made the front page.' It was headline news that I'd managed to get planning permission for the motel. This tempered my mood, as all wasn't well on the domestic front. I still wasn't content to be living in Stafford when I returned from America and wanted to move to the south of England again. Diane was adamant that she and the kids wanted to stay in the

Midlands and would not be moved under any circumstances. So, as a last resort, I called her bluff and told her that I wanted a divorce, a move that might make her think twice.

A week later, I took a call from a Stafford businesswoman who had seen the *Newsletter* headlines. She offered me a take-it-or-leave-it bid of £650,000 for the land. I told her I'd consider it and get back to her after contacting my solicitor, Chris Clark. He told me that he thought that it was a good offer. I subsequently instructed Chris to push the deal through and once it was finalised to make out two cheques, splitting the money down the middle between me and Diane. She and the kids now needed a new home, and she soon spotted an auction board advertising a large bungalow set in eight acres. The property was situated in Sandon, on the outskirts of Stafford, about one and a half miles away from Pool Cottage. I went over to meet the farmer who owned the site. He showed me around, and after the tour concluded I asked him how much he was looking for it. '£170,000,' he replied. I suggested that he take the property out of the auction and accept the asking price from me without having to pay any commission. 'I prefer to take my chances at the sale, thank you kindly,' he replied. I bade him farewell and good luck through gritted teeth, then waited for the auction day.

The farmer and I were both there on sale day, and I bought The Woodlands for bang on the reserve of £170,000. The cowpoke's face was a picture. He'd come off second best. Always remember that the first offer is usually the best. The bungalow was paid for out of Diane's share of the Pool Cottage fund. I left her all the furniture and antiques plus the Mercedes. I was free. All I took with me was a suitcase full of clothes. I headed for Marbella and bought a small beachfront flat. I decided to shuttle to New York from Spain as I got accustomed to my new bachelor lifestyle.

After about six months, Teresa rang me in Spain. 'Dad, Mum's worried. The money's dwindling away. She needs an income.' I told Teresa that I'd fly back over. I was looking forward to seeing the kids again but was met with a tale of woe. Diane had paid a builder £50,000 to convert the attic into bedrooms so that her parents could stay over, but it looked like she'd been ripped off. Add to that the additional costs associated with the bungalow, such as filling the large outside tank with heating fuel at £1,500 a throw, and it was easy to see where the money was going.

Teresa told me that Diane had seen a pet shop and thought she could make a living from it but couldn't actually afford to buy it, so I went down to secure the lease. I even bought £5,000 of stock to start her off. I returned to Spain, content that I had helped remedy the situation. However, during my many phone calls back to Stafford over the coming months, I got the feeling that the business wasn't setting the world alight. Diane was employing two staff, so wages and overheads were surpassing the profits. Back I came again. I sorted out the bills and even paid for a conservatory to be built on the side of The Woodlands. It was then that Diane asked me to drop the divorce request and come back home. To tell you the truth, I was really missing the girls and family life, so I decided to agree. At least that way I could keep my eye on Diane's spending, which would save me a fortune in the long run.

Diane liked to wear a fair bit of jewellery, and I realised that it wouldn't go unnoticed that I was away for long periods. This worried me, as a woman and three girls would be vulnerable to an attack or robbery. So, I acquired the latest gadgetry: a remote control to activate the double garage doors from anywhere in the house – it even worked under a pillow. If anybody drove into The Woodlands unannounced, the doors would be opened and the four Rottweilers that I'd also bought would make an appearance. Diane told me that on a number of occasions, people were left cowering in their cars with four dogs patrolling round them. While I was in New York, my family would be as safe as possible.

Even though I'd moved to The Woodlands, people still managed to contact me about business matters, including a guy called Tom Wainwright, who I'd helped out three years earlier. He'd worked for a large pensions firm as an investor and adviser. He was one of the best in the business and was making bundles for the company but never seemed to be given the credit he deserved, so he branched out on his own and started making big money. His new-found status came to the attention of a local crook, who conned him out of £100,000. He had asked for my help, and I got him his money back.

Well, now he needed me again, so I went to his new drum. He was renting a very large house near Slough. It must have been costing him a fortune, but he knew that first impressions counted. When I arrived, he recounted his current tale of woe. It concerned a diminutive Jewish-American guy named Leon Silver. The American had shown Tom extensive plans for a new condominium in Los Angeles. He then told him that his client, a Californian lady who was the wife of the vice president of a large international bank, was the main backer and that he was looking for another investor. Tom dotted all the i's and crossed all the t's and even phoned up the bank to confirm the lady's identity. Everything stacked up, and it looked like a golden opportunity. What Tom didn't know was that Leon Silver was a world-class con man and that the banker who'd vouched for his wife didn't know that she was having a steamy affair with a virile tennis professional. Silver and the errant wife were looking for a big payday, and Tom Wainwright was their target.

All in all, it looked like a very profitable venture, but Tom was shrewd. He swapped cheques with the wife, both dated ten days in the future for added security. However, unbeknown to Tom, the femme fatale cashed her cheque the very next morning through her husband's bank. This transaction wouldn't have been authorised at any other bank in the world, but she used her husband's position to her advantage. Silver, the banker's wife and the tennis pro then chartered a private jet to take them to France with a huge amount of money in tow.

After hearing Tom's account, I decided to telephone John Francis in America. He was returning to England on business anyway, and the following day I met him at Heathrow. We made the short journey back to Slough, where John perused the condominium plans and asked for the names of the three people involved. He phoned the USA, and within 30 minutes his men had located Leon Silver's partner in Philadelphia. They told the partner that he was in big trouble and that because Silver wasn't there he would be held responsible for paying back the money. Silver's partner was not the bravest man in the world and spluttered out, 'Leon's just phoned me. He's staying at the Paris Hilton, room 184.'

These details were relayed back to John in Slough, and I watched on as he then telephoned Silver in Paris. 'Don't do anything stupid. The money stays there. Somebody will be over to collect it tomorrow.' The three con artists must have been terrified. The Mafia had found them in a foreign country in just one day. They now had two choices: to stay or go. John phoned again later on that night. They had all checked out, choosing a life on the run, always looking over their shoulders. John never got Tom's money back, but this episode demonstrated how well connected he was and that it was wise not to fuck with him. You can't win them all, but John Francis used to win most of them.

John's visit coincided with a phone call from my old friend Serge Polinski, a man of influence in the Polish community. Anybody of Polish extraction with clout would phone Serge if they had a problem. He was like the Polish *Yellow Pages*. For instance, he'd just sorted out brilliant accommodation for the Polish Olympic boxing team. The multiple medal winners were in Britain for a tournament, and Serge made their stay as comfortable as possible.

He was now being pestered by the finance minister of a West African country, who happened to be Polish, to find anyone who would be willing to invest money in his stricken adopted nation. The country was in the grips of a revolution by the military who had put down the existing government in an audacious coup. That was the easy part. The long-term problem would be finding an organisation or country to recognise the new regime and offer support. The African country wouldn't be getting a brass farthing from the UK or USA, so the Polish finance minister was on a worldwide search to locate a friendly ally, good or bad. This was the reason I had received the call from Serge. My Mafia connections could solve all his associate's problems.

I told Serge that I would get back to him. I put the scenario to John, telling him that the beleaguered government would even give permission for the wise guys to open a bank. Laundering money would then become child's play. John said, 'Give me a day, Norm. I'll look into it.' He studied every aspect of the tin-pot state, including its economics, history, geography and politics, before deciding that the deal wasn't feasible. 'The country's just too unstable, Norman. There's too much risk involved.' John could always sniff out a moneymaking opportunity, but the logistics of this operation were just too difficult to take on. I telephoned Serge, who was disappointed with the news but thanked me for trying. Africa would have to look after itself.

John returned to the USA, and I followed him a day later. On my arrival, I was concerned to hear that Russell Bufalino had been indicted on a charge of conspiracy to murder, though he was still free on bail. The machinations of the arrest made for an amazing tale. Prior to Bufalino's indictment, a high-ranking Mafia boss by the name of Jimmy 'the Weasel' Fratianno had been taken down by the FBI, who flippantly told him that he would die in jail. Jimmy knew that he was going to get a long stretch, and with the FBI chipping away at him he eventually turned, becoming one of the first big-name bosses to be enlisted as an informer.

This went down like a dose of cholera with the families, and a contract was placed on Fratianno's head. He was a dead man walking. The FBI knew that Russell Bufalino was involved in ordering the hit but couldn't prove his culpability, so they arranged for Fratianno to call Bufalino to see if it could be called off. Fratianno phoned Bufalino from the FBI headquarters, and the telephone conversation was recorded. Fratianno asked Bufalino if he would call off the hit, but Bufalino, who was nobody's fool, merely replied, 'Give my regards to your family.' However, those six little words were interpreted by the FBI as Bufalino sanctioning the hit. Bufalino was then, unbelievably, charged with conspiracy to murder and was left to sweat it out while he waited for his trial.

On a previous visit to the States, I had undergone an operation on a cataract in my right eye that had been a resounding success. On my return to England, I had championed the American private health system, not mentioning to anybody that I was actually working over there. Terry Coombs, the ex-middleweight boxer and an old friend of mine, had a similar problem with one of his eyes and was impressed with the results of my operation. 'If you go over again, Scouse, can I come with you? I've got a bit of a cataract myself.' I'd known Terry for years, but I had to consider his request carefully. Even Diane didn't know a lot of what was going on, and everyone else was totally in the dark.

I took a chance on Terry. 'I'm going to visit my sisters in the States in a few weeks. You can come along if you want.'

'Cheers, Scouse.' He was over the moon, but I couldn't help wondering if I was making a mistake. You bet I was!

On our arrival in New York, we checked into The Wellington Hotel on Broadway. My plan was to get him back home as soon as possible. I liked Terry a lot. He had a reputation as a bit of a playboy but could have been a world-class boxer. A couple of years earlier, I had gone with him to the Thomas a Becket boxing gym in London. While Terry was talking to a young boxer called Danny Holland, Henry Cooper's cut man and trainer came over. He said, 'You know, Norm, Terry could have been one of the greats, but he never applied himself. What a waste.' I knew that Terry was good, but I didn't know that he could have risen to that standard. He had started boxing at fairgrounds and had married at a young age to his long-suffering wife Pat, who knew he had wandering eyes but had stayed with him through thick and thin.

Something that happened years later summed up Terry perfectly. He was a boyish 52 years old and had gone to Miami for a break. When he returned to England with his hair dyed blond, it was all I could do not to break into hysterical laughter. He told me that he'd met a woman over there who was besotted with him – Terry could charm the pants off the best of them. 'Scouse, she's got a string of hairdressing salons in Florida and is loaded. She wants me to stay with her permanently.'

'Are you going to go for it, Terry?' I asked.

'Nah, she's too old.' I imagined her to be a wrinkly 60 year old. 'She's 32.' Terry never did like the older woman.

Later that evening, John Francis rang me. He had arranged dinner with Russell Bufalino and some top mob faces. I told John I had my friend Terry Coombs over with me and that he was a sound guy, so John said to bring him along. On the way to dinner at Jimmy Weston's, Terry gave me some bad news: the earliest date possible for his eye surgery was three days' time. Well, it couldn't be helped, so I introduced Terry to the New Yorkers. He was a man of the world and soon sussed out that he wasn't at a reps meeting about double glazing. I think he was awe struck, especially as the amounts of money being mentioned were enough to bail out a third-world country.

Just before Terry was due to go for his surgery, I had a big falling-out with John Francis. He'd taken a right liberty with Sonny Newcombe, whom he'd previously been good friends with. John was bang out of order, and when I phoned him I told him so. He countered by saying, 'A deal's a deal.'

'No, John. Put it right.'

'Don't talk to me like that.'

I wasn't having that. 'Right, I want to see you. We're going to sort this out.' John informed me that he was out of town for a few days, which was no problem. I'd still be around when he returned. I'd left him in no doubt that I was very angry, and he definitely got the message that I wasn't playing about. I then slammed down the phone.

Terry had been listening to everything I'd said. 'Oh no, Scouse. You'll get us killed.' He'd been watching too many gangster movies.

'Fuck off, Terry,' I said in an attempt to reassure him, but he was still afraid. He went for his eye operation and returned to the hotel, full of trepidation. 'I'm definitely going home tomorrow, Scouse,' he said, 'but can we change hotels tonight? I'm really worried.'

For an easy life, and knowing that he would soon be out of my hair, we checked out and booked into the Hilton. It wasn't far away, and I could see the relief on Terry's face when we arrived. We both unpacked then Terry came into my room. 'Scouse, you're in my room. You should be in 42.'

'What's the difference?' I asked. 'They're both identical.'

'No, no, Scouse. Your name's booked in for my room.' I realised that Terry thought that the mob would come in the middle of the night to bump me off. The only problem was that he was sleeping in my bed. I wasn't swapping. I'd unpacked, and I wasn't going to play his games.

The sweat was pouring off him. I devilishly advised him, 'Keep your door bolted, just in case.' That didn't go down too well.

Without telling Terry, I decided to go on a recce at around midnight to see if John was back in town. I went out and about to his usual watering holes, but there was no sign of him, so I told three or four wise guys that I was looking for him. They could tell by my demeanour that we weren't the best of buddies at that precise moment.

I returned to the Hilton at about two in the morning. Before retiring, I tried Terry's door handle and knocked on his door. He must have shit himself. When I got back to my room, the phone rang. 'Scouse, there's somebody out there. I swear. They've just tried to get into my room.'

I told him gruffly, 'Go to sleep. You've just woken me up.'

I gave it 15 minutes and then repeated my earlier corridor caper, this time much louder. The phone rang again. 'Did you hear that? You must have heard that.'

'I heard jack shit. Open your door in ten seconds. We'll sort it.'

We both faced each other in the empty corridor. 'Will you go to sleep now, you cunt?' I slept like a baby, but poor old Terry told me that he didn't sleep a wink. He sat on a chair facing the door all night.

Terry flew out the next day and returned to London an enlightened man. The trouble was, though, that he was enlightening anyone who would listen about his American adventure.

I still had the hump with John Francis. I eventually arranged a meeting with him, and we managed to straighten everything out. I liked him but didn't agree with liberty taking. John said, 'We don't need to row, Norman. We've got too many things going on. It would be crazy to fall out.' It was business as usual for a few weeks, and then it was time for me to fly back to England again.

When I arrived home, the first thing that Diane said to me was, 'Who are these women in New York who are being laid on a plate for you?'

'What are you talking about?' I asked. She informed me that Terry's wife had phoned her and told her that Terry had said that women were readily available in New York. 'You know Terry's a wind-up merchant,' I said. 'He can't even lie down straight.' This put me on edge, though, as I wondered what else he had been saying. I'd been so discreet for years. I hoped Terry hadn't opened up a Pandora's box.

The next day, I received a further kick. Jimmy Tibbett, the friend who had worked for me at the pub disco, telephoned. 'Scouse, can you get down for a meeting with Freddie Foreman?' he said.

I thought, 'What the fuck does Fred want?' I then told Jimmy, 'I'll be at The Green Man in Catford at one o'clock tomorrow.' I had known Freddie for a while, but we hadn't worked together and our paths hadn't crossed that much, so I was intrigued to know what he wanted.

The next day, I joined Freddie and Jimmy in the bar at The Green Man. Fred kicked off the proceedings. 'I've heard you're involved with good people in America. Can we do something with them over here?'

I cut him short. 'No, Fred. They wouldn't be interested.' He seemed disappointed, but that was the least of my problems. Things were getting out of hand. 'Who told you that I was working in America, Fred?' I asked.

He was keeping his cards close to his chest. 'One or two people,' he replied. We had a few drinks then moved on to a club in Waterloo, where a few faces, including the Great Train Robber Charlie Wilson, were enjoying a liquid lunch.

Jimmy kept on referring to the USA, so I asked him straight, 'Who is talking about me and the Mafia?'

'Terry Coombs,' he said. 'He's telling all and sundry.'

I felt my hackles rise. Terry was endangering my position and prospects with his loose talk. I gave Jimmy instructions to contact Terry and tell him that I wanted to see him pronto. I was in the Smoke for two days before I got the call I was waiting for. Jimmy said, 'I'm down at Eddie Richardson's club, J. Arthur's in Catford. Terry's here with me.'

I stormed over and confronted him. 'What have you been saying, rent a gob? Say what you want about yourself, but don't spread gossip about me.'

Terry half-heartedly tried to deny what he'd said, but I was in his face. He didn't back down but knew that if it went off he was in big trouble. Luckily for him, Jimmy somehow got in between us. I hoped that Terry had got the message. A few months later, we made up. I'd known him for too many years to hold a grudge, but I wouldn't make the same mistake with my business affairs again.

21

· · · · · · ·

Brooklyn, Boxers and Bother

Five days later, I was again crossing the Atlantic, heading for the Stars and Bars. It was now as common for me to fly to America as for an office worker to commute to London on the train.

It didn't take me long after touchdown to hear that Russell Bufalino had been sent down for a very unjust ten years and was languishing in a Philadelphia prison. This had put John Francis under a lot of pressure. He was rushing back and forth, dealing with the mob's business interests, which meant that I had to deal with our own ventures.

On a quieter day, I had a social drink with Louis Rush. I told him that John Francis was under the cosh, trying to keep the mob's interests afloat, which was having a domino effect on me and our business affairs. Louis had heard about my earlier falling-out with John, and out of the blue casually remarked, 'Norman, if you ever want me to clip that Francis, just let me know. He's a slippery mother.'

Louis looked genuinely disappointed when I replied, 'It's OK, Louis. It's been sorted. It's water under the bridge.'

He shrugged his shoulders. 'The offer's there, Norman.'

I thanked him and thought, 'You're one cool customer.' He was talking about taking somebody out as if he was opening a bottle of wine, but I really appreciated that he valued our friendship that much.

Later that afternoon, a guy came into the bar whom I recognised immediately: Jake 'The Bronx Bull' LaMotta, one of the all-time great middleweights, who was brilliantly played by Robert DeNiro in the film *Raging Bull*. As I was an ardent fan of the noble art, Jake was one of the boxers whom I most admired, but it soon became clear that Louis didn't share my good opinion. He sighted Jake up at the bar and shouted across, 'Get out, you flat-nosed cocksucker. And don't come into any bar that I'm drinking in.' It was an incredible encounter: a small elderly man chastising a guy with very dangerous fists. Jake turned on his heels and slunk out without a word. He knew Louis was not a man to argue with. Louis turned to me and said, 'Norman, that creep's no good.'

'He was a great sportsman, Louis,' I insisted.

The little hit man began to reminisce. 'He could have been. He should have made us bundles of money but wouldn't ever take a fall. The dumb motherfucker's lucky not to be six feet under.' I knew I couldn't persuade Louis to change his mind, so I let it be.

I got to know Jake better later on when I found out where he drank. We became good friends and would regularly meet up for a beverage. He was frequently down on his luck, and I would regularly slip him $50. He always seemed to have a young lady on his arm, even though he wasn't a looker and was utterly potless. It's incredible what a powerful aphrodisiac fame is. Jake should have been staying away from young ladies, really, as earlier in his life he had been accused of having underage sex with the woman he eventually married.

Sometimes, while I was out with John Francis and the wise guys, we'd bump into Jake, and he'd always come across to say hello. John and the mobsters would all show their disgust, saying, 'Why are you talking to that bum? He's poison.'

I always stood up for Jake, though. 'I respect him as a boxer, and I will always talk to him.' This used to drive them all mad, but they knew that I had an affinity for boxers and took it on the chin.

Just after I met Jake, I became good friends with another former world boxing champion: New Yorker Rocky Graziano. He was a popular guy, and his story had also appeared on the silver screen in *Somebody Up There Likes Me* when he'd been played superbly by Paul Newman. One day, he told me a story about his dealings with the Mafia that reminded me of LaMotta's. Years before, he had earned himself an eliminator fight for a shot at the world title and was up against a boxer whom he was supremely confident of beating. In the changing-room before the fight, he was visited by two gentlemen from the Chicago underworld, namely the Al Capone gang. They presented Rocky with a five-carat, square-cut diamond ring. 'Regards from Al. He'd appreciate it if you didn't win this fight.' The wise guys were very polite, issuing no threats, and they wished him all the best before disappearing into the night.

Rocky was in a real quandary: should he take a fall or defy the mob and take his chances? Once the fight had started, he decided to see what the other boxer had to offer. Not a lot as it turned out. He had to take him out and duly stopped him. He now thought that he was going to be in a lot of trouble. Sure enough, when Rocky returned to the changing-rooms, the two hoods reappeared. Rocky was just about to make his excuses when one of the mobsters cut him short. 'Al is disappointed with the result of the fight, but maybe another time, Rocky. Congratulations, and please keep the ring.' He was relieved but still suspected that a bullet might come his way when he was not expecting it. However, nothing ever happened. The Chicago underworld were a lot more forgiving than LaMotta's New York associates.

Louis Rush knew Rocky well, but he didn't know that Graziano had once defied the Chicago Mafia. It was a good job, too, because years earlier he had been talking to Graziano about his up-and-coming fight against rock-hard middleweight boxing champion Tony Zale. (Between 1946 and 1948, Zale and Graziano had a monumental trilogy of fights that would go down in boxing folklore as all-time classics.) Louis loved a bet and asked Rocky if he could take the Polish-American Zale, who was then considered to be the finest pound-for-pound fighter in the world. At that time, Zale already had one decision over Graziano on his CV after a brutal showdown in New York. The return was scheduled for 1947 in Chicago, and Louis asked the New Yorker, 'Can you take him, Rocky?'

'I'll give him a good hiding,' said a confident Graziano.

Tony Zale, nicknamed 'The Man of Steel', was a heavy odds-on favourite, so Louis, with all the money he could get his hands on, was finding it easy to back Graziano. The trouble was that Louis was putting on more than he could afford to lose. He wasn't worried, though, as he thought that Rocky was a good investment. Louis and his personal driver, who was also a big fight fan, flew up to Chicago on the day before the fight and booked into a hotel, where they hired a car to drive to the arena. For good measure, Louis again asked Rocky if he could win. 'Are you sure, Rocky?'

Defeat was out of the question for Graziano. 'Sure I'm sure. I'll knock him out.' That would do for Louis, and he put more money on Rocky to win with his fellow hoods and illegal bookies at ringside. They couldn't take his bets quickly enough – Tony Zale was the Mike Tyson of his time. Louis and the driver then settled down to watch the fight. It was uncomfortable theatre. The first three rounds were a mismatch. Zale battered Graziano all around the ring. He had him on the canvas and closed one of his eyes. In short, he gave him a boxing lesson. It seemed to be only a matter of time before Rocky would be defeated. Louis couldn't take it any more and said to his driver, 'Get the car. We're going.' But not before offering the bloodied, battered boxer some words of encouragement as he got up from his seat. 'You low-down son of a bitch, Rocky. You've cost me plenty.'

They drove through the city towards the hotel, and the driver switched on the radio. 'He's put him down with a beautiful right,' said the commentator. 'One . . . two . . . three . . . four . . .'

'Cheapskate, fuckin' bum,' muttered Louis.

'Five . . . six . . . seven . . . eight . . .'

'Cocksucking, useless motherfucker,' he added.

'Nine . . . ten . . . out. And the new champion of the world . . . Rocky Graziano.'

'Quick,' said Louis. 'Turn the car around. I knew he could do it!'

They returned to the fight venue, and Louis picked up a fortune in winning bets. Rocky had pulled it out of the fire and knocked out Zale in the sixth round. The public couldn't get enough of Zale v. Graziano, and the third and final leg was fought in 1948 in New Jersey, Zale getting his revenge by knocking out his opponent. The three fights with Rocky must have taken their toll on Zale, as he was never the same fighter afterwards.

Rocky Graziano retired from the ring in 1952. He had made good money from the fight game but started spending as if the dollar had gone out of fashion. He was profligate with his gambling and drinking, and looked to be heading towards the gutter, but his friends rallied around him, including Frank Sinatra, who arranged for him to front an advertising campaign for, of all things, bread products. He slowly got back on his feet, but his long-suffering wife decided that now was the time to keep hold of the purse strings. Rocky reluctantly agreed that this was the right way to proceed, even though she only ever gave him a $20 daily allowance. This became a standing joke amongst the wise guys. Rocky would enter a bar, and they'd all chorus, 'How much you got today, Rocky?' From his top pocket, he'd produce a bill with president Andrew Jackson on it and hold it high in the air between his fingers. But the truth was that Rocky was so popular he never had to put his hand in his pocket anyway. People were always buying him drinks, including me, and we had many great conversations about life and boxing. He was a man born on the wrong side of the tracks who made good. He was a truly great boxer and a personal friend.

Sinatra could be a strange fish. One night, John Francis and I were having a meal in a restaurant on Third Avenue when he came in with his full entourage, including a couple of lookers. Sinatra sent a bottle of Dom Pérignon champagne over, as he knew John well. The waiter put the chilled ice bucket down on our table. 'Compliments of Mr Sinatra.' We both stood up and acknowledged the gesture, and Sinatra waved back. Later, as we were leaving, we waved goodbye and sent over a bottle of our own. A year later, in a different restaurant, John Francis told the maître d', 'Give them anything they want, with my compliments.' Sinatra didn't look up or even acknowledge that we were in the restaurant. John said, 'You never know what mood Frank will be in on the night.' He was certainly a man you couldn't take for granted!

John had a French mistress named Marie, who lived in a downtown Manhattan flat. She was a high-class madame, who had about 20 girls working for her. After I arrived in New York on one occasion, John and I headed for her address, and we were welcomed by Marie into her apartment. John whispered, 'Sweetheart, can you fetch me some cigarettes?' Marie knew the score. She got her coat and left. John used her flat for a lot of business meetings. It was a safe house away from the prying eyes and ears of the authorities.

Ten minutes after the Gallic girlfriend had gone, the front doorbell rang. John ushered in a very rotund wise guy, accompanied by a small, dapper, balding Italian mobster. I had previously met both men on my rounds with John and was relaxed in their company. John got them both a drink and got down to business. The smaller man did all the talking. 'John, the motherfucker's had our money and not delivered the goods. It's making us look bad. Son of a bitch.'

John was always the mediator. 'Let's have a serious word in his ear to see if we can bring him round.'

'Fuck that, John,' the small man screamed back. 'He's had his chances. No more. He's got to go. We can't be made to look weak.'

John was pensive. 'Do we really need to go down this road?'

The mafioso was adamant. 'Too right we do, John. The guy's history. I feel like strangling him with my own hands.'

'If we go down this route, we'll have to bring in somebody from out of town,' John replied.

The large wise guy, who hadn't spoken a word up to that point, now interjected, and he certainly got my attention. 'How about Norman?' he suggested nonchalantly.

John wasn't having that. 'Don't even go there. Norman's here as my partner.'

The big guy insisted. 'But it makes sense, John. Norman's not well known here. What could go wrong?'

I didn't know if I was being set up as a patsy, but I never ducked a challenge and took the bull by the horns. 'I'll do it,' I said coolly. You might think that I'd jumped into a viper pit, but I was earning mega bucks and living life to the full. It was the least I could do. If it was all done professionally, I could put it behind me with my reputation intact.

John wasn't happy, but the wise guys were made up. 'Norman, we'll meet up tomorrow in Giacomino's at 11 p.m. Leave all the arrangements to us.' They rose, shook our hands, hugged us and left.

John looked at me. 'I don't agree with this, Norman. It's a bad time, but I've got to go down to Miami tonight. You can still pull out. It wouldn't go against you.'

'I'm committed, John,' I replied and wondered if he was distancing himself from the heat. Like I've said before, he was a hard man to read.

The next evening, I caught a yellow cab over to Giacomino's, arriving a few minutes before 11 p.m. The smaller hood greeted me.

'Norman, this is the plan.' We went over an uncomplicated series of moves two or three times. We would use three cars, with me travelling in the middle one. The front and rear vehicles were back-up in case anything went wrong. Shorty bade me farewell, and I jumped into the back seat of the middle motor as arranged. There was a driver in the front and a wise guy in the back. He handed me a .38 calibre Beretta. 'The catch is off. The piece is ready to fire.'

I put the gun in my pocket, and we made our way to Queens, one of the five boroughs of New York. We drove for about 15 minutes before sidling into a back street. In the near distance, a man in an overcoat and homburg was standing under a club's neon sign with his hands in his pockets. He was the only sign of life; the street was otherwise deserted. I got out and walked 100 yards. I went behind and past him and suddenly swivelled back round. I pushed the gun into the back of his head and pulled the trigger four times: click, click, click, click. I thought, 'Oh no, fuck me,' and sprinted back to the car as quick as a flash. I dived into the back seat, threw the gun at the hood and screamed, 'What's this piece of shit? The fucking magazine's empty.'

He put his hands in the air defensively. 'I swear I don't know anything about it. That's how the gun was given to me.'

We sped back to Giacomino's, and I strode purposely over to the wise guy's table, but before I could say anything the small hood welcomed me back. 'Norman, we needed to see if you were the man John Francis said you were. Have some champagne. You've exceeded all of our expectations.'

I wasn't having that. 'Keep your champagne. Don't take me for a mug. I'm too old to play games.' And with that, I stormed out.

The next day, John returned to New York. I phoned him and said, 'John, I want to see you, now.'

He turned up an hour later. He had the gall to tell me that he had known what was going on, although he hadn't endorsed it. He said, 'They wanted to know if you had the balls, and you've come through with flying colours.' I told him that I still wasn't happy about being duped, but he just shrugged his shoulders and said, 'Don't worry about it.' That didn't placate me, as I hated the saying. It really got up my nose, because I heard it mentioned every day. At that moment, I felt like chinning him – then I wouldn't be worrying about it!

Later that year, just before Christmas, Diane telephoned me to ask if she could come over for a week before I returned to England. I gave her the thumbs up, and she arrived at JFK Airport wearing a summer dress and cardigan. You couldn't miss her on the concourse, surrounded by sheepskins and fur hats. Whenever I returned home, at whatever time of year, I was always tanned. The main reason for this was that John and I had regular business meetings on Paradise Island in the Bahamas. We would fly across at least eight times a year, hence the Mediterranean look. Diane had never been to New York and thought that it must be like Florida, weather-wise, as I'd never told her that my tan came from having a whale of a time in the Caribbean. She said, 'I can't believe how cold it is. How come you're so brown?' I quickly changed the subject with a suggestion that we go shopping, and after buying her some suitable clothes we headed for the jewellery quarter, where she started spending for Britain. At a little Jewish establishment, the owner handed her some complimentary cashmere sweaters and designer handbags for her and the kids. If he was giving these away, she must have been giving my credit cards a right workout on his other goods, as you wouldn't have got those sorts of freebies at Ratners. As we were leaving, I noticed him whisper something in her ear, but at that moment I thought no more of it. Next stop: Bloomingdale's.

As I drove across New York, Diane changed into one of the cashmere sweaters and swapped the contents of her handbag into a new designer one. When we arrived at the world-famous department store, we made a grand entrance into the building, but when we were three steps in a cacophony of alarms went off. A large security guy came over and apologised. He suggested walking out and re-entering. Outside, Diane had a sheepish look on her face. 'Norman, I've just remembered what the jeweller told me. He said not to go into any shops.'

'Brilliant,' I thought. The clothes and handbags still had their security tags on them and were setting off the alarms. By that point, the Bloomingdale's staff were giving us quizzical looks, so I feigned umbrage and walked off, declaring that their alarms must be faulty. Back at the hotel, we found all the tiny plastic tags and removed them.

During the week, I gave Diane the full tour of New York, showing her all the sights. She was introduced to all the faces, including Rocky and the wise guys. At the weekend, we were dining at a restaurant with Louis Rush. John and Kathy were due to join us later. When they eventually arrived, Kathy turned everybody's head. She was wearing a full-length mink fur coat, made from top-quality female fur. Diane gasped. Louis saw her reaction and said, 'Would you like one, Diane?'

She said, 'No, I just think it's so beautiful.' This was a time when fur wasn't such a taboo and politically incorrect subject.

Louis persisted. 'Do you like it, Diane?' She nodded enthusiastically, so he went to the use the phone and came back after making a call. 'Ten o'clock, tomorrow morning, at this factory I know. They are opening up especially for us.' Diane's face was a picture.

The next day, Louis picked us up personally. Champagne was laid on, and Diane was fitted. The lady furrier told us that it would take about half an hour to take in the alterations, so we spent a pleasant 30 minutes chatting and quaffing bubbly. When the lady returned with the coat, I asked how much I owed her. She said, 'That'll be $3,000.' I knew for sure that the coat should not have been a dime under $10,000. It was obvious that Louis had used his influence and done me a great favour. He wasn't finished. 'I'll get the bill, Norman.'

But I wasn't having that. 'No you won't, Louis. Thank you, but you've done more than enough.' I paid the lady, and as I helped Diane on with the coat I noticed that her name was stitched into the lining. At the same time, the furrier popped the receipt into the breast pocket of my sports jacket.

The next day, we flew back to Heathrow. Diane was feeling like the empress of the universe until we reached the 'Anything to declare' aisle, where an overzealous female Customs officer, who was either jealous or malicious, started quizzing Diane about the fur. 'How long have you had this garment?' she asked.

Quick as a flash, Diane said, 'Eighteen months.'

The Customs woman then turned to me and repeated the same question. 'If she says 18 months, then it's 18 months,' I replied.

She proceeded to put her face into the luxuriant fur. 'It smells new to me. Would you mind if we search your cases?' It wouldn't have mattered if I had minded, and before long one of the dipsticks had found the receipt in my jacket pocket.

The alpha Customs officer came over. He was the kind of man who should have had the word 'bastard' tattooed on his forehead. It was obvious that he'd been in the same situation many times before and was getting a perverse pleasure out of it, as he said, 'One, you can go to Uxbridge Magistrates tomorrow, where you'll be fined £1,500 for smuggling and £2,500 for unpaid taxes. Two, we can keep the coat. Or three, you can part with £4,000 now and take the coat with you.' He certainly had me snookered behind the black ball.

I'd been inside too many court rooms and knew that number one wasn't even an option. I didn't consider option two – they were certainly not going to get the coat – so I decided to plump for option three, which was the best of a bad bunch. It was like going to hospital and being told that both your legs would need amputating but the bloke in the next bed wanted to buy your carpet slippers. I pulled out a huge roll of dollars to show that I wouldn't miss four big ones, although I was secretly seething at the legalised robbery. 'I'm sorry, sir, but we can't accept foreign currency. Sterling only.'

'You're taking the piss,' I said, but he wasn't and accompanied me to the nearest NatWest. I passed the wad to the Customs officer. 'You can have a good fucking Christmas party now,' I said, but he didn't even crack a smile. The coat had ended up costing me a lot more than the original price. Her Majesty's Customs and Excise had seen to that.

Back in Stafford, I discovered that the Old Bill were up to their old tricks again. I was relaxing at home when Diane said, 'There's a man at the door who wants to have a word.'

I got to my feet and went to the door, where I came face to face with a stocky blond-haired man. 'What do you want, pal?' I asked.

He said, 'My name's Mick Glover. Can I come in? I've got something to tell you.' It transpired that Mick, a local hard man but a decent guy, had heard some interesting information concerning me from his wife, who worked in the local NatWest branch. That morning, she had been summoned into the manager's office, where two of Scotland Yard's finest had been waiting. 'I want you to assist these two officers,' the manager had told her. 'Take out Norman

Johnson's files.' That evening, she'd returned home and told Mick that there was going to be an investigation into a local man over money laundering. Mick had asked her who it was, and she had told him Norman Johnson. The name rang a bell with Mick, and he'd made his way to Pool Cottage. He had also heard that all of Stafford's travel agents had been advised to call a police contact number whenever I booked a flight. I gave Mick £100 for his trouble. He's since died, but at that time I really appreciated his help.

'What a fiasco,' I thought. I didn't know why the English authorities were on my back. I hadn't bothered them for years, but once they got their claws into you, they never let go. I very rarely used travel agents, anyway, but I didn't need all this aggro, so it was back to the USA, a country not riddled with jealousy and spite.

Once I'd returned to the States, I found that Louis Rush was again on top form. The pair of us were drinking in Mickey Quinn's bar on Third Avenue with John Francis and a couple of other wise guys when a small Jewish fellow came into the bar. He was the ace accountant for the Joe 'Bananas' Bonanno family, and over the years this important little cog in their money wheel had saved them millions of dollars. He acknowledged the two wise guys in our company before making his way to the toilet. Louis asked one of the mobsters, 'Who's that dumb fuck?'

'Dumb fuck? That little mother's never got less than $20,000 on him. He's a top accountant.'

Louis' eyes lit up. 'Is that so?' He then got to his feet and followed the accountant into the toilet. Five minutes later, the pen pusher burst back through the toilet door and fled from the bar. Louis calmly returned to the table, and as he straightened his tie he said, 'Twenty grand, eh? I made him take off all his clothes, and he didn't have a bent nickel on him.'

Louis sat down, and I said to him, 'He left a bit sharpish, didn't he?'

The little hit man nodded solemnly. 'So he should. I told him, "You've wasted my time. I want ten grand. If you don't bring it back here, I'll kill you."' Louis started laughing. It was infectious, and the table was rocking. I knew he was only joking and wouldn't have carried out the threat, and we carried on drinking all afternoon.

In the early evening, two large mafiosi came into the bar. The bigger of these walking juggernauts said to Louis, 'Can we have a word?' They moved to the end of the bar to talk.

All of a sudden, Louis exploded. 'Get out, you bums. I'll put one in him now, you motherfuckers.' They shuffled out with their tails between their legs. Louis said to me, 'I was only joking, Norman, but now I'm serious. I'm gonna clip that piece of shit.'

Worse was to follow. An hour later, two more of the Joe Bonanno mob appeared. One was a capo. 'Louis, cut this crap out. It stops here, right now. Joe Bonanno won't tolerate it.'

Louis wouldn't be intimidated. 'Fuck you and fuck Joe Bananas.'

John was concerned. He thought that Louis was playing a very dangerous game and said to me, 'He's pushing his luck, Norman. I'm going. I'll see if I can find out what's happening.' Later that night, John rang me. 'Bad news, Norman. There's a contract out on Louis. To be on the safe side, stay away from him. I'll ask Russell to get the hit lifted, but in the meantime be careful.' I had no intention of steering clear of Louis, but I must admit that during the following days we did a lot of drinking with our backs against the wall.

Russell Bufalino telephoned Joe Bananas from prison. 'Louis has always been a stand-up guy and has done good work for all of the families, Joe. I want you to lift the contract as a favour to me.'

Bonanno begrudgingly ceded to Bufalino. 'OK, Russell, but keep the little maniac in line. He's becoming a loose cannon.' The accountant never drank in Mickey Quinn's again, and Louis wouldn't be getting a payday from any Bonanno associate.

John was still under pressure with Bufalino behind bars, even though the boss was still dictating everything from prison. He had his finger on the pulse from his cell, but John was being delegated more and more work, while I was finding myself under the cosh from Diane, who was pleading for me to return to England for good. My American business affairs were becoming intolerable without the shared input from John, and things came to a head when we had another big falling-out. I decided to turn my back on the States, although I knew I could return at anytime to continue my American experience. I sold my New York flat for $60,000, and John wrapped up our other business deals, which netted me another $300,000.

Instead of heading for Britain, I flew directly to Spain. With the amount of money I had on me, I didn't fancy British Customs again.

As I was flying over the Atlantic, it suddenly dawned on me that I might not see Jake or Rocky again. Neither of them were getting any younger, and who could say when I'd be back in New York. If I'd have carried on my professional boxing career, I would have ended up a middleweight, and the two guys I admired most were all-time greats at that level. I was leaving them with a heavy heart, but I had worked in two of the world's great cities, and the memories would never fade away.

22

·······

Wrong Place, Wrong Time

I walked out of Malaga Airport into the Spanish sunshine. I was wedged up with a godly amount, but there was no trouble getting the money into Spain, as they had very lax border controls. I caught a cab to Marbessa, where an old acquaintance of mine called Tom Smith resided. Tom had run a pub in Kent at the same time that I was proprietor of The King's Lodge. He was now retired and had previously given me an open-ended invitation to stay with him any time I liked.

I told Tom that I was looking for a villa, to which he replied, 'Look no more, Norman. There's an absolute beauty down the road.' The next morning, we went to take a look at it. It was a modern three-bedroomed villa with a large swimming pool and an underground garage. I thought, 'This is the dog's bollocks.' Tom knew the owner, who lived in the exclusive Puerto Banús area, so we went down to see him. I asked him if he would accept cash; it was a silly question, really.

We drove down to his solicitors, and I threw a huge wad of $100 notes onto his desk, which he and his secretary counted with relish. 'This looks like Mafia money,' he innocently remarked and flashed me a cheesy grin. Who says that solicitors never tell the truth? It was a done deal in less than a fortnight, and in the meantime I furnished the villa with top-quality furniture.

I phoned Diane and the girls back in England and told them to come over. They loved it, especially the youngest two, Victoria and Rachel. Diane and Teresa were keen on the villa but reluctant to move to Spain permanently, as they were still very attached to family and their horses back in England, so we made it our holiday home, and it turned out to be a good investment.

I started trawling the bars. Ronnie Knight and Freddie Foreman were still up and about, and I was always bumping into them. One day Fred said to me, 'You know Gordon, don't you, Scouse?' He pointed to a gaunt, balding guy at the bar.

'Not that I know of,' I replied.

'No, you do,' Fred insisted. 'He's just been talking about you.'

I went over. 'Norman, it's me, Gordon. We used to knock about at Theo's nightclub.' The penny dropped. I realised that it was Gordon Goody, the Great Train Robber. The long years spent in jail hadn't been kind to him. I remembered a smart Crombie-clad Jack the Lad with a crop of blond hair. Then again, I hadn't seen him for 30 years, which was nearly half a lifetime. It was great to see him, and we arranged to meet again later on that week.

On the day I was to due to see Gordon, I walked into the bar we'd arranged to meet at and bumped into a little Jewish girl, who used to drink with all the faces. 'That thing over there insulted me,' she cried, pointing to a large swarthy guy of Middle Eastern appearance.

I hardly knew her, so I said, 'What do you want me to do about it? Leave it out.'

She cocked me a dirty one and left the bar. I ordered a Scotch and Coke, and the Arab said, 'I get that.'

'No, pal. It's OK.'

'You live here?' he asked.

'Just bought a villa,' I said, trying to keep the conversation to a minimum.

I was just moving in the direction of away when he asked me what business I was in. I don't know why, but the words 'import and export' came out of my mouth. Big mistake. He delightedly proclaimed, 'I also import and export. Maybe we work together?'

'No, I don't think so. I've already got a partner.'

He was all ears, and his eyes were wide with anticipation, so I decided to play him along. 'He's from the Middle East. His name is Dr Zawawi,' I said, plucking a name from the ether.

He nearly had a coronary. 'I know him, I know him.' Arabs are the most suspicious people on the planet until they know you well, and he kept grilling me, asking me where Zawawi lived, what he looked like and so on. Of course, I knew all the answers from my time with the princess. 'Do you know Sheikh Mustahail?' he asked.

'Very well,' I replied.

'Surely not Sultan Qaboos?' I nodded in the affirmative. It looked like he was going to explode with excitement until Gordon walked in and rescued me.

Gordon and I left and had a great time in the local bars, finishing the night off at a club with a late licence. The large Arab whom I'd met earlier was at a table surrounded by four dolly birds and even more champagne buckets. He moved exceedingly quickly for a big man and ran over to greet me like I was his long-lost brother. 'Norman, my friend. It is so good to see you again.' He had me clamped in a sweaty bear hug. I don't know who was more embarrassed, Gordon or me. The Arab let go and said, 'You must come to my house later on tonight. I live on the hilltop.' Puerto Banús was the millionaires' playground, and to live up on the hill meant that you had serious amounts of wonga. He pressed his calling card into my palm, and I made my excuses and left. Back at the villa, I ripped it up. I'd had my fill of Arabs for the time being.

Over the months, the Spanish property was being used less and less, as I found myself taking the family on expensive holidays to Tenerife, Bermuda and the Bahamas. I still wanted a base in Spain so decided to sell the villa and get a smaller apartment that I could use for business and pleasure. I purchased a first-floor flat in an exclusive part of Marbella that would serve me better than the large villa that wasn't being used to its optimum.

I sold the house for a tidy profit to a Swiss guy named Philippe. It was the start of a series of events that would culminate in his death. He was a big cheese in the music industry and duly converted the underground garage into a music room, where he could conduct his business affairs as well as relax in his leisure time. He also installed a spiral staircase that led directly up to his living quarters.

One night, he befriended some English guys and invited them back for a drink. The next day, Philippe was found murdered. The two guys must have been mugs, as they started cruising round Marbella in Philippe's BMW, using his credit cards and generally spending money like water. It didn't take long for them to be arrested. One was wearing the dead man's Cartier watch and the other his leather jacket. Even the Spanish police couldn't fuck that one up!

I'd completed my business affairs for the time being in Spain and was on the verge of flying back to England when the phone rang. It was club owner Bobby McEwen, who'd received an invite to a wedding in Morocco, courtesy of the actor Richard Harris, whose son was getting married to the daughter of a wealthy local. Bobby knew that I got on with Richard, whom I had met on quite a few occasions, so asked me over to the wedding. I didn't have much on that week and consequently booked a flight to Tangiers. They don't stand on ceremony in that part of the world, and the celebrations continued for five days and nights. They certainly knew how to throw a party.

Most of my time was spent drinking and talking to Bobby and Richard Harris, who had a worldwide reputation for bending the elbow. A quality actor and intelligent raconteur, Harris kept us all entertained while the staff filled our glasses with a never-ending supply of local wines and spirits. I flew back to Marbella in an alcohol-induced trance, tired but happy. I slept for the next 24 hours, unaware that events beyond my control that would jeopardise my future happiness were just around the corner.

Before I returned to England, I had one more thing to take care of. I popped into a local bar owned by an English guy called Ernie, who had borrowed three grand from me a month earlier. After my exertions in Morocco, where I had spent money like I was the Sultan of Brunei, the folding stuff would come in handy. Ernie was in the company of three well-known London faces from Eltham, whom I was familiar with. It looked like they were discussing business, so I went to the bar for a drink.

Ernie came over. 'Scouse, I've got some work going down. I'll have your money in a fortnight. Is that OK?' I nodded. The three grand would have to wait, so I left him my Stafford phone number. Ernie added, 'I'll arrange to get it over to you.' He was obviously in cahoots with the faces, which was no skin off my nose, as long as I got my three grand back. It was of no interest to me how Ernie was making his money.

I'd had an uneventful week back in Stafford when Sid Murphy called round to the house. Sid had just moved to Stafford; he seemed to follow me wherever I went. Our conversation was interrupted by the telephone. A male voice said, 'This is Simon. I'm at Hilton Park services, north bound, with my wife and baby. We've broken down. Could you pick us all up?' Before I could reply, the line went dead.

I looked at Sid quizzically. 'That was a fucking strange phone call, Sid. Somebody called Simon.'

'Well, he's got your number, Norm. He must know you.'

I was baffled. 'I can't for the life of me place him. Says he's broken down at Hilton Park. Wants me to pick him up.'

Sid suggested nipping down there and offered to come with me, so we jumped into the Merc and drove to the service station, which was about 12 miles south of Stafford on the M6. We had a good walk round the car park and searched the restaurants and toilets, but nobody caught our eye, even though it wasn't that busy. I said to Sid, 'We'll give it ten minutes. Let's have a couple of Cokes.'

We finished our drinks, and Sid remarked, 'Somebody's taking the piss, Norm. It's a wind-up. Let's fuck off. If it's gen, he'll contact you again.'

We cruised out of the services and were just about to hit the motorway when we heard tyres screeching and men shouting. Four cars surrounded our motor, and at least a dozen men, screaming at the top of their voices, pointed firearms at us. We were then dragged out of the Mercedes. Three men threw me over the bonnet, and I was handcuffed behind my back. When they straightened me up and hauled me round, I was face to face with a bespectacled plain-clothes detective. 'Norman Johnson, you are charged with the importation of a controlled substance. Anything you say . . .' Blah, blah, blah. I gave him my standard response: total silence.

My mind was racing. Surely they weren't fitting me up again. I'd never had any dealings with drugs in my life. I'd never even smoked so much as a spliff. I'd had plenty of offers and chances to get involved, and I knew that narcotics could bring incredible wealth, but I'd amassed ample assets and savings without ever having to resort to that level. Besides, the British judiciary took a very stern view of people who dealt in the naughty stuff.

Sid and I were taken to Cannock Police Station and placed in separate cells, while Customs sent six men to search my house.

Another half dozen went to Sid's. Unluckily for him, they found an Italian double-barrelled shotgun in his bedroom. Nobody was in at my place, but still they turned it upside down. No drawer was left unopened, and every nook and cranny was thoroughly inspected. They even dug up the gardens.

I had a miraculous piece of luck. There was a large oil painting on the wall of my lounge that the Customs officers unbelievably didn't lay a finger on. If they had looked behind it, they would have found a wall safe containing £8,000 in cash, a .38 calibre Magnum and numerous dum-dum bullets from my time with the Arabs. Thank God the house came up clean. I didn't need any extra charges to add to my current predicament.

We spent the night at Cannock, which was a punishment in itself, and the next morning were taken to Exeter Prison. Sid and I were transported in separate vehicles, and on arrival we were put in separate cells and placed under heavy security. At that moment, I was completely in the dark, but it later transpired that the ongoing shenanigans were down to my association with Ernie back in Spain. The day I'd popped into his bar, he'd been discussing with the Eltham mob a way of bringing Moroccan hashish, which was easily and readily available, into Britain from Spain. Again, I repeat, it had nothing to do with me. I just wanted my three grand back. Also in the bar that day was a young, penniless English lad named Simon. His girlfriend had just had a baby, and he was out to improve his low financial standing.

As a drug-smuggling operation, it didn't exactly rival *The French Connection* for finesse. Simon, his girlfriend and baby took a ferry to Portsmouth, where they stood out like a sore thumb the moment they drove off the boat in a battered, old banger. They were immediately stopped and searched by a Customs officer, who opened the boot to find 34 kilos of Morocco's finest staring back at him. They hadn't even attempted to hide it. Customs knew that the young lad was only the courier and not one of the top dogs, so they performed their usual scare tactics on him and his girlfriend. They told them that they were looking at a very long stretch at Her Majesty's pleasure but that they would serve less time if they came clean and cooperated. Simon was promised that he would be a free man by the time the case came to court as long as he played ball with the authorities. He talked and talked but dropped none of the protagonists in it. However, yours truly was still implicated.

The drug run had gone wrong before it had even started. Ernie had lost the contact number for the Eltham boys, who were all back in the mother country. He'd searched high and low but had been forced to admit defeat, so he'd sent Simon over in his dope-carrying rust bucket with the scrap of paper with my name and number on it. Ernie had given him instructions to ring me as soon as he landed in England, as he knew that I'd be able to tell Simon where the Eltham boys drank. Ernie had inadvertently involved me in this fiasco, even though the drug deal was something I'd always have steered a million miles away from.

Customs couldn't believe their luck and were jerking off on the fact that my name had suddenly appeared in the middle of a large cannabis confiscation. They knew I'd been careful before so must have thought that I'd cracked up. Regardless, they were going to try and make me pay the price, by hook or by crook.

The phone number Simon had on him was mine, and he could even recognise me from my visit to Ernie's bar. He had also seen the Eltham men but didn't know any of their names or addresses, so it looked to all and sundry like I was the mastermind behind the scabby operation. My visit to Morocco the previous week didn't help me, either. Customs had definitely fingered me for Mr Big. They drove the wrecker up to Hilton Park without Simon and phoned me themselves in an attempt to try and incriminate me. When I turned up with Sid, we parked only four bays away from the old drug car but walked straight past it and into the service station. We weren't to know that it was involved in a drug run, but Customs must have presumed that we were just being shrewd and arrested us on the presumption that we had come down to collect the cannabis anyway. I knew that I hadn't done anything wrong, so I was concerned but not overly worried. Sid, on the other hand, was totally in the dark and desperately waiting for somebody to tell him he could go home. That option never materialised.

Simon got very close to us in Exeter Prison and was always hanging about. We took him under our wing because we felt sorry for him. I assured him that things weren't too bad. Little did I know that he was a rat and had been ordered to report secretly to Customs once a week, informing them about our conversations and actions. It turned out that he was prepared to save his own skin by lying and saying anything to drop me and Sid in the mire.

After a period, we were taken from Exeter Prison to the local magistrates' court, where Sid, shady Simon and I all applied for bail. Sid told me that the main Customs officer involved in the case was taking it personally and had told him, 'Johnson will never get bail. I'll rot in hell before he does. Take that as read.'

'He sounds like a nice bloke,' I thought. 'I bet he gasses badgers in his spare time.' Sure enough, our bail requests were all knocked back by the magistrates, on recommendation from the Customs Gestapo. We must have had five or six visits to the courts while we were festering on remand, which stretched to eighteen months waiting to be committed to Crown court. The delay was deliberately fashioned by Customs. Even though their case was weak, they could nick a couple of years off our lives in this way. It might appear vindictive and cruel, but it is common practice for the authorities to do this to criminals whom they cannot put behind bars with a guilty decision.

Behind the scenes, my defence solicitor, a certain Miss Davis from London, and I were pushing hard to clear me of all the accusations. The prosecution was adamant that I had gone to Morocco to set up the hashish deal, so Miss Davis flew over to Tangiers to interview Adsam, the father of the bride. He categorically told her that I had been at the wedding for the whole five days, had not talked to any strangers and had not mentioned drugs to anybody. He reiterated that there was no possible time or place that I could have set up a large drugs deal. The solicitor prepared a statement that Adsam signed. He was even prepared to come over to Exeter Crown Court to give evidence and clear my name.

As soon as Miss Davis relayed the good news to me, I followed suit and repeated it to Sid and Simon, confident at least that Sid and I would be distanced from the accusations. But Simon couldn't wait to fill in the authorities with the information that would cripple their prosecution. Subsequently, they took immediate action and sent over the heavy mob to Morocco, where they terrified Adsam with threats. They told him that if he attempted to testify, he would be arrested as soon as he landed in the country and charged with conspiracy.

Two days later, Bobby McEwen visited me. He brought bad news with him. 'Scouse, Adsam's not coming over. He's been got at.'

I still didn't realise we had a rat in the camp and thought that Customs had contacted Adsam through my black book, which they had confiscated. That book was very important to me and contained the names and numbers of many associates. It was taken when Customs raided my house. There was forty years' worth of contacts in it, and when the book wasn't returned later it was a mortal blow. It was like walking down the high street naked. The authorities said that they had lost it. It's amazing how many things disappear, including evidence, that could harm the prosecution.

When we were eventually committed to Crown court, Sid got bail and was able to spend some quality time with his family. Simon didn't, as he was bang to rights, and, as the senior Customs officer had promised, there was more chance of the Boston Strangler getting bail than me. By the time the trial came round, I had been in Exeter for what seemed like an eternity, and I was ready for the day of reckoning. The trial lasted nearly one week, and I was reunited with Sid on the first day. We both pleaded not guilty.

Simon had pleaded guilty at an earlier hearing so was not present at court; in fact, he had just been released, as he had served his entire sentence on remand. He had received a surprisingly lenient sentence, considering the amount of hash he had couriered to Britain. I thought he'd got a right result, as I'd expected him to get four or five years. Of course, I still hadn't sussed out that he'd been grassing me and Sid up.

Quite a few of the old lags in Exeter who were experienced in the drug game told us that the most we could expect to get for what we had done was two or three years. We should have never listened to those barrack-room lawyers.

As the court case got under way, I wasn't unduly worried as long as we received a fair hearing – I must have been going soft to think that was possible. The prosecution brought in a top barrister, who was determined to squeeze me until the pips squeaked. He maintained that I had travelled to Morocco to set up the deal and was present in the Spanish bar at the time of the discussions with the Eltham mob, which was corroborated with written evidence from Simon. The prosecution stressed to the jury that I had responded straight away to the phone call and had come down to the service station to pick up the cannabis. Of course, it was all circumstantial evidence: I'd been to Morocco to attend a wedding, visited the Spanish bar to collect a debt and didn't know Simon from the Elephant Man. All of these killer facts were put to the jury by my barrister, who, to be brutally frank, seemed to be outclassed by the prosecution brief. I sometimes thought that he was batting for the other side, he was so ineffective.

Sid's QC was equally mediocre, and as the days passed I knew that we had more chance of getting a knighthood than a not-guilty verdict. To add insult to injury, the judge seemed to be overruling for the prosecution most of the time. It was nice to know that British justice was alive and kicking.

After six tortuous days, the jury retired to consider its verdict. I knew we were going to be found guilty, but I just hoped that we would get a fair sentence, especially with Simon getting less than two years for being caught in possession of the drugs.

The jury returned, and the foreman was asked, 'How do you find Sid Murphy?'

The answer was an unsurprising: 'Guilty.' I copped the same verdict.

It was now down to the judge. He sentenced Sid first. 'For the importation of drugs: two years in prison. For the possession of an unlicensed firearm with ammunition: a further two years. Both sentences to run consecutively.'

I thought, 'Christ, that's a bit stiff. Four years.' I felt sorry for Sid. All he'd done was be in the wrong place at the wrong time.

The judge sentenced me next. 'Norman Johnson, over the years you have been an habitual criminal, but I will take account of your age [I was 63 at the time]. You will serve five years for the importation of cannabis.' It shook me. It was twice the sentence anybody was expecting.

Back in the holding cell, my barrister informed me that Customs had got to Simon. It left a bitter taste in my mouth, but I was determined not to let the authorities think I was down and out.

Sid and I returned to Exeter Prison. The enormity of it all sunk in as I sat in my solitary cell. I realised that Sid and I were looking at the best part of nine years between us. We hadn't been involved in drug dealing in any way, shape or form, yet here we were, rotting at the rough end of British justice.

My mind returned to the time of the shotgun offence at the Old Bailey, when the police produced an incriminating statement that I was supposed to have made and I was told that I was going down. Those words were now ringing in my ears again. I had to stay strong, put it all behind me and do the only thing I could: look to the future. As it was, I'd served a large chunk of time on remand, so I concentrated on breaking the back of the sentence.

However, before my time was up, I lost my eldest and youngest sisters in the States to illness, and, to cap it all, Rose passed away in London. I'd lost three sisters in a short period. A part of me had gone for ever.

A few months later, I was transferred to Channings Wood Prison, near Newton Abbot, four miles north of Torquay, where I stayed for a year. I finished my sentence at Sudbury Open Prison near Uttoxeter. It was the only time in my life that I'd ever served time in an open nick, even though it was only a few weeks.

I returned to Stafford. It was a pleasure to see my daughters and grandchildren. With my black book gone, I felt naked. My whole life was on those pages, and it was like starting from scratch. I set off for the Smoke, because people in London owed me money. Even though I was liberated, I needed to make a living. A few faces were delighted to see me, others not so.

I was struck by how many people had passed away. It made me aware of my own mortality. Not only that, but the old London was disappearing fast. Anyone who had lived in the capital after the war would know the feeling. It was in a state of flux. I know everything changes and nothing goes on for ever, but it was disappointing all the same.

With regret, I returned to Stafford and became friendly with a local publican named Micky O'Rourke, who ran an establishment called The Jolly Jockey. As you can tell by the name, Micky was mad for the horses. I made it my local and enjoyed his company.

One day out of the blue, he informed me that he had acquired a bookmaker's licence. 'How would you like to work at the racetracks, Norm?' In my younger days, I'd been keen on visiting the racetracks around London for a punt. I knew some good people in the racing game and frequently had a bet at courses such as Kempton and Lingfield. I also had experience with my gaming clubs, so I didn't need to be asked twice.

We bought bookmaker pitches at racecourses such as Chester, Wolverhampton and Southwell. At the three-day meeting at Chester, we decided to stay at the Adelphi Hotel in Liverpool, rather than make six trips up and down the motorway to Stafford.

I wanted to show Micky where I was brought up. After we caught a cab to the south end of Liverpool around Toxteth, we bent an elbow or two in the local establishments. In the third pub, I recognised a voice. 'Hello, Norman.' It was Christine Corrigan, who had visited me in Brixton Prison. She said, 'I know someone who would like to talk to you.' She passed me her mobile, and on the other end was an old flame, Joan Walker. We chatted and exchanged phone numbers and started to meet up again.

The racing was going well, and if either Micky or I was unavailable, we had people to cover for us. I had an overwhelming urge to return to the States. I knew I had to go back sooner rather than later. I told Micky my intention, and he said to take as long as I wanted.

I flew into New York again, minus the black book. I hadn't been Stateside for over a decade. I eventually tracked down Mickey Quinn, who was still a bar owner. If anything, New York had changed even quicker than London. Places had closed and old haunts had fallen into disrepair. Rocky Graziano was dead, and Russell Bufalino and Louis Rush were also long gone. It made me realise that I was a septuagenarian.

Mickey Quinn piled on the misery. 'Even John Francis has been clipped coming out of a restaurant.' New York was a young man's town. Even though the heart was willing, my body was telling me to finish that chapter of my life.

New York and London were now impostors, and I decided to get on with the real reason why I had crossed the herring pond. I flew to Kansas City to visit my niece, Lisa Lamport, who had gathered the family members of my late sister Minnie together in the old house. They had all thrived and prospered. It was a million miles from the struggles of yesteryear. America was certainly the land of opportunity. I spent a pleasant fortnight with them, contented that all was well with the Lamports.

The next stop was Florida. I wanted to see if life had been as kind to Sylvia's family, the Desotells. My niece Tracey Desotell couldn't have been happier, and Des and Tina flew down from Virginia for the family gathering. I needn't have worried. They were all on the up, so after a short stay I flew back to England. I have returned time and again, and I am affectionately known as Uncle Norman.

I now see Joan Walker quite a bit. She's always been there for me, and we take turns seeing each other. Joan lives in Ellesmere Port, where she runs a hairdresser's, and we both pop up and down the M6 as often as we can.

I've been around for eight decades, and I've certainly not led a mundane or ordinary life. Rightly or wrongly, I did it my way.